Exam Ref 70-347 Enabling Office 365 Services

Orin Thomas

PUBLISHED BY
Microsoft Press
A Division of Microsoft Corporation
One Microsoft Way
Redmond, Washington 98052-6399

Library of Congress Control Number: 2015936019
ISBN: 978-1-5093-0067-9

Printed and bound in the United States of America.

First Printing

Microsoft Press books are available through booksellers and distributors worldwide. If you need support related to this book, email Microsoft Press Book Support at mspinput@microsoft.com. Please tell us what you think of this book at *http://aka.ms/tellpress*.

This book is provided "as-is" and expresses the author's views and opinions. The views, opinions and information expressed in this book, including URL and other Internet Web site references, may change without notice.

Some examples depicted herein are provided for illustration only and are fictitious. No real association or connection is intended or should be inferred.

Microsoft and the trademarks listed at *http://www.microsoft.com* on the "Trademarks" Web page are trademarks of the Microsoft group of companies. All other marks are property of their respective owners.

Acquisitions Editor: Karen Szall
Developmental Editor: Karen Szall
Editorial Production: Troy Mott, Ellie Volckhausen
Technical Reviewers: Mike Toot; Technical Review services provided by Content Master, a member of CM Group, Ltd.
Copyeditor: Eryn Leavens
Indexer: Julie Grady
Cover: Twist Creative • Seattle

Contents at a glance

Contents

What do you think of this book? We want to hear from you!

Microsoft is interested in hearing your feedback so we can continually improve our books and learning resources for you. To participate in a brief online survey, please visit:

www.microsoft.com/learning/booksurvey/

**Chapter 4   Plan for Exchange Online and Skype for
            Business Online   229**

What do you think of this book? We want to hear from you!

Microsoft is interested in hearing your feedback so we can continually improve our books and learning resources for you. To participate in a brief online survey, please visit:

www.microsoft.com/learning/booksurvey/

Introduction

The 70-347 exam deals with advanced topics that require candidates to have an excellent working knowledge of Office 365, Exchange Online, SharePoint Online, and Skype for Business Online. Some of the exam comprises topics that even experienced Office 365, Exchange Online, SharePoint Online, and Skype for Business Online administrators may rarely encounter unless they are consultants who deploy new Office 365 tenancies on a regular basis.

Candidates for this exam are Information Technology (IT) Professionals who want to validate their advanced Office 365, Exchange Online, SharePoint Online, and Skype for Business Online management skills, configuration skills, and knowledge. To pass this exam, candidates require a strong understanding of how to manage and configure Office 365 clients and user devices, provision SharePoint Online site collections, configure Exchange Online and Skype for Business Online for users, and manage, migrate to, and administer Exchange Online and Skype for Business Online. To pass, candidates require a thorough theoretical understanding, as well as meaningful practical experience implementing the technologies involved.

This book covers every exam objective, but it does not cover every exam question. Only the Microsoft exam team has access to the exam questions themselves and Microsoft regularly adds new questions to the exam, making it impossible to cover specific questions. You should consider this book a supplement to your relevant real-world experience and other study materials. If you encounter a topic in this book that you do not feel completely comfortable with, use the links you'll find in text to find more information and take the time to research and study the topic. Great information is available on TechNet, through MVA courses, and in blogs and forums.

Microsoft certifications

Microsoft certifications distinguish you by proving your command of a broad set of skills and experience with current Microsoft products and technologies. The exams and corresponding certifications are developed to validate your mastery of critical competencies as you design and develop, or implement and support, solutions with Microsoft products and technologies both on-premises and in the cloud. Certification brings a variety of benefits to the individual and to employers and organizations.

> **MORE INFO**   **ALL MICROSOFT CERTIFICATIONS**
>
> For information about Microsoft certifications, including a full list of available certifications, go to *http://www.microsoft.com/learning/en/us/certification/cert-default.aspx.*

Free ebooks from Microsoft Press

From technical overviews to in-depth information on special topics, the free ebooks from Microsoft Press cover a wide range of topics. These ebooks are available in PDF, EPUB, and Mobi for Kindle formats, and are ready for you to download at:

http://aka.ms/mspressfree

Check back often to see what is new!

Errata, updates, & book support

We've made every effort to ensure the accuracy of this book and its companion content. You can access updates to this book—in the form of a list of submitted errata and their related corrections—at:

http://aka.ms/ER347/errata

If you discover an error that is not already listed, please submit it to us at the same page.

If you need additional support, email Microsoft Press Book Support at *mspinput@microsoft.com.*

Please note that product support for Microsoft software and hardware is not offered through the previous addresses. For help with Microsoft software or hardware, go to *http://support.microsoft.com.*

We want to hear from you

At Microsoft Press, your satisfaction is our top priority, and your feedback our most valuable asset. Please tell us what you think of this book at:

http://aka.ms/tellpress

The survey is short, and we read every one of your comments and ideas. Thanks in advance for your input!

Stay in touch

Let's keep the conversation going! We're on Twitter: *http://twitter.com/MicrosoftPress.*

Preparing for the exam

Microsoft certification exams are a great way to build your resume and let the world know about your level of expertise. Certification exams validate your on-the-job experience and product knowledge. Although there is no substitute for on-the-job experience, preparation through study and hands-on practice can help you prepare for the exam. We recommend that you augment your exam preparation plan by using a combination of available study materials and courses. For example, you might use the Exam ref and another study guide for your "at home" preparation, and take a Microsoft Official Curriculum course for the classroom experience. Choose the combination that you think works best for you.

Note that this Exam Ref is based on publicly available information about the exam and the author's experience. To safeguard the integrity of the exam, authors do not have access to the live exam.

CHAPTER 1

Manage clients and end-user devices

One of the challenges in deploying and managing Office 365 for traditional IT departments is that Office 365 is designed around the idea that users are able to install and configure their own applications, rather than having the deployment and management of applications occur centrally by an IT department. In this chapter, you'll be reminded of not only how you can enable or restrict users from performing their own deployments, but how you can manage the deployment of Office 365 applications centrally, monitor the

> **IMPORTANT**
> ## Have you read page xv?
> **It contains valuable information regarding the skills you need to pass the exam.**

functionality of those applications, as well as allow for the configuration of Office applications. You'll also be reminded of some of the differences between the volume license versions of Office 2013 traditionally deployed and managed by IT departments and Office 365 ProPlus, the version available through Office 365.

Objectives in this chapter:

- Objective 1.1: Manage user-driven client deployments
- Objective 1.2: Manage IT deployments of Office 365 ProPlus
- Objective 1.3: Set up telemetry and reporting
- Objective 1.4: Plan for Office clients

Objective 1.1: Manage user-driven client deployments

One of the great advantages of Office 365 is that it provides end users with the opportunity to perform self-service deployment of software to their own devices. While this has definite advantages, empowering users to this degree can also lead to problems, such as users exceeding their allocation of Office 365 ProPlus licenses. This objective deals with how you can restrict self-provisioning of Office 365 ProPlus, Windows Store apps and mobile apps, how to manage and revoke activation, as well as Office for Mac.

This objective covers the following topics:

- Restrict self-provisioning of Office 365 ProPlus
- Windows Store apps and mobile apps
- Manage activation
- Office for Mac

Restrict self-provisioning of Office 365 ProPlus

Depending on the policies of your organization, you might want to allow users to install software directly from the Office 365 portal, to restrict this ability entirely, or to allow users to install some applications but restrict them from installing others. Office 365 ProPlus is the version of Microsoft Office that is available to appropriately licensed users in an Office 365 tenancy. Office 365 ProPlus includes the following software products:

- Access
- Excel
- InfoPath
- OneNote
- Outlook
- PowerPoint
- Publisher
- Word

Depending on the Office 365 subscription associated with a tenancy, the Skype for Business, Project, and Visio applications might also be available.

To configure which Office software users are able to install from the portal, perform the following steps:

1. When signed in to Office 365 with a user account that has Administrator permissions, open the Office Admin Center, and then select User Software under Service Settings, as shown in Figure 1-1.

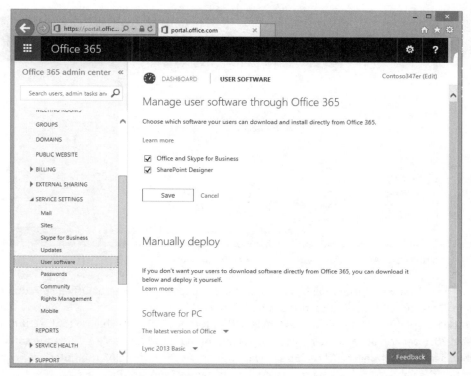

FIGURE 1-1 Manage user software

The options that are available here will depend on the Office 365 subscription that you have.

2. To restrict users from deploying software from the Office 365 portal, clear the check box next to the listed software.

For example, in Figure 1-2 the check box next to SharePoint designer has been cleared. Users in this tenancy will only be able to install the apps that are available as part of the Office and Skype for Business category.

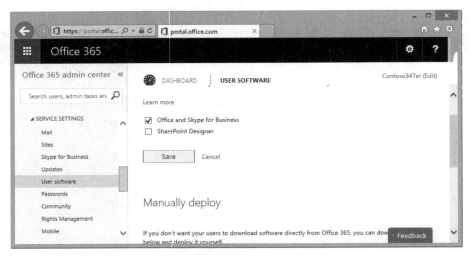

FIGURE 1-2 Allowing only Office and Skype for Business

The software that users will be able to install depends on the type of Office 365 subscription. Different Office 365 subscriptions have different software options. It is also likely that software options will change. For example, Office for Mac 2011 will change to the Office for Mac 2016 version at some point after the release of that product. Table 1-1 lists the software that is available for each Office 365 software option. As the Office 365 user interface is updated, the name "Lync" will be replaced with the name "Skype for Business."

TABLE 1-1: Software available with each Office 365 software option

Software option	Software made available to users
Office	■ Office 365 ProPlus ■ Office for Mac 2011/Office for Mac 2016
Office and Skype for Business	■ Office 365 ProPlus ■ Office for Mac 2011/ Office for Mac 2016 ■ Skype for Business ■ Lync for Mac 2011
Skype for Business	■ Skype for Business ■ Lync for Mac 2011
Project	■ Project Pro for Office 365
Visio	■ Visio Pro for Office 365
SharePoint Designer	■ SharePoint Designer 2013

While you can make Office 365 software available to users through the Office 365 portal, this doesn't mean that users will automatically be able to successfully install this software. When allowing users to self-provision software from the Office 365 portal, keep the following in mind.

- To successfully run Office 365, users will need an Office 365 license.

- For users to be able to install the software they downloaded from the Office 365 portal, they will need to have local administrator privileges on their computer. This means that self-provisioning of software through the Office 365 portal is a suitable strategy in Bring Your Own Device (BYOD) scenarios where the user is the owner of the computer and is responsible for its configuration. Self-provisioning of software is less of a concern for most environments where each user is assigned a computer with a Standard Operating Environment (SOE), as users in these environments rarely have local administrator credentials.

- If you do not make Office software available to users, they will see a message that informs them that Office installations have been disabled when they navigate to the Software page in the Office 365 portal.

- Office 365 ProPlus is only run on the following operating systems (with support available for Windows 10 and Windows Server 2016 when those operating systems are available):
  - Windows 7
  - Windows 8
  - Windows 8.1
  - Windows Server 2008 R2
  - Windows Server 2012
  - Windows Server 2012 R2

> **MORE INFO CONTROL WHICH SOFTWARE USERS CAN INSTALL FROM THE PORTAL**
>
> You can learn more about controlling the Office software users can install from the Office 365 portal at *https://technet.microsoft.com/en-us/library/jj219421.aspx*.

By default, if a user installs Office 365 ProPlus from the Office 365 portal, all programs included with Office 365 ProPlus (Access, Excel, InfoPath, OneNote, Outlook, PowerPoint, Publisher, and Word) will also install. Administrators can configure deployments so that only some, not all, of these programs will install. You can configure which programs are excluded from Office 365 ProPlus using the Office Deployment Tool. You will learn more about configuring the Office Deployment Tool later in this chapter.

MORE INFO **EXCLUDE PROGRAMS FROM OFFICE 365 PROPLUS**

You can learn more about excluding programs from Office 365 ProPlus at *https://technet. microsoft.com/en-us/library/dn745895.aspx*.

Office 365 and mobile devices

Microsoft has made Word, Excel, PowerPoint, and OneNote apps available for the Windows Phone, iOS, Android, and Windows RT mobile platforms. There are several ways that you can install these apps on these devices.

The first is to navigate to the Office 365 portal using the mobile device on which you want to install each application and select the app that you want to install from the list that is available. Figure 1-3 shows the apps that are available for an iPad from the Office 365 portal.

FIGURE 1-3 List of apps available for the iPad platform

Selecting an app opens the app's page in the appropriate vendor's app store. Figure 1-4 shows the Apple App Store page that opens when the Excel link on the Office 365 portal is opened. The application can then be downloaded from the App Store and installed on the device.

FIGURE 1-4 Excel app in the Apple App Store

These applications can also be installed directly from each mobile device operating system vendor's app store. To use all the available features of each app, such as accessing documents in OneDrive for Business that are associated with your organization's Office 365 subscription, it will be necessary to sign in to the app using your Office 365 user account credentials. Premium features include:

- The ability to track changes, change page orientation, insert chart elements, and add WordArt and picture effects in the Word app.
- Use Pivot Tables, add and modify chart elements in the Excel app.
- Use Presenter View with speaker notes, perform audio and video edits, and use picture styles in the PowerPoint app.
- Technical support options from Microsoft.

Select the Sign In option of an app, shown in Figure 1-5, to connect the app to an Office 365 subscription.

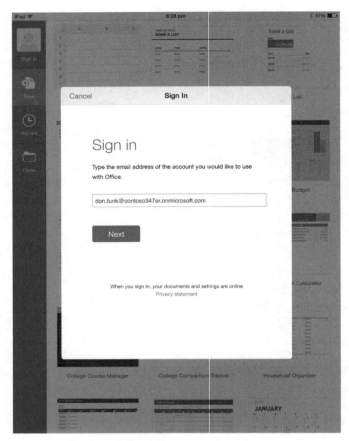

FIGURE 1-5 Sign In to Office 365

MORE INFO **OFFICE 365 AND MOBILE DEVICES**

You can learn more about deploying at *https://support.office.com/en-us/article/Office-365-mobile-setup---Help-7dabb6cb-0046-40b6-81fe-767e0b1f014f.*

Manage activation

Office 365 ProPlus must be activated for users to be able to create and edit documents. While this can vary depending on the subscription level, each Office 365 user account generally allows for the activation of five concurrent instances of Office 365 ProPlus. Activation usually occurs automatically when a user downloads and installs Office 365 ProPlus from the Office 365 portal.

Reduced functionality mode

If Office 365 ProPlus is not in an activated state, it enters reduced functionality mode. Reduced functionality mode allows users to open and view documents, but restricts them from creating new documents or making modifications to existing documents. When Office 365 ProPlus is in reduced functionality mode, users are prompted to reactivate the product on a regular basis.

Regular reactivation

After Office 365 ProPlus has been activated on a computer, additional activation checks must be performed every 30 days. These automatic activation checks occur automatically when the computer connects to the Internet. If the computer does not connect to the Internet for more than 30 days, Office 365 ProPlus will enter reduced functionality mode. This 30-day period is an important consideration for certain types of scenarios and will determine whether it's okay to deploy Office 365 ProPlus or if it is necessary to deploy an appropriate edition of Office 2013.

For example, imagine that you are responsible for selecting a version of Office for the laptop computers of a scientific team that is going to work in Antarctica. As part of this scenario, you learn that the scientific team will be away from the main base for a period of 45 days, and during this 45-day period, those laptops will be unable to make an Internet connection. In this scenario, you should not choose to deploy Office 365 ProPlus because you don't want members of the scientific team to have Office 365 ProPlus go into reduced functionality mode while away from the base.

You can check which licenses have been assigned to a user from the User Properties page in the Office 365 portal as shown in Figure 1-6.

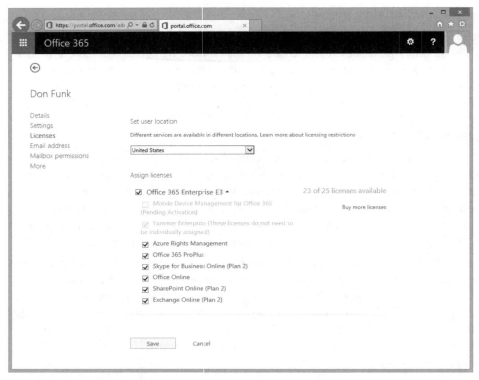

FIGURE 1-6 Software Licenses

Deactivating Office 365 ProPlus

A user can have a maximum of five installations tied to their Office 365 account. Should a user who has reached their five-installation limit need to install Office 365 ProPlus on a new computer, they can deactivate one of their existing installations as a way of reclaiming the license. Deactivating an installation does not remove the software from the computer on which it is installed. While it is possible to run the software after it has been deactivated, the software will be in reduced functionality mode.

To deactivate an existing Office 365 ProPlus activation, a user must perform the following steps:

1. Sign in to the Office 365 portal with their Office 365 user account.

2. Navigate to the software page at *https://portal.office.com/OLS/MySoftware.aspx*.

3. On the software page, shown in Figure 1-7, locate the computer for which you want to deactivate an existing activation and then click Deactivate.

FIGURE 1-7 Deactivate installation

4. You will be prompted to confirm that you want to deactivate the installation, as shown in Figure 1-8. Click Yes.

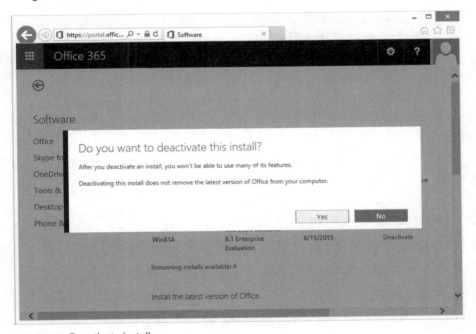

FIGURE 1-8 Deactivate install

5. If you attempt to start an Office 365 ProPlus application after the product activation has been deactivated, you will be presented with the Product Deactivated dialog box, shown in Figure 1-9.

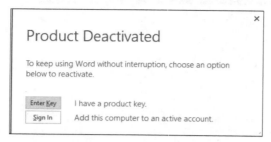

FIGURE 1-9 Product Deactivated

6. You can either manually enter an Office product key to reactivate the installation, or sign in with your Office 365 subscription and attempt to perform activation, as shown in Figure 1-10.

FIGURE 1-10 Activate Office

7. If you have not reached your activation limit, you will be able to successfully activate the deactivated copy of Office 365 ProPlus, as shown in Figure 1-11.

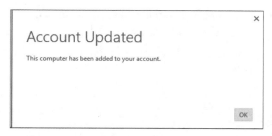

FIGURE 1-11 Account Updated

MORE INFO OFFICE 365 PROPLUS LICENSING AND ACTIVATION

You can learn more about Office 365 ProPlus licensing and activation at
https://technet.microsoft.com/en-us/library/gg982959.aspx.

Office for Mac

Office 365 ProPlus is currently only available for computers running Windows operating systems. Until Office 365 ProPlus is also available for OS X, users with computers running the Mac OS X operating system can obtain Office for Mac 2011 from the Office 365 portal and activate the program using their Office 365 credentials. Office for Mac 2011 includes Word, PowerPoint, Excel, and Outlook. Activating Office 2011 for Mac with the Office 365 user credentials consumes one of the five available licenses, as shown in Figure 1-12.

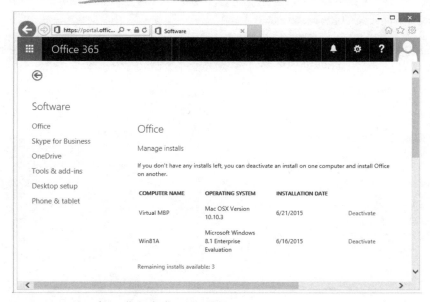

FIGURE 1-12 List of installs including Mac OS X

To install Office for Mac 2011, sign on to a computer running Mac OS X with a user account that has administrator credentials and perform the following steps:

1. Using a web browser, navigate to *https://portal.office.com* and sign in with your Office 365 user credentials shown in Figure 1-13.

FIGURE 1-13 Signing in to Office 365 on a Mac

2. On the Office 365 Welcome page, shown in Figure 1-14, click Install.

FIGURE 1-14 Office 365 console

3. The computer operating system will automatically be detected and Office for Mac 2011 will be offered. Click Install to trigger a download of the disk image containing the Office for Mac 2011 installation files (see Figure 1-15).

FIGURE 1-15 Install Office For Mac 2011

4. When the disk image file containing the Office for Mac 2011 has downloaded, open it and double-click the Office Installer shown in Figure 1-16. This launches the Microsoft Office for Mac 2011 installer.

FIGURE 1-16 Office for Mac 2011 installer

5. On the Welcome page of the Microsoft Office For Mac 2011 Installer, shown in Figure 1-17, click Continue.

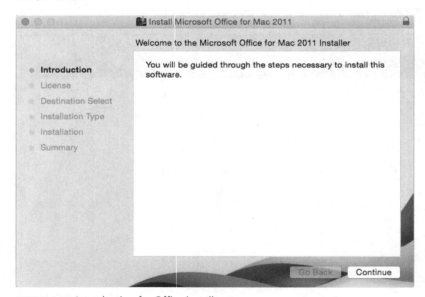

FIGURE 1-17 Introduction for Office installer

6. Review the Software License Agreement, as shown in Figure 1-18, and click Continue.

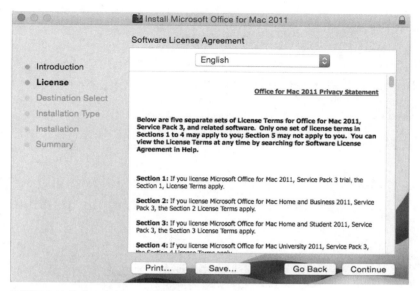

FIGURE 1-18 Software License Agreement

7. When prompted to agree with the license agreement, you will need to click Agree, as shown in Figure 1-19, to continue with the installation.

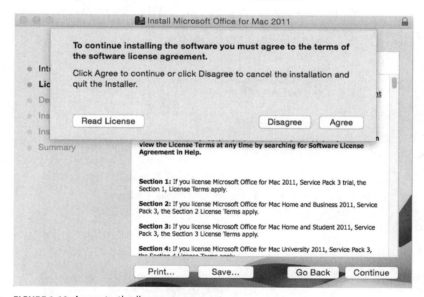

FIGURE 1-19 Agree to the license agreement

8. On the Installation Type page, click Install. Click Customize to change the installation options, such as placing the files on a separate disk.

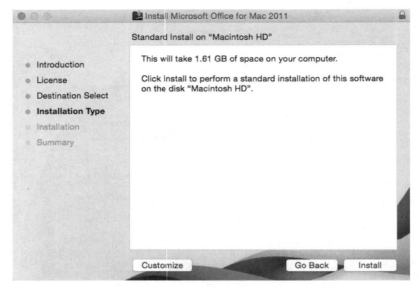

FIGURE 1-20 Standard installation

9. The installer prompts you for the credentials. (Remember, you must have the credentials of a user who has permission to install software on the Mac OS X computer.) Provide your credentials, as shown in Figure 1-21, and then click Install Software.

FIGURE 1-21 Provide administrative permission

10. After a period of time, the installer will report the installation has completed successfully. Click Close to exit the wizard, as shown in Figure 1-22.

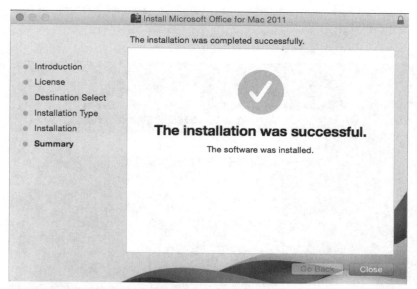

FIGURE 1-22 Successful installation

11. Exiting the installation wizard will trigger the Get Started With Office 2011 wizard shown in Figure 1-23. Click Sign In To An Existing Office 365 Subscription to initiate the activation process.

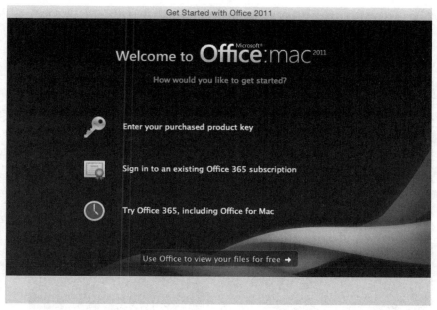

FIGURE 1-23 Sign in to activate

12. Enter the email address associated with the Office 365 account, as shown in Figure 1-24, and click Next.

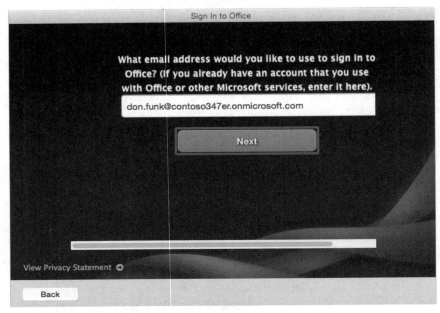

FIGURE 1-24 Sign In To Office

13. When prompted, enter the password associated with the Office 365 account, as shown in Figure 1-25, and click Sign In.

FIGURE 1-25 Provide Office 365 credentials

14. You might be prompted to give Office access to your contacts, as shown in Figure 1-26. Choosing not to provide access to contacts will still allow the installation to complete normally.

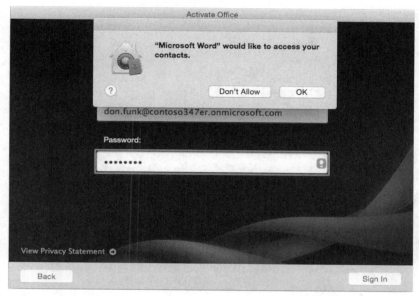

FIGURE 1-26 Access to contacts

15. Provide the first name, last name, and company name that you want to associate with this Office for Mac installation, as shown in Figure 1-28, and then click Continue.

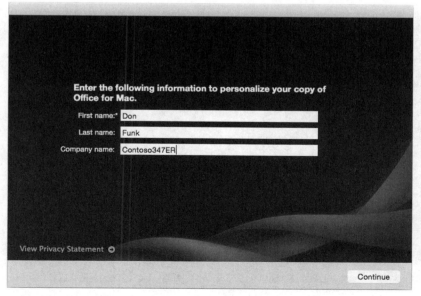

FIGURE 1-27 Personalize Your Copy Of Office For Mac

16. On the Help Improve Microsoft Office page, choose whether you want Office for Mac to automatically download updates and whether you want to join the Customer Experience Improvement Program, as shown in Figure 1-28. After your choices have been made, click Continue.

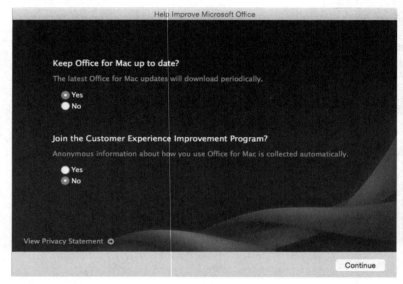

FIGURE 1-28 Configure updates

17. When activation has been completed successfully, you will see a message congratulating you, as shown in Figure 1-29. Click Done to complete the installation process.

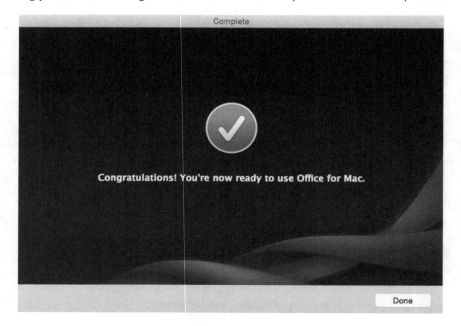

FIGURE 1-29 Installation complete

EXAM TIP

Remember that users can deactivate an Office 365 ProPlus activation through the Office 365 portal.

Thought experiment

Mobile apps and Office 365 at Adatum

In this thought experiment, apply what you learned about this objective. You can find answers to these questions in the "Answers" section at the end of this chapter.

There are an increasing number of iPad and Android tablet users at Adatum who want to use these mobile devices to perform work tasks. Several of the users of Android tablets have already installed apps from the Google Play Store, but are unable to access documents stored in SharePoint online. Some of the iPad users have heard that Office apps are available, but don't know where to start when it comes to obtaining them. With this information in mind, answer the following questions:

1. What instruction should you give to iPad users about locating Office apps?

2. What instruction should you give to Android tablet users who have already installed apps from the Google Play Store?

Objective summary

- You can use the Office 365 Admin Console to restrict the applications that users can self-deploy. However, you can only allow or block them from Office 365 ProPlus. You cannot allow or block individual programs within Office 365 ProPlus such as Word and Excel.

- Users can self-provision apps for mobile devices from the Office 365 portal. Selecting an application in the portal will open the device vendor's app store to the chosen application.

- Each Office 365 user can run five activated copies of Office 365 ProPlus and/or Office for Mac 2011.

- Unactivated copies of Office 365 ProPlus run in reduced functionality mode.

- Reduced functionality mode allows documents to be viewed, but does not allow new documents to be created or existing documents to be modified.

- Users can deactivate existing activations. When a user does this, the application enters reduced functionality mode.

- An activated copy of Office 365 ProPlus must be able to communicate with Microsoft servers on the Internet every 30 days. If this communication does not occur, Office 365 ProPlus will enter reduced functionality mode.

Objective review

Answer the following questions to test your knowledge of the information in this objective. You can find the answers to these questions and explanations of why each answer choice is correct or incorrect in the "Answers" section at the end of the chapter.

1. Don wants to install Office 365 ProPlus on a new laptop he purchased from a consumer electronics store. Don has already installed Office 365 from his organization's Office 365 portal tenancy on several other computers. Don has never performed a deactivation of an existing Office 365 ProPlus activation. How many existing activations must Don have already performed before he must manually deactivate an activation, allowing him to install and activate Office 365 ProPlus on his new laptop?

   A. Four

   B. Five

   C. Nine

   D. Ten

2. You have a variety of computers in your environment running a variety of operating systems. On which of the following operating systems is Office 365 ProPlus supported? (Choose all that apply.)

   A. Windows Vista

   B. Windows XP

   C. Windows Server 2008 R2

   D. Windows 8.1

3. After Office 365 ProPlus is activated, what is the maximum amount of time that a computer can be disconnected from the Internet before Office 365 ProPlus will enter reduced functionality mode?

   A. 15 days

   B. 30 days

   C. 90 days

   D. 180 days

Objective 1.2: Manage IT deployments of Office 365 ProPlus

In most organizations, the IT department is still responsible for installing and maintaining software on the computers used by that organization. Just because Office 365 ProPlus is traditionally installed manually by a user doesn't mean that it can't be installed and managed centrally by an IT department. This objective deals with managing the deployment of Office 365, including managing streaming updates, the Office deployment tool, and how to customize deployment.

> **This objective covers the following topics:**
> - Manage deployment
> - Manage streaming updates
> - Use the Office deployment tool
> - Customize deployment

Manual deployment

The typical method of deploying Office 365 ProPlus on a computer is for a user to access the installation files from the Office 365 portal. You can install Office 365 ProPlus on a computer by performing the following steps:

1. Sign in to the computer with a user account that is a member of the local administrators group.

2. Open a web browser and sign in to the Office 365 portal at *https://portal.office.com*.

3. On the Office 365 Home page, shown in Figure 1-31, click Install Now.

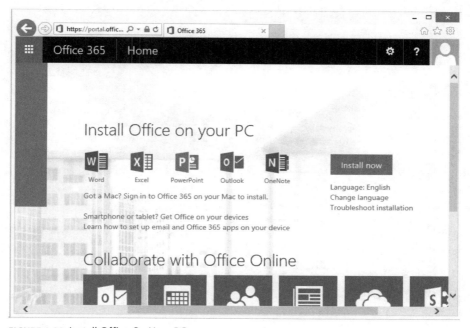

FIGURE 1-30 Install Office On Your PC

4. On the Do You Want To Run Or Save dialog box, shown in Figure 1-31, click Run.

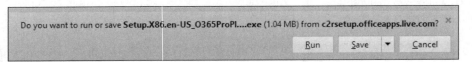

FIGURE 1-31 Run Or Save dialog box

5. On the User Account Control dialog box, verify that the Program name is set to Microsoft Office Click-to-Run, as shown in Figure 1-32, and then click Yes.

FIGURE 1-32 User Account Control

6. On the Welcome To Your New Office page, shown in Figure 1-33, click Next.

FIGURE 1-33 Welcome to Office

7. On the First Things First page, select Use Recommended Settings and then click Accept.

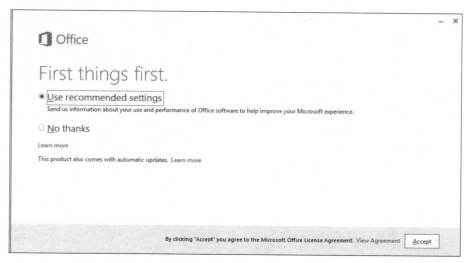

FIGURE 1-34 Use Recommended Settings

8. On the Meet OneDrive page, shown in Figure 1-35, click Next.

FIGURE 1-35 Meet OneDrive

9. On the How Would You Like Your Office To Look page, shown in Figure 1-36, select the theme to be used with Office 365 ProPlus.

FIGURE 1-36 Choose background

10. On the Take A Look At What's New page, shown in Figure 1-37, click No Thanks.

FIGURE 1-37 Take A Look At What's New

11. On the You're Good To Go page, shown in Figure 1-38, click All Done.

FIGURE 1-38 Good To Go

MORE INFO **MANUALLY INSTALLING OFFICE 365 PROPLUS**

You can learn more about installing Office 365 ProPlus at *https://support.office.com/en-us/article/Download-and-install-Office-using-Office-365-for-business-on-your-PC-or-Mac-72977511-dfd1-4d8b-856f-405cfb76839c.*

Central deployment

With special preparation, Office 365 ProPlus can be downloaded to a local shared folder and then deployed centrally. To use this central deployment method, the IT department must use the Office Deployment Tool to download the Office 365 ProPlus software from Microsoft servers on the Internet. While it is possible to deploy Office 365 ProPlus centrally, successful installation of Office 365 ProPlus requires the ability for the software to activate against Microsoft Office 365 servers on the Internet. You can't use a volume licensing solution, such as a Key Management Services (KMS) server, to activate Office 365 ProPlus even when you are deploying it centrally.

Office Deployment Tool

The Office Deployment Tool allows IT departments to perform the following tasks:

- **Generate a Click-to-Run for Office 365 installation source**   This allows administrators to create a local installation source for Office 365 rather than requiring that the files be downloaded for each client from the Internet.

- **Generate Click-to-Run for Office 365 clients**   This allows administrators to configure how Office 365 ProPlus is installed. For example, blocking the installation of PowerPoint.

- **Creating an App-V package**   Allows administrators to configure Office 365 ProPlus to work with application virtualization.

To install the Office Deployment Tool, perform the following steps:

1. On the computer on which you want to deploy the Office Deployment Tool, open a web browser and navigate to the following address: *https://www.microsoft.com/en-us/download/details.aspx?id=36778*.

2. On the Office Deployment Tool For Click-To-Run webpage, shown in Figure 1-39, click Download.

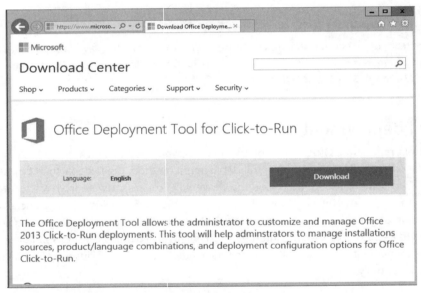

FIGURE 1-39 Office Deployment Tool For Click-To-Run

3. Save the installer file to a location on the computer, as shown in Figure 1-40.

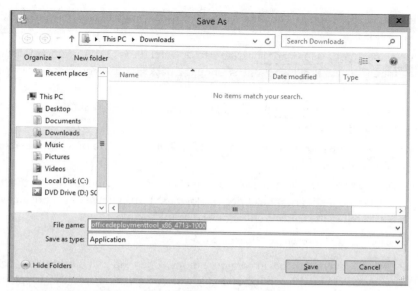

FIGURE 1-40 Save Office Deployment Tool For Click-To-Run

4. After the deployment tool has downloaded, double-click it to start the deployment tool setup.

5. On the Microsoft Software License Terms page, select the Click Here To Accept The Microsoft Software License Terms option and click Continue.

6. On the Browse For Folder page, select the folder in which to store the files associated with the tool. While these files can be extracted anywhere, you will need to interact with the tool frequently so you should create a folder in the root folder of a volume.

7. Two files will be extracted: Configuration.xml and Setup.exe, as shown in Figure 1-41.

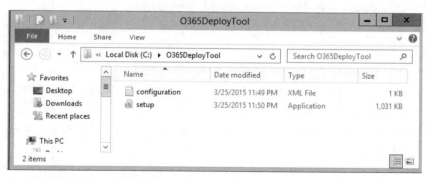

FIGURE 1-41 Deployment Tool folder

The Office Deployment Tool is a command line utility that provides administrators with three general options:

- The download mode allows administrators to download the Click-to-Run installation source for Office 365 ProPlus as well as language pack files to a central on-premises location.
- The configure mode allows for the configuration and installation of Click-to-Run Office products and language packs.
- The packager mode allows for the creation of an App-V package from downloaded Click-to-Run installation files.

The Office Deployment Tool must be run from an elevated command prompt in the /configure and /packager modes. To run the Office Deployment tool in download mode against a configuration file stored in the c:\ClickToRun folder, use the syntax:

```
Setup.exe /download c:\ClickToRun\configuration.xml
```

To run the Office Deployment Tool in configure mode, when the tool is hosted on the share \\SYD-Deploy\O365 and the configuration file is stored on the share \\SYD-Deploy\Configs, run the command:

```
\\SYD-Deploy\O365\Setup.exe /configure \\SYD-Deploy\Configs\Configuration.xml
```

> **MORE INFO OFFICE DEPLOYMENT TOOL**
>
> You can learn more about the Office Deployment Tool at *https://technet.microsoft.com/en-us/library/jj219422.aspx.*

Configuration.xml

You use the Configuration.xml file to perform the following tasks:

- Add or remove Office products from an installation.
- Add or remove languages from the installation.
- Specify display options, such as whether the installation occurs silently.
- Configure logging options, such as how much information will be recorded in the log.
- Specify how software updates will work with Click-to-Run.

Figure 1-42 shows the example Configuration.xml file that is available with the Office Deployment Tool.

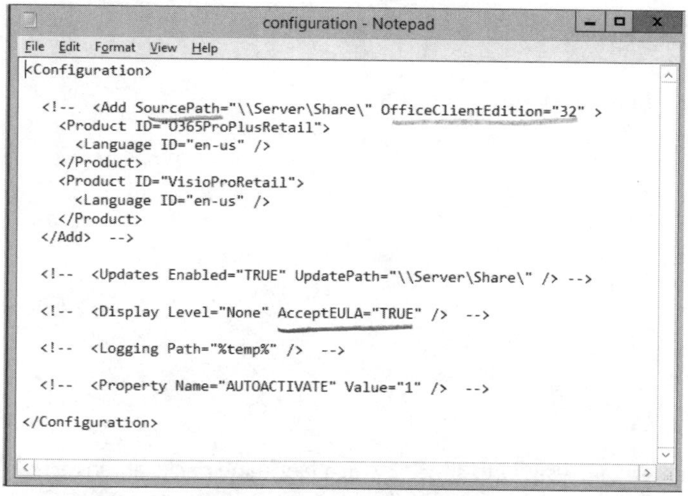

FIGURE 1-42 Configuration.xml

Important attributes include:

- **SourcePath** When you run the tool in download mode, the SourcePath attribute determines the location where the Click-to-Run files will be stored. When you run the tool in configure mode, the SourcePath attribute determines the installation source.

- **OfficeClientEdition** This value is required and either must be set to 32 or 64. This determines whether the x86 or x64 version of Office applications are retrieved or installed.

- **Version** If this element is not set, the most recent version of files will be either downloaded or installed. If a version is set, then that version of the files will either be downloaded or installed.

- **Display** The display element allows you to specify what information the user sees during deployment. The options are:

  - **Level=None** The user sees no UI, completion screen, error dialog boxes, or first run UI.

  - **Level=FULL** The user sees the normal Click-to-Run user interface, application splash screen, and error dialog boxes.

  - **AcceptEULA=True** The user does not see the Microsoft Software License Terms dialog box.

  - **AcceptEULA=False** The user will see the Microsoft Software License Terms dialog box.

- **ExcludeApp** You use this element to exclude applications from being installed. Valid values of this attribute are as follows:

  - Access

  - Excel

- Groove (used for OneDrive for Business)
- InfoPath
- Lync (used for Skype for Business)
- OneNote
- Outlook
- PowerPoint
- Project
- Publisher
- SharePoint Designer
- Visio
- Word

- **Language ID** This element allows you to specify which language packs are installed. For example, en-us for US English. You can have multiple Language ID elements, one for each language that you are installing.
- **Logging** This element allows you to disable logging, enable logging, and specify the path where the log file is to be written.
- **Product ID** This element allows you to specify which products to install. The available options are:
  - **O365ProPlusRetail** Office 365 ProPlus
  - **VisioProRetail** Visio Pro
  - **ProjectProRetail** Project Professional
  - **SPDRetail** SharePoint Designer
- **Remove** If this element is set ALL=TRUE then all The Click-to-Run products are removed.
- **Updates** The updates element allows you to configure how updates are managed and includes the following options:
  - **Enabled** When set to true, Click-to-Run update system will check for updates.
  - **UpdatePath** If this element is not set, updates will be retrieved from Microsoft servers on the Internet. If the element is set to a network, local, or HTTP path, then updates will be sourced from the specified path.
  - **TargetVersion** Allows you to have updates applied to a specific Office build version. If not specified, the most recent version is updated.
  - **Deadline** Specifies the deadline by which updates must be applied. You can use Deadline with Target Version to force Office applications to be updated to a specific version by a specific date. The Deadline will only apply to a single set of updates. To ensure that Office applications are always up-to-date, it is necessary to revise the deadline when new updates are available.

Thought experiment

Central deployment at Tailspin Toys

In this thought experiment, apply what you learned about this objective. You can find answers to these questions in the "Answers" section at the end of this chapter.

You are interested in centrally deploying Office 365 ProPlus at Tailspin Toys, but have to do some research to determine how to accomplish this task. With this in mind, you need to find answers to the following questions:

1. Which tool should you use to obtain the Office 365 ProPlus Click-to-Run files from the Microsoft servers on the Internet?

2. Which file should you edit to retrieve a specific version of the Office 365 ProPlus Click-to-Run files?

Objective summary

- The Office Deployment Tool is a command line utility used if you want to centralize the deployment of Office 365 Click-to-Run files from a location on your local area network.

- You can use the Office Deployment Tool to download the Office 365 Click-to-Run files and language pack files from Microsoft servers on the Internet.

- You use the Office Deployment Tool in download mode to retrieve files from the Microsoft servers on the Internet.

- You use the Office Deployment Tool in configure mode to install Office 365 using an installation source on the local area network.

- The configuration.xml file is used with the Office Deployment Tool in both download and configure mode. In download mode it allows you to specify which files are downloaded. In configure mode it allows you to specify how Office Click-to-Run applications and language packs are installed and how updates are applied.

Objective review

Answer the following questions to test your knowledge of the information in this objective. You can find the answers to these questions and explanations of why each answer choice is correct or incorrect in the "Answers" section at the end of the chapter.

1. Which element in the configuration.xml file for the Office Deployment Tool for Click-to-Run should you configure to prevent the installation of PowerPoint?

   A. ExcludeApp

   B. Updates

   C. Product ID

   D. OfficeClientEdition

2. Which element in the configuration.xml file for the Office Deployment Tool for Click-to-Run should you configure to retrieve the x64 Click-to-Run installation files from Microsoft servers on the Internet?

   A. ExcludeApp

   B. OfficeClientEdition

   C. Updates

   D. Product ID

3. Which element in the configuration.xml file for the Office Deployment Tool for Click-to-Run should you configure to specify how updates are managed?

   A. Updates

   B. Product ID

   C. ExcludeApp

   D. OfficeClientEdition

Objective 1.3: Set up telemetry and reporting

Office 365 ProPlus and Office 2013 both support gathering of telemetry data about how Office applications are being used in an environment. This objective deals with how you configure the collection of telemetry through Group Policy, how you configure a central repository for telemetry issues, how you can view local telemetry data, and what steps you can take to deploy the Telemetry Agent to computers that have versions of Office that do not automatically include telemetry functionality.

Set up telemetry service

Office Telemetry is a compatibility-monitoring framework. You can use it to assess Office compatibility issues. Office Telemetry provides similar functionality to the following Office 2010 compatibility tools:

- Office Migration Planning Manager
- Office Code Compatibility Inspector
- Office Environment Assessment Tool

Office Telemetry works with both Office 2013 and Office ProPlus and is included with the applications. Some Office Telemetry features are available for earlier versions of Office if the Office Telemetry Agent is installed on each computer running the previous version of Office.

> **MORE INFO** **OFFICE TELEMETRY**
>
> You can learn more about Office Telemetry at *https://technet.microsoft.com/en-us/library/jj863580.aspx.*

Deploy Telemetry Dashboard

The Telemetry Dashboard allows you to view information collected by the Telemetry Processor, a special server that you deploy on the network to collect telemetry information. The Telemetry Dashboard is installed automatically when you install Office 365 ProPlus, Office Professional Plus 2013, and Office Standard 2013. The Telemetry Dashboard is a specially configured Excel worksheet that connects to a database hosted on a supported SQL instance. You can start the Telemetry Dashboard in the following manner:

- On computers running Windows 7, Windows Server 2008, or Windows Server 2008 R2, click Telemetry Dashboard for Office 2013 in the Office 2013 Tools folder under Microsoft Office 2013.

- On computers running Windows 8 or Windows 8.1, type Telemetry Dashboard on the Start Screen.

- On computers running Windows Server 2012 or Windows Server 2012 R2, open the Search charm from the Start menu and type "Telemetry Dashboard for Office 2013," as shown in Figure 1-44.

FIGURE 1-43 Search for Telemetry Dashboard

Note that the name Telemetry Dashboard For Office 2013 applies even when the installed product is Office 365 ProPlus. You must have Excel installed to open the Telemetry Dashboard For Office 2013.

To use the Telemetry Dashboard for Office 2013, you need to configure a computer to function as the Telemetry Processor and a computer to host the SQL Server database used by the Telemetry Dashboard for Office 2013. The computer that functions as the Telemetry Processor and the computer that hosts the SQL Server database used by the Telemetry Dashboard can be the same computer.

You can use the following versions of SQL server to host the back-end database for the Telemetry Dashboard for Office 2013:

- SQL Server 2005
- SQL Server 2005 Express Edition
- SQL Server 2008
- SQL Server 2008 Express Edition
- SQL Server 2008 R2
- SQL Server 2008 R2 Express Edition
- SQL Server 2012
- SQL Server 2012 Express
- SQL Server 2014
- SQL Server 2014 Express

The Telemetry Dashboard for Office 2013 contains links from which you can download SQL Server Express.

Microsoft recommends that you host the Telemetry Processor role on a computer running one of the following operating systems:

- Windows Server 2008
- Windows Server 2008 R2
- Windows Server 2012
- Windows Server 2012 R2

After Windows Server 2016 is released, it is likely that it will be added to this list of recommended operating systems. Before deploying the Telemetry Processor, ensure that you have the following information:

- Name of the SQL Server Instance on which the Telemetry Dashboard will be created or where the database is already present.
- Permission to create and configure the database on the SQL Server. This needs to be a domain account that has been assigned the systems administrator role on the SQL Server instance.
- Permission to create a shared folder or the UNC path of an existing folder.
- 11 GB or more of free hard drive space on the computer that hosts the Telemetry Processor role.

To deploy the Telemetry Processor, perform the following steps:

1. Open the Telemetry Dashboard for Office 2013 spreadsheet and then click the Getting Started worksheet in the workbook.
2. Click the arrow next to Install Telemetry Processor, as shown in Figure 1-45.

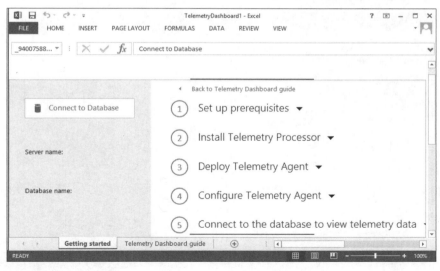

FIGURE 1-44 Getting Started

3. Under Install Telemetry Processor, click either the x86 or x64 link, as shown in Figure 1-45. For deployment of the Telemetry Processor on Windows Server 2012 R2, select the x64 option. While the x86 version will run, Windows Server 2012 R2 requires an x64 processor.

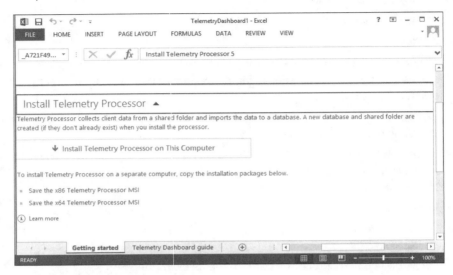

FIGURE 1-45 Install Telemetry Processor

4. Save the file to a location where you will be able to retrieve it. Figure 1-46 shows the file osmdp64.msi being saved to the desktop.

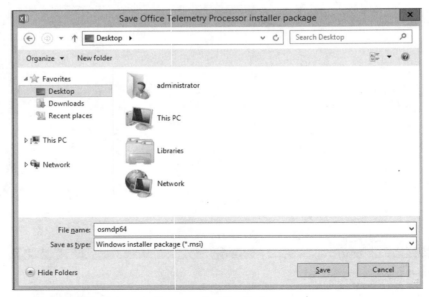

FIGURE 1-46 Office Telemetry Processor Installer Package

5. After the file has saved, double-click it to run the Telemetry Processor Installer.

6. On the Welcome To The Microsoft Office Telemetry Processor page of the Setup Wizard, shown in Figure 1-47, click Next.

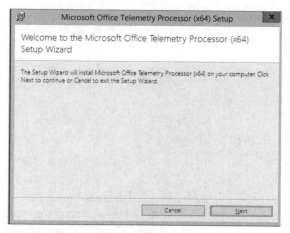

FIGURE 1-47 Welcome page

7. On the Completed the Microsoft Office Telemetry Processor page, ensure that Run The Office Telemetry Processor Settings Wizard Now option is selected, as shown in Figure 1-48, and click Finish.

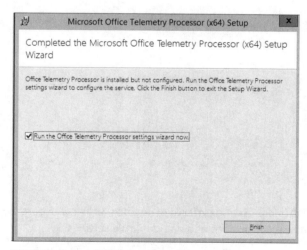

FIGURE 1-48 Installation complete, now run setup

8. On the Getting Started page of the Office Telemetry Processor Settings Wizard, review the information, as shown in Figure 1-49, and then click Next.

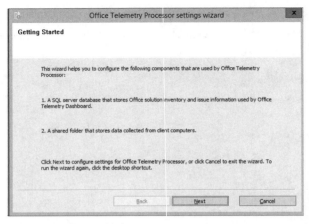

FIGURE 1-49 Setup requirements

9. On the Database Settings page, enter the name of the database server and click Connect. The connection will be made using the credentials of the currently signed-on user. Enter a name for the database and then click Create. Figure 1-50 shows a database named OfficeTelemetry. When the database is created, click Next.

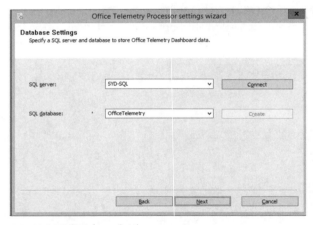

FIGURE 1-50 Database Settings

10. On the Office Telemetry Processor Settings Wizard dialog box, shown in Figure 1-51, click Yes to configure database permissions and database role settings.

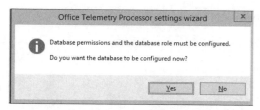

FIGURE 1-51 Database Permissions configuration

11. On the Shared Folder page, shown in Figure 1-52, click Browse.

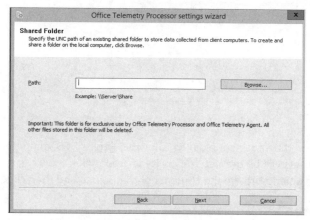

FIGURE 1-52 Shared Folder configuration

12. Create and select a shared folder, as shown in Figure 1-53. If you are going to use an existing folder, ensure that it is empty.

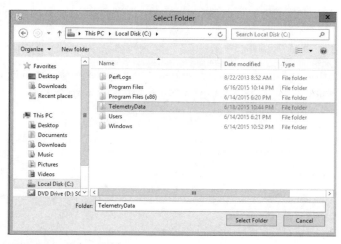

FIGURE 1-53 Select Folder

13. On the Shared Folder page, shown in Figure 1-54, click Next.

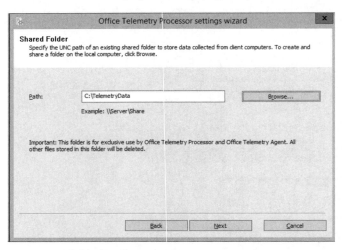

FIGURE 1-54 Folder location

14. Review the information on the information dialog, shown in Figure 1-55, that informs you that authenticated users will be granted the ability to create files and write data in the folder without being able to browse the contents of that folder, and then click Yes.

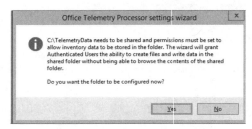

FIGURE 1-55 Permissions warning

15. On the Microsoft Customer Experience Improvement Program page, shown in Figure 1-56, decide if you want to participate in the Customer Experience Program.

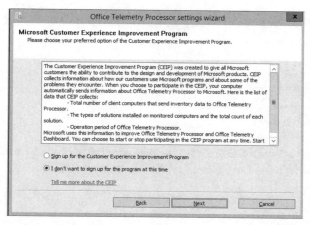

FIGURE 1-56 Customer Experience Improvement Program

16. On the Configuration Successful page, click Finish.

17. After the Telemetry Processor is deployed, return to the Telemetry Dashboard spreadsheet and on the Getting Started tab, under section 5: Connect To The Database To View Telemetry Data, as shown in Figure 1-57, click Connect To Database.

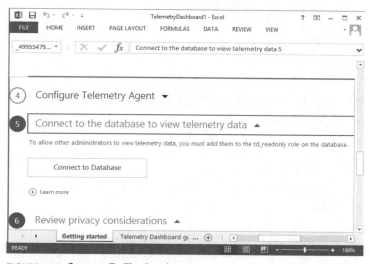

FIGURE 1-57 Connect To The Database

18. The Data Connection Settings dialog box, shown in Figure 1-58 should be automatically populated with the name of the SQL instance and the name of the database. Click Connect.

FIGURE 1-58 Data Connection Settings

19. Until you have configured telemetry collection, the Telemetry Dashboard will display a message informing you that there is no telemetry data, as shown in Figure 1-59.

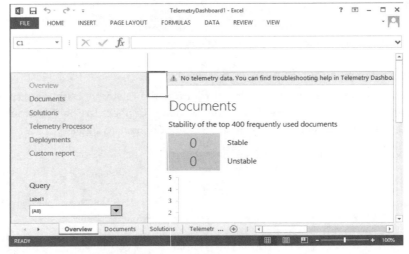

FIGURE 1-59 Telemetry information

> **MORE INFO DEPLOY TELEMETRY DASHBOARD**
>
> You can learn more about deploying the Telemetry Dashboard at *https://technet.microsoft.com/library/f69cde72-689d-421f-99b8-c51676c77717*.

Enable telemetry through Group Policy

Before you can enable telemetry through Group Policy, you need to install the Office 2013 Group Policy administrative template.

You can download the administrative template from the Microsoft website at *http://www.microsoft.com/en-us/download/details.aspx?id=35554*.

You'll need to download the file to a domain controller and then run it. If you are deploying to a Windows Server 2012 R2 domain controller, ensure that you download the 64-bit version of the administrative template file. This is because Windows Server 2012 R2 is an x64 platform. While the x86 version will likely also run, you should choose the architecture that matches the platform on which you will install the template.

When running the file downloaded from the Internet, you will be asked to agree to the license terms, as shown in Figure 1-60. When you have agreed to the license terms, click Continue.

FIGURE 1-60 Software License Terms

You will be asked to choose a temporary directory in which to extract the template files. After you have extracted the files, you will need to do the following:

- Copy the file Office15.admx to the C:\Windows\PolicyDefinitions folder.
- Copy the language appropriate Office15.adml file to the C:\Windows\PolicyDefinitions\ Language folder. For example, if using EN-US for US English, copy the Office15.adml file from the EN-US folder where you extracted the templates to the C:\Windows\Poli-cyDefinitions\en-US folder, as shown in Figure 1-61.

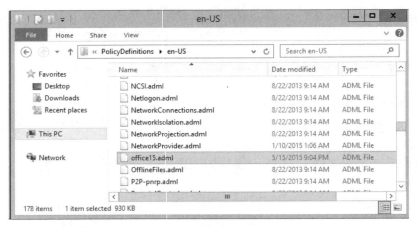

FIGURE 1-61 Office15.adml

When the ADMX and ADML files are copied across to the appropriate folders, you'll be able to edit the following policies, which are located in the User Configuration\Policies\Administrative Templates\Microsoft Office 2013\Telemetry Dashboard node shown in Figure 1-62.

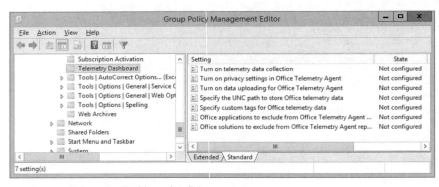

FIGURE 1-62 Telemetry Dashboard policies

TURN ON TELEMETRY DATA COLLECTION

The Turn On Telemetry Data Collection policy must be enabled, as shown in Figure 1-63, for telemetry data collection to be enabled. If this policy is not enabled, Office telemetry data collection will not occur.

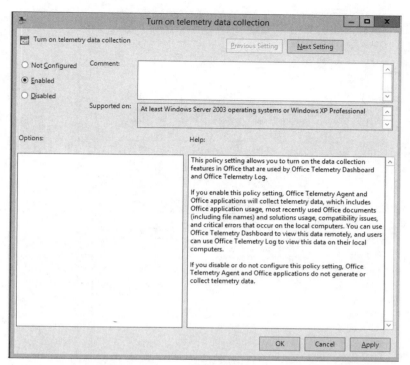

FIGURE 1-63 Turn On Telemetry Data Collection

TURN ON DATA UPLOADING FOR THE TELEMETRY AGENT

When you enable this policy, shown in Figure 1-64 Office telemetry data is uploaded to a shared folder specified in another policy. If you don't enable this policy, Office telemetry data is stored on the client and cannot be accessed at a central location through the Telemetry Dashboard.

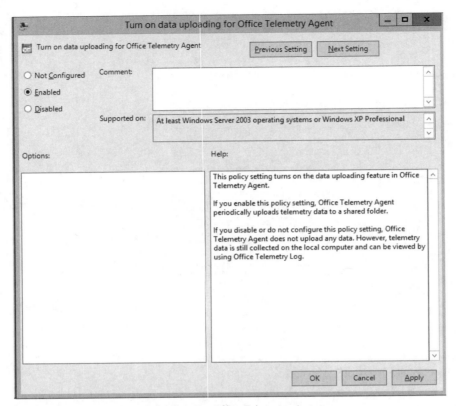

FIGURE 1-64 Turn On Data Uploading For Office Telemetry Agent

SPECIFY THE UNC PATH TO STORE OFFICE TELEMETRY DATA

If you have configured telemetry data to be uploaded to a shared folder using the Turn On Data Uploading For The Telemetry Agent policy, you'll need to configure this policy, shown in Figure 1-65, to specify the address to which the data will be uploaded.

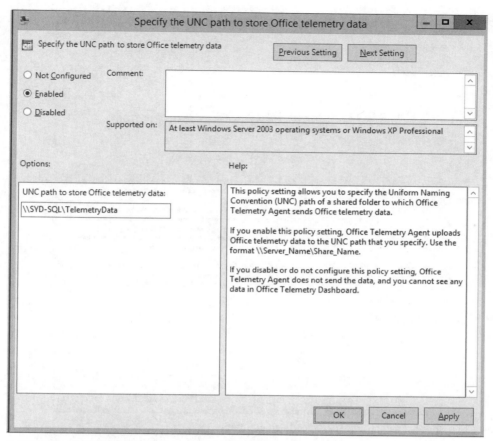

FIGURE 1-65 Specify The UNC Path To Store Office Telemetry Data

SPECIFY CUSTOM TAGS FOR OFFICE TELEMETRY DATA

The Specify Custom Tags For Office Telemetry Data allows you to apply tags to telemetry data forwarded to the shared folder used by the Telemetry Processor. You can specify up to four separate tags, as shown in Figure 1-66.

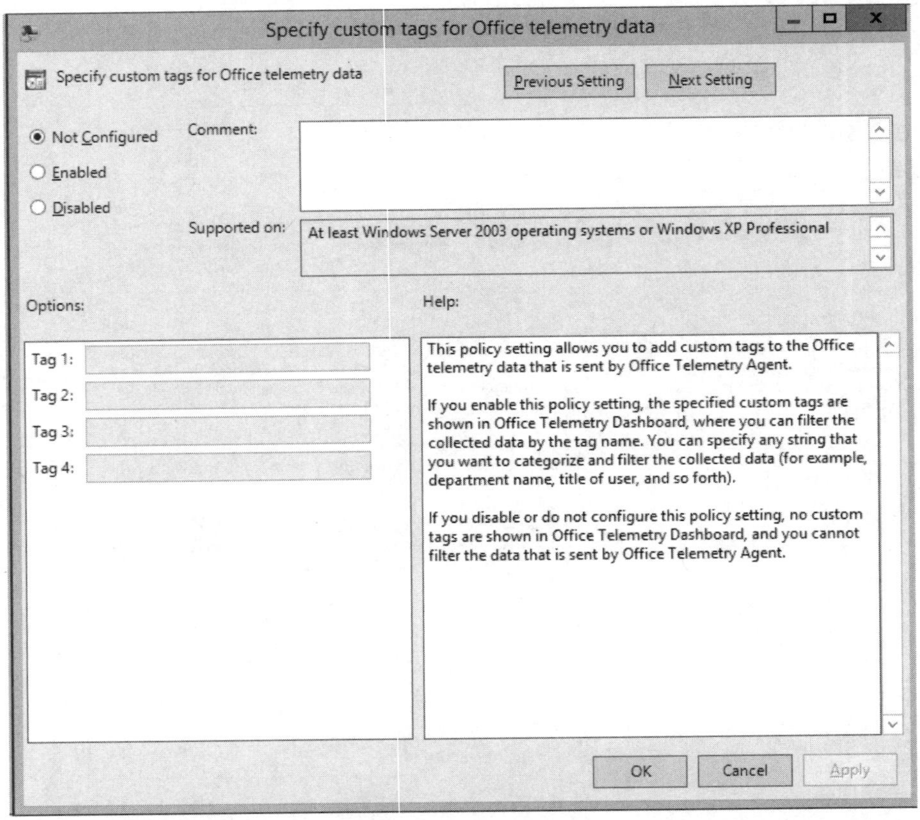

FIGURE 1-66 Specify Custom Tags For Office Telemetry Data

TURN ON PRIVACY SETTINGS IN TELEMETRY AGENT

Enabling this policy, shown in Figure 1-67, obfuscates the file name, file path, and title of Office documents before telemetry data uploads into the shared folder. If this policy is not enabled, the file name, path, and title of documents remain visible.

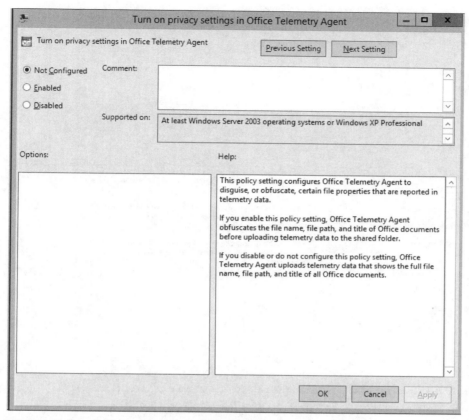

FIGURE 1-67 Turn On Privacy Settings In Office Telemetry Agent

OFFICE APPLICATIONS TO EXCLUDE FROM TELEMETRY AGENT REPORTING

You can use the Office Applications To Exclude From Office Telemetry Agent Reporting policy to exclude telemetry data from specific applications from being forwarded to the shared folder used by the Telemetry Processor. Figure 1-68 shows a configuration where telemetry from the Publisher and Visio applications will be excluded from being sent to the Telemetry Processor.

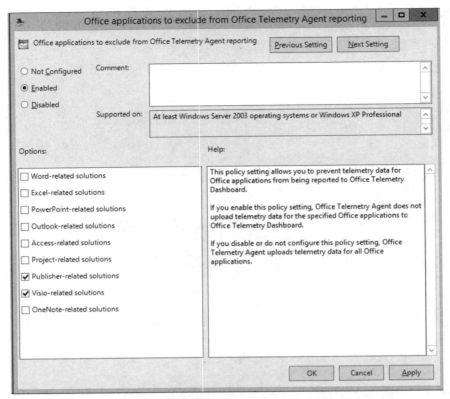

FIGURE 1-68 Office Applications To Exclude From Office Telemetry Agent Reporting

OFFICE SOLUTIONS TO EXCLUDE FROM TELEMETRY AGENT REPORTING

Configuring the Office Solutions To Exclude From Telemetry Agent Reporting policy allows you to stop telemetry data from the following Office solution categories from being forwarded to the Telemetry Processor:

- Office document files
- Office template files
- COM add-ins
- Application-specific add-ins
- Apps for Office

Figure 1-69 shows this policy configured so that telemetry from Office template files and COM add-ins won't be forwarded to the Telemetry Processor.

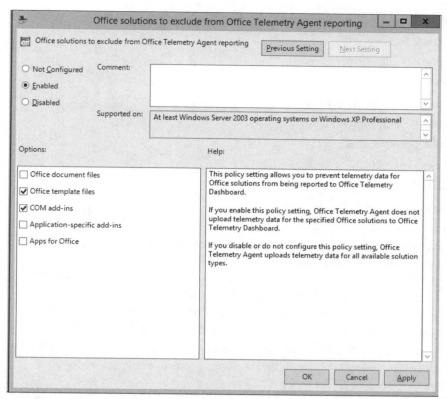

FIGURE 1-69 Office Solutions To Exclude From Office Telemetry Agent Reporting

> **MORE INFO** **TELEMETRY AGENT POLICY**
>
> You can learn more about configuring group policies related to the Telemetry Agent at *https://technet.microsoft.com/library/f69cde72-689d-421f-99b8-c51676c77717#agentpolicy*.

Deploy agent

Office Telemetry works natively with Office 2013 and Office ProPlus. This is because the Office Telemetry Agent is built into the Office 2013 and Office 365 ProPlus software. Office Telemetry will also work with newer versions of Office, including Office 2016.

To use Office Telemetry with Office 2003, Office 2007, and Office 2010 it is necessary to deploy special agent software. This agent will collect data about any installed Office add-ins as well as any documents that have been recently accessed. The Office Telemetry Agent for previous versions of Office collects inventory and usage data only. The Office Telemetry Agent for previous versions of Office does not collect application event data.

The Telemetry Agent is supported on the following 32-bit and 64-bit versions of Windows:

- Windows 8.1
- Windows 8
- Windows 7
- Windows Vista with Service Pack 2
- Windows XP with Service Pack 3
- Windows Server 2012 R2
- Windows Server 2012
- Windows Server 208 R2
- Windows Server 2008
- Windows Server 2003

While the Telemetry Agent is likely to be supported on Windows 10 and Windows Server 2016 when those products are released, it is important to remember that the separate Telemetry Agent software is only required if versions of Office prior to Office 2013 and Office ProPlus are in use. While Office 2010 and earlier can work on Windows 10 and Windows Server 2016, you will need to check the Microsoft website to determine whether Office 2010 or earlier is supported on the operating systems after they are released.

You can get the MSI files that allow for the installation of the Telemetry Agent through the Deploy Telemetry Agent section of the Getting Started worksheet of the Telemetry Dashboard, as shown in Figure 1-70.

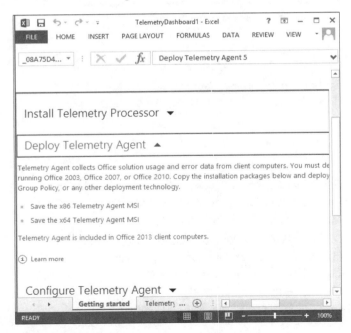

FIGURE 1-70 Deploy Telemetry Agent

Clicking on either the x86 or x64 Telemetry Agent MSI links will prompt you to save the Telemetry Agent Installer Package, as shown in Figure 1-71. These MSI files can then be deployed to computers using Group Policy, Microsoft Intune, System Center 2012 R2 Configuration Manager, or any other software deployment solution.

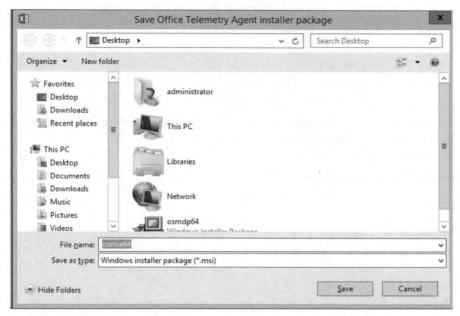

FIGURE 1-71 Save Telemetry Agent Installer Package

Telemetry Dashboard details

When connected to the telemetry database, the Telemetry Dashboard includes the following worksheets:

- **Overview worksheet**   This worksheet provides information about how documents and solutions are functioning on monitored computers. This worksheet provides a high-level view of solution and document stability.

- **Documents worksheet**   This worksheet provides a list of documents collected by Telemetry Agent scans and telemetry documents. This worksheet will provide you with information about the most frequently used documents in your organization.

  - **Document details worksheet**   Available through the documents worksheet, allows you to see which users are accessing a document.

  - **Document issues worksheet**   Available through the documents worksheet, allows you to learn about unique events related to a specific document, such as if the document was open during an application crash.

- **Document sessions worksheet** Available through the documents worksheet, shows session information during which issues occurred including data, user name, computer name, and domain information.

- **Solutions worksheet** Provides information about solutions collected by the Telemetry Log and Telemetry Agent scans. Solutions include COM add-ins, application specific add-ins, and apps for Office.

  - **Solution details worksheet** Available through the solutions worksheet, allows you to see which users are using a solution.

  - **Solution issues worksheet** Available through the solutions worksheet, allows you to discover the details of unique events related to a solution.

  - **Solution sessions worksheet** Available through the solutions worksheet, allows you to determine session information about events related to a solution, such as when it occurred, the user, and computer on which the event occurred.

- **Telemetry Processor worksheet** Provides information about the health of the Office Telemetry infrastructure. This worksheet is shown in Figure 1-73.

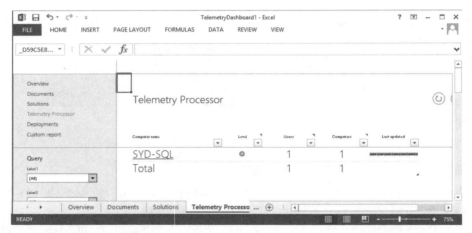

FIGURE 1-72 Telemetry Processor

- **Agents worksheet** Provides information about the users who have computers forwarding data to the Telemetry Processor.

- **Deployments worksheet** Provides information about the number of Office clients deployed in the organization.

- **Custom report worksheet** Creates relationships based on data in the database in a pivot table.

Configure Telemetry Agent through registry

In some scenarios, you will want to enable the collection of telemetry data from computers that are not members of an Active Directory domain and hence are not subject to Group Policy. In this scenario, you can create and import registry settings that will configure the Telemetry Agent. You can do this by using a text file with the .reg extension and then importing it into the registry. The example below shows the settings required to configure a computer to upload its data to the shared folder \\SYD-SQL\TelemetryData.

```
[HKEY_CURRENT_USER\Software\Policies\Microsoft\Office\15.0\osm]
"CommonFileShare"="\\\\SYD-SQL\\TelemetryData"
"Tag1"="<TAG1>"
"Tag2"="<TAG2>"
"Tag3"="<TAG3>"
"Tag4"="<TAG4>"
"AgentInitWait"=dword:00000258
"Enablelogging"=dword:00000001
"EnableUpload"=dword:00000001
"EnableFileObfuscation"=dword:00000000
"AgentRandomDelay"=dword:000000F0
```

Report user issues

The Office Telemetry Log is a local log file that is automatically installed when you install Office 2013 or Office 365 Pro Plus. The Office Telemetry Log tracks the solution types listed in Table 1-2 for Office 2013 and Office 365 ProPlus applications:

TABLE 1-2 Office Telemetry Log properties

Solution type	Applications	Description
Task pane apps	Excel, Word, Project	Apps located in the task pane of the client application
Content apps	Excel	Apps integrated into an Office document
Mail apps	Outlook	Apps that appear in Outlook, often when a message contains specific words or phrases
Active documents	Word, PowerPoint, Excel	<ul><li>Office binary files (.doc, .ppt, .pps, .xls)</li><li>Office OpenXML files (.docx, .pptx, .ppsx, .xlsx)</li><li>Macro-enabled files with Visual Basic for Applications (VBA) code (.docm, .dotm, .pptm, .potm, .xlsm, .xltm)</li><li>Files with ActiveX controls</li><li>Files with external data connections</li></ul>

COM add-ins	Word, PowerPoint, Excel, Outlook	COM add-ins, including Office development tools in Visual Studio application-level add-ins
Excel Automation add-ins	Excel	Excel-supported automation add-ins built on COM add-ins
Excel XLS RTD add-ins	Excel	Excels worksheets that use the RealTimeData worksheet function
Word WLL add-ins	Word	WLL are work-specific add-ins built with compilers that support the creation of DLLs
Application add-ins	Word, PowerPoint, Excel	Application-specific files that contain VBA code (.dotm, .xla, .xlam, .ppa, .ppam)
Templates	Word, PowerPoint, Excel	Application-specific templates (.dot, .dotx, .xlt, .xltx, .pot, .potx)

A file or solution must be either loaded or opened within the local Office application before information about it will be present in the Telemetry Log.

To open the Telemetry Log, on the start menu type "Telemetry Log For Office 2013," as shown in Figure 1-73. Use the name Telemetry Log For Office 2013 for both Office 2013 and Office 365 Pro Plus.

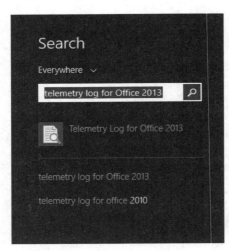

FIGURE 1-73 Telemetry Log Search

The events worksheet of the Telemetry Log shows event information (see Figure 1-74). This is the primary view of the log that you would use if attempting to diagnose user issues using the Telemetry Log.

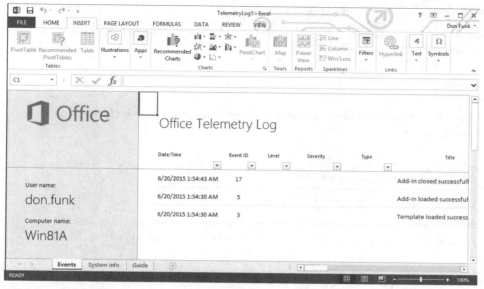

FIGURE 1-74 Telemetry Log

The System Info worksheet provides you with information about the computer on which the Telemetry Log is being run, including user name, computer name, system type, Windows edition, time zone, Telemetry Log version, and Office edition (see Figure 1-75).

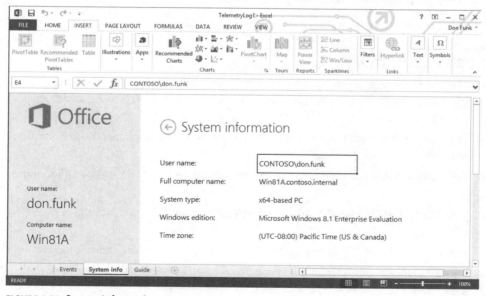

FIGURE 1-75 System Information

MORE INFO **OFFICE TELEMETRY LOG**

You can learn more about the Office Telemetry Log at *https://msdn.microsoft.com/en-us/library/office/jj230106.aspx.*

EXAM TIP

Remember which policies must be enabled to allow telemetry data to be forwarded to the Telemetry Processor.

Thought experiment

Telemetry Dashboard at Margie's Travel

In this thought experiment, apply what you learned about this objective. You can find answers to these questions in the "Answers" section at the end of this chapter.

You are in the process of preparing to use the Telemetry Dashboard to monitor your organization's Office 365 ProPlus deployment. As a part of this preparation, you need to find the answers to the following questions:

1. What is the role of the Telemetry Processor?

2. How do you configure a non-domain joined computer with Office 365 ProPlus to forward telemetry data to a specific specially configured shared folder used with the Telemetry Dashboard?

Objective summary

- The Telemetry Dashboard is a specially configured Excel workbook that connects to a SQL Server database and displays telemetry information from Office 2013 and Office 365 ProPlus.

- The Telemetry Processor is a computer that collects telemetry data and writes information to a SQL Server database.

- Telemetry collection settings are configured through Group Policy or by configuring the registry.

- Office 2013 and Office 365 ProPlus have telemetry collection built into the applications.

- Previous versions of Office require the deployment of a telemetry collection agent.

- A local version of the Telemetry Log can be accessed to help in the diagnosis of problems related to Office.

Objective review

Answer the following questions to test your knowledge of the information in this objective. You can find the answers to these questions and explanations of why each answer choice is correct or incorrect in the "Answers" section at the end of the chapter.

1. You want to determine on which computers and to which users issues with documents occurred. Which worksheet in the Telemetry Dashboard should you consult to determine this information?

   A. Solution sessions worksheet

   B. Solution issues worksheet

   C. Document sessions worksheet

   D. Document details worksheet

2. You want to determine which users are using a specific COM add-in. Which worksheet in the Telemetry Dashboard would allow you to determine this information?

   A. Solution sessions worksheet

   B. Solution details worksheet

   C. Document sessions worksheet

   D. Document details worksheet

3. You want to determine which users are accessing a specific document. Which worksheet in the Telemetry Dashboard would you use to determine this information?

   A. Document details worksheet

   B. Solution sessions worksheet

   C. Document sessions worksheet

   D. Solution details worksheet

4. You want to determine when problems with a specific COM add-in occurred, the computer the problem occurred on, as well as who was using the computer at the time. Which of the following worksheets in the Telemetry Dashboard would you use to determine this information?

   A. Document sessions worksheet

   B. Solution details worksheet

   C. Document details worksheet

   D. Solution sessions worksheet

Objective 1.4: Plan for Office clients

Just installing Outlook from the Office 365 portal doesn't configure it with a person's Office 365 user name and password. This objective deals with configuring Outlook and Skype for Business clients to use Office 365 accounts. It also deals with the Office Web Apps, known as Office Online, and the differences between Click-to-Run and MSI deployment formats.

> **This objective covers the following topics:**
> - Outlook client
> - Skype for Business Online client
> - Office on Demand
> - Office Web Apps
> - Click-to-Run versus MSI

Outlook client

The main task that is necessary to complete after Outlook is installed on a client computer is configuring access to the Exchange Online mailbox. You can add an Office 365 email account to the Outlook client by performing the following steps:

1. Open Outlook from the Start menu.
2. On the Welcome to Outlook 2013 page, shown in Figure 1-76, click Next.

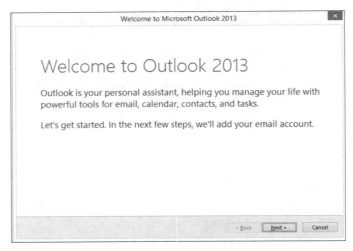

FIGURE 1-76 Welcome To Outlook 2013

3. On the Add An Email Account page, shown in Figure 1-77, select Yes and click Next.

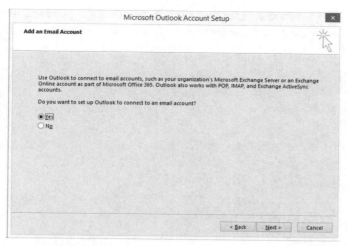

FIGURE 1-77 Add An Email Account

4. On the Auto Account Setup page, shown in Figure 1-78, provide the following information and click Next:

- Your name: user's real name.

- Email address: user's Office 365 email address. This will be the same as the user's Office 365 sign on name.

- Password: user's Office 365 password.

- Retype password: user's Office 365 password.

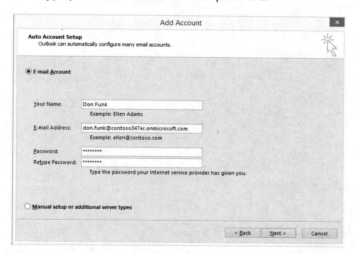

FIGURE 1-78 Auto Account Setup

5. You can be prompted a second time for the user's password on the Windows Security dialog box shown in Figure 1-79. Ensure that you select the Remember My Credentials option.

FIGURE 1-79 Windows Security

6. When the dialog box reports that Outlook has been able to successfully log on to the mail server, as shown in Figure 1-80, click Finish.

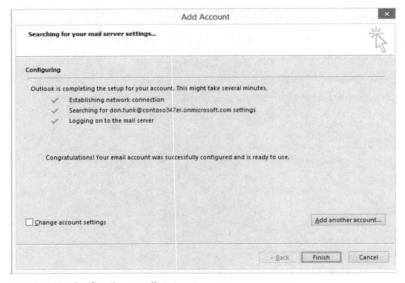

FIGURE 1-80 Configuring email account

> **MORE INFO USING OUTLOOK WITH OFFICE 365**
>
> You can learn more about Configuring Outlook for Office 365 at *https://support.office.com/ en-us/article/Set-up-email-in-Outlook-2013-or-2010-for-Office-365-6e27792a-9267-4aa4- 8bb6-c84ef146101b.*

Skype for Business Online client

The Skype for Business Online (previously known as Lync Online) client allows users to connect to Skype for Business Online to host or join meetings and instant message other Skype for Business Online users. To connect to Skype for Business Online, the user must enter their Office 365 email address, as shown in Figure 1-81 and then click Sign In.

FIGURE 1-81 Skype For Business

Users can be prompted for their Office 365 password. After they have successfully authenticated with the Skype for Business Online servers, they will be able to add contacts and join meetings from the client. Figure 1-82 shows the Skype for Business Online client.

FIGURE 1-82 Skype For Business Groups

MORE INFO **SKYPE FOR BUSINESS ONLINE**

You can learn more about the Skype for Business Online client at *https://technet.microsoft. com/enus/library/dn362805(v=ocs.15).aspx.*

Office on Demand

Office on Demand was a feature of Office 365 ProPlus that allowed users to download and temporarily install Office desktop applications. This installation did not count towards the typical five-installation activation limit for each Office 365 user. The idea of Office on Demand was to allow users to access the most recent version of Office applications when the latest version of Office was not available. Office on Demand applications were launched from a web browser after a special add-on was installed. The Office on Demand applications were streamed from Microsoft servers on the Internet and could only be used on computers that had an Internet connection. While the browser was used to launch the application, the application ran in a manner similar to the way a locally installed application ran, and was not like using Office Web Apps. Office on Demand was retired by Microsoft in November 2014.

> **MORE INFO OFFICE ON DEMAND**
>
> You can learn more about the retirement of Office on Demand at *https://community.of-fice365.com/en-us/f/172/t/259931*.

Office Web Apps

Office Web Apps allow you to access the basic functionality of a variety of Microsoft Office applications through a supported web browser. You can open Word Online, Excel Online, PowerPoint Online, and OneNote Online directly from the Office 365 portal, as shown in Figure 1-83.

FIGURE 1-83 Office Web Apps

People with Office 365 User Accounts will be able to access documents stored in organizational locations such as OneDrive for Business and SharePoint Online. Documents will also be able to be opened directly from the Outlook Web App or Lync Web App. Office Web Apps also support Azure RMS functionality on supported web browsers. Figure 1-84 shows the interface of the Word Online Office Web App.

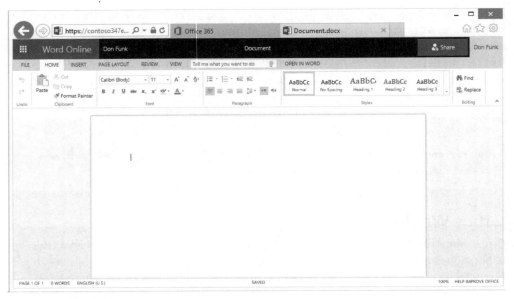

FIGURE 1-84 Word Online

MORE INFO **OFFICE WEB APPS**

You can learn more about Office Web Apps at *https://support.office.com/en-us/article/Get-started-with-Office-Online-in-Office-365-5622c7c9-721d-4b3d-8cb9-a7276c2470e5.*

Click-to-Run vs. MSI

Click-to-Run and MSI are two different formats through which Office applications can be distributed to users. Click-to-Run offers the following features:

- **Streaming installation** Streaming installation allows an application to be run before installation has completed. When the installation of an application is streamed, the first part of the application installed provides the minimum functionality necessary to get the application running. This allows the user to begin working with the application while installation completes.

- **Slipstreamed Servicing** The Click-to-Run functionality of Office 365 ProPlus means that updates are included in the installation. Rather than installing Office in a traditional manner and then running a Windows Update check to locate and install any relevant updates, relevant updates are already included within the Click-to-Run installation files. Slipstreamed Servicing means that end users have the most secure and up-to-date version of the application immediately, rather than having to wait for the post-deployment update cycle to complete.

- **User-based licensing**   User-based licensing means that the Office 365 ProPlus license is associated with the Office 365 user account, not the computer that the user is signed on to. Depending on the type of license associated with the user and the tenancy, the user is able to install Office 365 ProPlus on up to five different computers. It is possible to remove licenses from computers that have had Office 365 ProPlus installed on them at an earlier point in time.

- **Retail activation**   Office 365 ProPlus is activated using retail rather than volume license methods. Activation occurs over the Internet. As you learned earlier, this means that the computer must connect to the Internet every 30 days, otherwise Office ProPlus will enter reduced functionality mode.

- **SKU-level application suites**   Unless an administrator configures an appropriate configuration file, Office 365 ProPlus installs all products in the suite. The products that are installed will depend on the specifics of the Office 365 subscription, but this usually means Access, Excel, InfoPath, OneNote, Outlook, PowerPoint, Publisher, and Word. The products that are installed will be installed to all users in the tenancy. It is not possible to choose to install the PowerPoint program to some users but not to others when all users are using the same Click-to-Run installation file and configuration file. It is possible to have separate sets of applications deployed to users, but this requires separate configuration files for each set of applications.

- **Scenario limitations**   You cannot use Office 365 ProPlus with Remote Desktop Services, Windows To Go, or on networks that do not have a connection to the Internet.

MSI files are a method through which applications are packaged. MSI files allow organizational IT departments to automate the deployment applications, such as Office, using tools such as Microsoft Intune and System Center 2012 R2 Configuration Manager. MSI files are appropriate for organizations that have a managed desktop environment and are less suitable for the types of "Bring Your Own Device" scenarios in which Click-to-Run products, such as Office 365 ProPlus, are suitable. MSI files offer the following features:

- **Classic installation**   MSI files can be installed by double-clicking on the installer file, can be deployed using Group Policy, Microsoft Intune, System Center 2012 R2 Configuration Manager, or third-party application deployment products. The application is not available to the user until the installation of the application is complete. This differs from the Click-to-Run method's streaming technology which allows a user to begin using an application with a reduced set of features before the installation of the application completes.

- **Layered servicing**   MSI files represent the application at the time that it was packaged as an MSI file. This means that after deployment it will be necessary for the IT department to apply any necessary software updates to the application. Depending on the age of the MSI file and the number of software updates that have been released since the application was first packaged, it can take quite some time for the application to be updated to the current patch level after the application is deployed. This substantially increases the amount of time between an application being deployed and the user being able to use the application to perform their job role. IT departments can update MSI files with the latest updates and patches, but this is a complex, usually manual, process which requires deploying the application to a reference computer, updating the application, and then performing a technique known as a capture that creates the new updated MSI file. With Click-to-Run technology, the application updates are slipstreamed into the application by Microsoft, meaning that the application is current with updates as soon as it is deployed.

- **Volume licensing**   The versions of Office that you can deploy from an MSI file, including Office 2013 and Office 2016, have editions that support volume licensing. Volume licensing gives you the option of using a volume license key. Volume licensing is not something that is automatically supported by the MSI format and depends on the properties of the deployed software. Office 365 ProPlus does not support volume licensing. Volume licensing is only available to organizations that have volume licensing agreements with Microsoft.

- **Volume activation**   Like volume licensing, volume activation is not a property of an MSI file, but a feature that is supported by some versions of Office that use this packaging format. Volume activation allows large numbers of products to be activated, either through use of a special activation key used each time the installation is performed, or through technologies such as a Key Management Services (KMS) server on the organization's internal network. Volume activation is only available to organizations that have volume-licensing agreements.

- **Selective application installation**   Rather than deploying all products in the Office suite, the MSI-based deployment method makes it simple for organizations to deploy individual products in the suite. For example, it is possible to choose to deploy Word and Excel to some users, and PowerPoint to others.

- **Scenario limitations**   Unlike Click-to-Run Office 365 ProPlus, which uses retail activation,, the volume-licensed versions of Office 2013 can be used on Remote Desktop Services servers, can be deployed on Windows To Go USB devices, and can be deployed on networks that do not have Internet connectivity.

While there are differences between the Click-to-Run Office 365 ProPlus and MSI-based Office 2013, there are also certain similarities:

- Both can be configured through Group Policy.

- Both provide telemetry visible through the Telemetry Dashboard.

- Extensions designed for the Office 2013 version of a product will work with the Office 365 version of that product.

***MORE INFO* CLICK-TO-RUN VS. MSI**

You can learn more about Click-to-Run versus MSI at *http://blogs.technet.com/b/office_re-source_kit/archive/2013/03/05/the-new-office-garage-series-who-moved-my-msi.aspx*.

EXAM TIP

Remember that volume-licensing scenarios require MSI rather than Click-to-Run.

Thought experiment

Client configuration at Contoso

In this thought experiment, apply what you learned about this objective. You can find answers to these questions in the "Answers" section at the end of this chapter.

Don Funk is a user at Contoso. Don has just purchased a new consumer laptop for use at home and wants to set up Outlook and Skype for Business. Don signs in to his domain joined work computer using the contoso\don.funk user name. Don signs in to Office 365 using the don.funk@contoso.com user name. Single sign-on is configured with Office 365. With this in mind, answer the following questions:

1. Which user name should Don use when configuring Outlook email on the new computer?

2. Which user name should Don use when configuring Skype for Business on the new computer?

Objective summary

- Outlook can be configured by providing a user's Office 365 user name, which also functions as their email address and password.

- Skype for Business Online can be configured by providing a user's Office 365 user name, which also functions as their email address and password.

- Office on Demand allowed users to run temporary copies of Office launched through a special browser add-in. Office on Demand was discontinued by Microsoft in November 2014.

- Office Web Apps, also known as Office Online, provides browser-based versions of Word, Excel, PowerPoint, and OneNote. These versions provide only basic functionality.

- The Click-to-Run format has limitations that make it unsuitable for organizations that need to use volume licensing or do not allow client computers to connect to the Internet.

Objective review

Answer the following questions to test your knowledge of the information in this objective. You can find the answers to these questions and explanations of why each answer choice is correct or incorrect in the "Answers" section at the end of the chapter.

1. In which of the following scenarios are you unable to deploy Office 365 ProPlus through Click-to-Run?

   A. Installation on a Windows Server 2012 R2 Remote Desktop Services server

   B. Installation on a Windows To Go USB device

   C. Installation on an Internet-connected tablet running the Windows 8.1 Pro operating system

   D. On computers located on a network isolated from the Internet

2. Which of the following applications are available as Office Web Apps?

   A. Word

   B. Visio

   C. PowerPoint

   D. InfoPath

3. Which of the following statements about Office 365 ProPlus is true?

   A. Can be activated using a KMS server

   B. Supports Slipstreamed Servicing

   C. Supports computer-based licensing

   D. Applications can be run before installation completes

Answers

This section contains the solutions to the thought experiments and answers to the objective review questions in this chapter.

Objective 1.1: Thought experiment

1. You should tell the iPad users to sign in to the Office 365 portal. This will allow them to view the available Office 365-related apps for iPad. It will also provide them with direct links to those apps in the app store.

2. You should instruct them to sign in to their Office 365 accounts in each app so that they can gain access to documents stored in enterprise locations.

Objective 1.1: Review

1. **Correct answer:** B

   A. **Incorrect**: If Don had only performed four activations, he would be able to perform the activation required to successfully install and activate Office 365 ProPlus on his new laptop without deactivating any existing activation.

   B. **Correct:** If Don had performed five activations already, he would need to deactivate an existing activation to be able to successfully install and activate Office 365 ProPlus on his new laptop.

   C. **Incorrect**: Office 365 ProPlus can only be activated five times before deactivation becomes necessary. The only way that Don could have performed nine activations is if he had performed four deactivations.

   D. **Incorrect:** Office 365 ProPlus can only be activated five times before deactivation becomes necessary. The only way that Don could have performed ten activations is if he had performed five deactivations.

2. **Correct answers:** C and D

   A. **Incorrect:** Office 365 ProPlus is not supported on Windows Vista.

   B. **Incorrect:** Office 365 ProPlus is not supported on Windows XP.

   C. **Correct:** Office 365 ProPlus is supported on Windows Server 2008 R2, but not in a Remote Desktop Services configuration.

   D. **Correct:** Office 365 ProPlus is supported on Windows 8.1.

3. **Correct answer:** B

   A. **Incorrect:** A computer must be able to make a connection to the Office 365 servers on the Internet at least after every 30, not every 15, days.

   B. **Correct:** A computer must be able to make a connection to the Office 365 servers on the Internet at least after every 30 days.

   C. **Incorrect:** A computer must be able to make a connection to the Office 365 servers on the Internet at least after every 30, not every 90, days.

   D. **Incorrect:** A computer must be able to make a connection to the Office 365 servers on the Internet at least after every 30, not every 180, days.

Objective 1.2: Thought experiment

1. You should use the Office Deployment Tool, also known as the Office Deployment Tool for Click-to-Run, to obtain the Office 365 ProPlus Click-to-Run files from the Internet.

2. You must edit the configuration.xml files to specify a specific version of the Office 365 ProPlus files.

Objective 1.2: Review

1. **Correct answer:** A

   A. **Correct:** You use this element to exclude applications from being installed.

   B. **Incorrect:** The updates element allows you to configure how updates are managed.

   C. **Incorrect:** This element allows you to specify which products to install.

   D. **Incorrect:** This value determines whether the x86 or x64 version of Office applications are retrieved or installed.

2. **Correct answer:** B

   A. **Incorrect:** You use this element to exclude applications from being installed.

   B. **Correct:** This value determines whether the x86 or x64 version of Office applications are retrieved or installed.

   C. **Incorrect:** The updates element allows you to configure how updates are managed.

   D. **Incorrect:** This element allows you to specify which products to install.

3. **Correct answer:** A

   A. **Correct:** The updates element allows you to configure how updates are managed.

   B. **Incorrect:** This element allows you to specify which products to install.

   C. **Incorrect:** You use this element to exclude applications from being installed.

   D. **Incorrect:** This value determines whether the x86 or x64 version of Office applications are retrieved or installed.

Objective 1.3: Thought experiment

1. The Telemetry Processor takes data forwarded to the shared folder and processes it, forwarding it to the SQL Server database.

2. You need to edit the registry of the non-domain joined computer to configure it to forward telemetry data to a specific specially configured shared folder used with the Telemetry Dashboard.

Objective 1.3: Review

1. **Correct answer:** C

   A. **Incorrect:** This worksheet allows you to determine session information about events related to a solution, such as when it occurred, the user, and computer on which the event occurred.

   B. **Incorrect:** The solutions worksheet allows you to discover the details of unique events related to a solution.

   C. **Correct:** This worksheet shows session information during which issues occurred including data, user name, computer name, and domain information.

   D. **Incorrect:** This worksheet allows you to see which users are accessing a document.

2. **Correct answer:** B

   A. **Incorrect:** This worksheet allows you to determine session information about events related to a solution, such as when it occurred, the user, and computer on which the event occurred.

   B. **Correct:** This worksheet allows you to see which users are using a solution.

   C. **Incorrect:** This worksheet shows session information during which issues occurred including data, user name, computer name, and domain information.

   D. **Incorrect:** This worksheet, allows you to see which users are accessing a document.

3. **Correct answer:** A

   A. **Correct:** This worksheet, allows you to see which users are accessing a document.

   B. **Incorrect:** This worksheet allows you to determine session information about events related to a solution, such as when it occurred, the user, and computer on which the event occurred.

   C. **Incorrect:** This worksheet shows session information during which issues occurred including data, user name, computer name, and domain information.

   D. **Incorrect:** This worksheet allows you to see which users are using a solution.

4. **Correct answer:** D

   A. **Incorrect:** This worksheet shows session information during which issues occurred including data, user name, computer name, and domain information.

   B. **Incorrect:** This worksheet allows you to see which users are using a solution.

   C. **Incorrect:** This worksheet allows you to see which users are accessing a document.

   D. **Correct:** This worksheet allows you to determine session information about events related to a solution, such as when it occurred, the user, and computer on which the event occurred.

Objective 1.4: Thought experiment

1. Don Funk should use the user name don.funk@contoso.com when configuring Outlook email on the new computer.

2. Don Funk should use the user name don.funk@contoso.com when configuring Skype for Business on the new computer.

Objective 1.4: Review

1. **Correct answers**: A, B and D

   A. **Correct:** You cannot deploy Office 365 ProPlus through Click-to-Run on a Remote Desktop Services server. You can only use a version of Office that supports volume activation on a Remote Desktop Services server.

   B. **Correct:** You cannot deploy Office 365 ProPlus through Click-to-Run on a Windows To Go USB device. You can only use a version of Office that supports volume activation on a Windows To Go USB device.

   C. **Incorrect:** You can deploy Office 365 ProPlus on an Internet-connected tablet running the Windows 8.1 Pro operating system.

   D. **Correct:** You cannot deploy Office 365 ProPlus through Click-to-Run on a network isolated from the Internet as Office 365 ProPlus requires a connection to the Internet for activation to occur.

2. **Correct answers:** A and C

   A. **Correct:** Word is available as an Office Web App.

   B. **Incorrect:** Visio is not available as an Office Web App.

   C. **Correct:** PowerPoint is available as an Office Web App.

   D. **Incorrect:** InfoPath is not available as an Office Web App.

3. **Correct answers:** B and D

  A. **Incorrect:** Office 365 ProPlus must activate against Microsoft servers on the Internet.

  B. **Correct:** Office 365 ProPlus supports Slipstreamed Servicing.

  C. **Incorrect:** Office 365 ProPlus only supports user-based licensing.

  D. **Correct:** Office 365 ProPlus supports streaming installation, meaning that applications can be used with a minimal set of functionality prior to the completion of application installation.

CHAPTER 2

Provision SharePoint Online site collections

SharePoint Online allows collaboration for people within an organization, and also allows collaboration with people who are external to the organization. For many organizations, SharePoint Online has taken the place of the traditional shared file server when it comes to sharing documents. Understanding how to configure and manage SharePoint Online site collections is critical for an Office 365 administrator. Administrators must ensure that resources are externally shared when appropriate, and that access to resources is restricted when required.

Objectives in this chapter:

- Objective 2.1: Configure external user sharing
- Objective 2.2: Create SharePoint site collection
- Objective 2.3: Plan a collaboration solution

Objective 2.1: Configure external user sharing

This objective deals with the settings related to allowing people external to your organization's Office 365 tenancy access to content stored within SharePoint Online. There are a variety of sharing options, from allowing read and edit access to people with Microsoft accounts, to allowing read and edit access to anyone who has the correct URL for a document.

> **This objective covers the following topics:**
> - Enable external user sharing globally
> - Enable external user sharing per site collection
> - Share with external users
> - Remove external user access

Understanding external users

External users are people who need to collaborate with people in your organization using content hosted on SharePoint Online, but who haven't been provisioned with an organizational Office 365 or SharePoint Online license.

The use rights available to external users depend on the features available to the SharePoint Online tenancy with which they will collaborate. For example, if your organization has an E3 Enterprise Plan, and a SharePoint site uses enterprise features, the external user will be able to use and view those enterprise features.

External users can perform the following tasks:

- Can use Office Online to view and edit documents in the browser. Can use their own version of Office to interact with content hosted in SharePoint Online, but are not eligible for licenses to the tenancy's Office 365 Office ProPlus software.

- Perform tasks on the site commensurate with their permission level. For example, adding an external user to the Members group grants that user Edit permissions. They will be able to add, edit, and delete lists, list items, and documents.

- View other site content, including navigating to subsites to which they have been invited, and view site feeds.

External users are restricted from being able to perform the following tasks:

- Create personal sites
- Edit their profiles
- View the company-wide newsfeed
- Add storage to the tenant storage pool
- Enact searches against "everything" or access the Search Center
- Access site mailbox
- Access PowerBI features, including Power View, Power Pivot, Quick Explore, and Timeline Slicer
- Use eDiscovery
- Open downloaded documents protected by Azure Rights Management (it is still possible to open these documents using Office Online)
- Access SharePoint Online data connection libraries
- Use Excel Services features, such as Calculated Measures and Calculated Members, decoupled Pivot Tables and PivotCharts, Field List and Field support, filter enhancements, and Search Filters
- Use Visio Services

Enabling external user sharing globally

The external sharing options configured at the SharePoint Online tenancy level override those configured at the site collection level. You can configure the following global external sharing options shown in Figure 2-1:

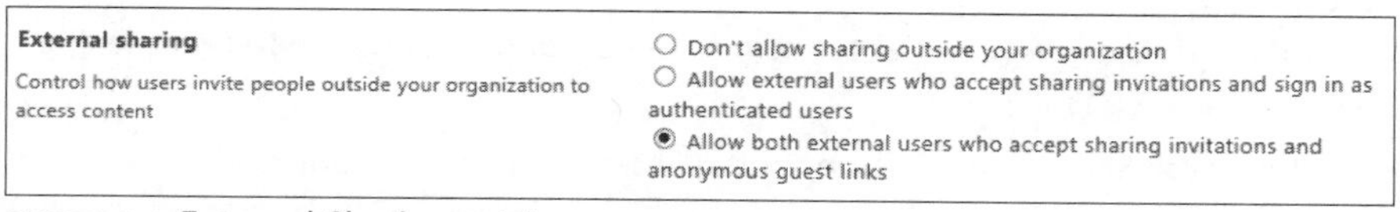

FIGURE 2-1 External Sharing settings

- Don't Allow Sharing Outside Your Organization.

    - Choosing this option prevents all users on all sites within the SharePoint Online tenancy from sharing sites or content with external users.

- Allow External Users Who Accept Sharing Invitations And Sign In As Authenticated Users.

    - Choosing this option requires external users who have invitations to view content or sites to sign in with a Microsoft account, such as an Outlook.com account.

    - Site owners and users with Full Control permissions are able to share sites with external users.

    - Site owners and users can choose to allow external users View or Edit permissions on documents.

    - All external users must sign in with a Microsoft account before they can access content.

    - Invitations to view content can only be redeemed once, and then are tied to the Microsoft account used for access. After an invitation has been used, it cannot be used by someone else to gain access with a separate set of Microsoft account priviledges.

- Allow Both External Users Who Accept Sharing Invitations And Guest Links.

    - Choose this option if you want to allow content to be shared with people who sign in with Microsoft accounts as well as allow anonymous guest links. Anonymous guest links allow access without any form of authentication.

    - Site owners and users with Full Control permission are able to share sites with external users.

    - Site owners and users with Full Control permission are able to choose between requiring sign-in or sending an anonymous guest link when sharing documents.

    - When sharing a document, site owners and users can select between granting View and Edit permissions.

    - All external users will be required to sign in with a Microsoft account before accessing content.

- Anonymous links can be shared and forwarded, meaning that unauthorized people can be granted the permission assigned when the document is shared with the anonymous guest link.

To configure external user sharing for the SharePoint Online tenancy, perform the following steps:

1. Sign in to the Office 365 Admin Center with a user account that has SharePoint Online administrator privileges.

2. Under Admin, click SharePoint. This opens the SharePoint Admin Center.

3. In the SharePoint Admin Center, click Settings, as shown in Figure 2-2.

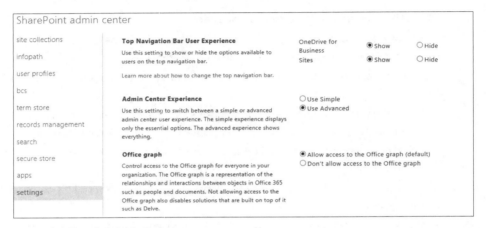

FIGURE 2-2 SharePoint Admin Center

4. Scroll down within the settings area until you get to the External Sharing section and choose between one of the three following options shown in Figure 2-3:

- Don't Allow Sharing Outside Your Organization
- Allow External Users Who Accept Sharing Invitations And Sign In As Authenticated Users
- Allow Both External Users Who Accept Sharing Invitations And Anonymous Guest Links

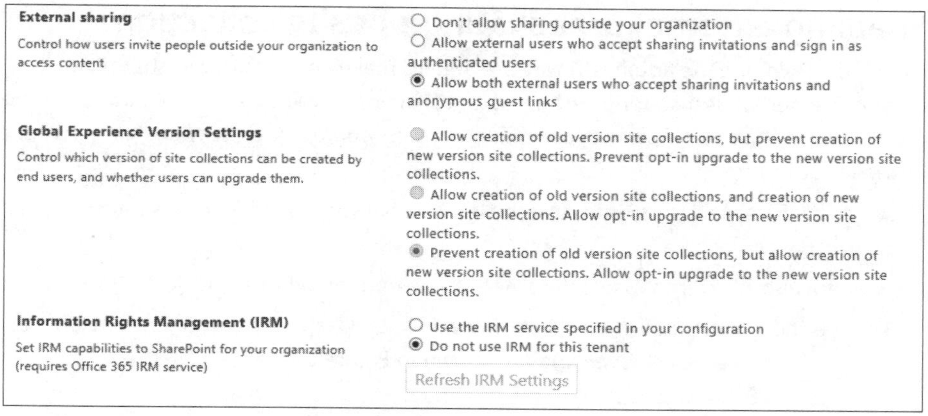

External sharing	○ Don't allow sharing outside your organization
Control how users invite people outside your organization to access content	○ Allow external users who accept sharing invitations and sign in as authenticated users
	● Allow both external users who accept sharing invitations and anonymous guest links
Global Experience Version Settings	○ Allow creation of old version site collections, but prevent creation of new version site collections. Prevent opt-in upgrade to the new version site collections.
Control which version of site collections can be created by end users, and whether users can upgrade them.	○ Allow creation of old version site collections, and creation of new version site collections. Allow opt-in upgrade to the new version site collections.
	● Prevent creation of old version site collections, but allow creation of new version site collections. Allow opt-in upgrade to the new version site collections.
Information Rights Management (IRM)	○ Use the IRM service specified in your configuration
Set IRM capabilities to SharePoint for your organization (requires Office 365 IRM service)	● Do not use IRM for this tenant
	Refresh IRM Settings

FIGURE 2-3 External Sharing settings

Turning off external sharing has the following consequences:

- If you disable and then re-enable external sharing, external users who have been granted access to content will regain access.

- If you disable and then re-enable external sharing, site collections that had sharing enabled will have sharing re-enabled.

- If you want to block specific site collections from having sharing re-enabled, disable external sharing on a per site collection basis prior to re-enabling external sharing.

- When you disable external sharing on a specific site collection, any configured External User permissions for that site collection are permanently deleted.

- Turning off external sharing at the site collection level disables guest links, but does not remove them. To remove access to specific documents, you need to disable anonymous guest links.

- Changes made to external access do not occur immediately, and might take up to 60 minutes.

MORE INFO **EXTERNAL SHARING**

You can learn more about external sharing at *https://support.office.com/en-us/article/ Manage-external-sharing-for-your-SharePoint-Online-environment-c8a462eb-0723-4b0b-8d0a-70feafe4be85*.

Enabling external user sharing per site collection

Only SharePoint Online administrators are able to make changes to the SharePoint Online tenancy's external user sharing settings. Site collection administrators are allowed to configure sharing settings on a per site collection basis as long as external user sharing is set to one of the following options:

- Allow External Users Who Accept Sharing Invitations And Sign In As Authenticated Users.

- Allow Both External Users Who Accept Sharing Invitations And Anonymous Guest Links

The sharing options at a site collection level are similar to those that are available at the SharePoint Online tenancy level, and are shown in Figure 2-4.

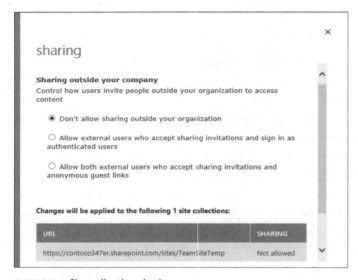

FIGURE 2-4 Site collection sharing

These options have the following properties:

- Don't Allow Sharing Outside Your Organization

  - Prevents all users on all sites in the collection from sharing sites or content with external users.

  - Users are unable to share content or sites with users who are not members of their organization's Office 365 tenancy.

  - If sharing had been enabled previously, any permissions assigned to external users will be deleted.

- Allow External Users Who Accept Sharing Invitations And Sign In As Authenticated Users

- Allow users with Microsoft accounts who have been sent invitations to access sites and content in a site collection.
- Site owners and users with Full permission can share sites and documents with external users who sign in with a Microsoft account.
- Invitations that are redeemed by external users are tied to the redeeming Microsoft account, and access cannot be shared with other Microsoft accounts.

- Allow Both External Users Who Accept Sharing Invitations And Anonymous Guest Links
  - Site owners and users will Full Control permissions are able to share sites and documents with external users.
  - Allows sites within a site collection that have been authenticated with Microsoft accounts to be shared with users.
  - Invitations that are redeemed by external users are tied to the redeeming Microsoft account. Access cannot be shared with other Microsoft accounts.
  - Site owners and users with Full Control permissions are able to share documents through an anonymous link.
  - When sharing documents with external users or through anonymous links, View or Edit permission can be assigned.
  - Anonymous links can be shared with the original sharer, having no control over which external parties access anonymously shared content after the guest link has been forwarded.

Settings configured at the SharePoint Online tenancy level determine those available at the individual site collection level. If sharing is only allowed for external users at the SharePoint Online tenancy level, the option to allow anonymous guest links to be sent at the site collection level will not be available. If sharing is blocked at the SharePoint Online tenancy level, then sharing will not be possible at the site collection level. Modifications to the external sharing settings for the My Site site collection apply to any existing personal sites as well as any personal sites created in the future.

To configure sharing at the site collection level, perform the following steps:

1. Sign in to the Office 365 Admin Center with a user account that has SharePoint Online administrator privileges.

2. Under Admin, click SharePoint. This will open the SharePoint Admin Center.

3. In the Site Collections area, select the site collection for which you want to configure sharing, and click Sharing in the Site Collections toolbar shown in Figure 2-5.

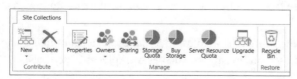

FIGURE 2-5 Site Collections

4. On the Sharing dialog box, shown in Figure 2-6, specify the type of sharing you want to enable, and click Save.

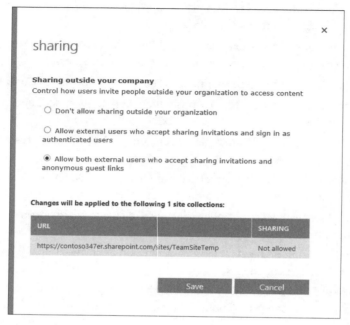

FIGURE 2-6 Sharing options

Sharing settings configured at the site collection level determine the sharing options available at the document level. If sending anonymous links is not allowed at the site collection level, it will not be allowed from a document hosted within a site in that collection.

> **MORE INFO SITE COLLECTION SHARING**
>
> You can learn more about sharing at the site collection level at *https://support.office. com/en-us/article/Manage-external-sharing-for-your-SharePoint-Online-environment-c8a462eb-0723-4b0b-8d0a-70feafe4be85*.

Sharing with external users

After sharing is appropriately configured at the SharePoint Online tenancy level and at the site collection level, there are three basic methods that allow you to share content with external users:

- Share an entire site and invite users to sign in using a Microsoft account (including Office 365 accounts from separate organizations, such as workplaces or schools).
- Share individual documents by inviting external users to sign in using a Microsoft account.

- Send users a guest link that allows users external to the organization access to each individual document that you want to share anonymously.

Sharing a site

To share a site with an external user, perform the following steps:

1. Sign in to Office 365 with an account that has permission to share the site. Select Sites from the list of My Apps as shown in Figure 2-7.

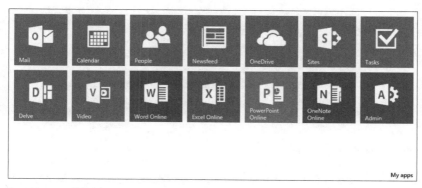

FIGURE 2-7 Office 365 Apps

2. In the list of sites, select the site that you want to share.

3. In the upper right-hand corner of the Site page, click Share, as shown in Figure 2-8.

FIGURE 2-8 Share

4. On the Share Site dialog box, shown in Figure 2-9, provide the name of the person with whom you want to share the site, specify the permission level, and click Share. You can choose between the following levels:
   - Excel Services Viewers [View Only]
   - Team Site Members [Edit]
   - Team Site Owners [Full Control]
   - Team Site Visitors [Read]

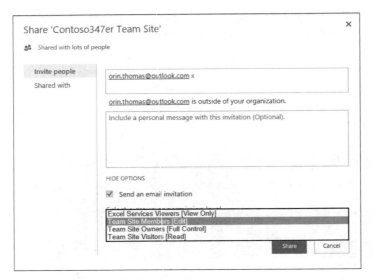

FIGURE 2-9 Team Site sharing

An invitation will automatically be sent to the person or people who you invited. If the invitation isn't accepted within seven days, it will expire. Users accepting an invitation must sign in with a Microsoft account, such as an Outlook.com or Hotmail.com account, or an Office 365 account.

You can determine which external users a SharePoint Online site collection has been shared with by performing the following steps:

1. Sign in to Office 365 with an account that has permission to share the site and select Sites from the list of My Apps.

2. In the list of sites, select the site that you want to share.

3. In the upper right-hand corner of the Site page, click Share, as shown in Figure 2-10.

FIGURE 2-10 Share

4. On the Share Site dialog box, click Shared With, as shown in Figure 2-11. The dialog box will list all users with whom the site collection has been shared.

FIGURE 2-11 Shared With

Sharing a document

There are two ways to share a document: sharing with an external user who must authenticate and sharing through an anonymous guest link.

To share with an external user who must authenticate using a Microsoft account, which includes the option of using an Office 365 account, perform the following steps:

1. Sign in to Office 365 with an account that has permission to share the site, and select Sites from the list of My Apps.

2. In the list of sites, select the site that hosts the document that you want to to share.

3. Next to the document that you want to share, click the ellipses and then click Share, as shown in Figure 2-12.

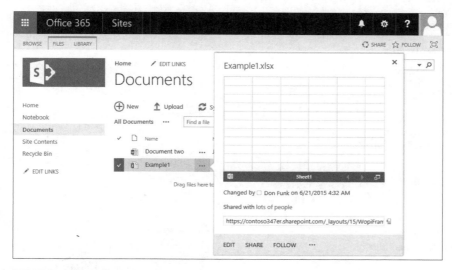

FIGURE 2-12 Share Document

4. On the Share page, select Invite People and then type the Microsoft account addresses of the people with whom you want to share the document. You can choose between the permissions Can Edit and Can View. Select the Require Sign-In check box to require the account be used to sign in. If this option is not selected, a link will be generated and forwarded to the email address provided. Figure 2-13 shows the document Example1 shared to the Microsoft account orin.thomas@outlook.com, with the permission that allows the user of that account to edit the document.

FIGURE 2-13 Share document

5. Click Share to share the document.

You can view the Shared With section of the Shared dialog box to view a list of users who have access to this shared document. Figure 2-14 shows the document Example1 shared with Orin Thomas.

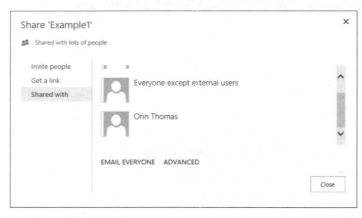

FIGURE 2-14 Shared With

The process of creating a shared link is similar. Sign in to Office 365, locate the document that you want to share, and then open the Sharing dialog box by clicking the ellipses next to the file and clicking Share. On the Get A Link section, you have the option of creating a View Only link, an Edit link, or both. Figure 2-15 shows a document where a View Only link and an Edit link have been created. You can click Disable on this dialog box to disable one or both links.

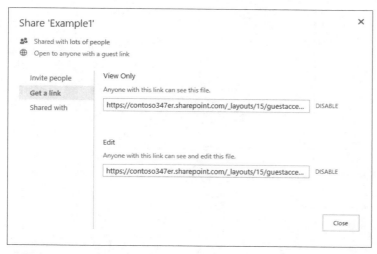

FIGURE 2-15 Get A Link

MORE INFO **SHARE SITES OR DOCUMENTS WITH EXTERNAL USERS**

You can learn more about sharing sites or documents with external users at *https://support. office.com/en-us/article/Share-sites-or-documents-with-people-outside-your-organiza- tion-80e49744-e30f-44db-8d51-16661b1d4232*.

Removing external user access

You can revoke external user access to a site only after a user has accepted their invitation. You can revoke access by removing the external user's permission to the site. To revoke ac- cess, perform the following steps:

1. Sign in to Office 365 with an account that has permission to share the site and select Sites from the list of My Apps.

2. In the list of sites, select the site that you want to share.

3. Select Settings, which is represented as a cogwheel, and then click Site Settings, as shown in Figure 2-16.

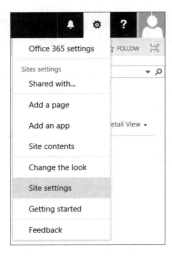

FIGURE 2-16 Site Settings

4. Under Users And Permissions, click People And Groups, as shown in Figure 2-17.

FIGURE 2-17 Site Settings

5. Select the external user from whom you want to revoke access. Figure 2-18 shows the Orin Thomas external user selected.

FIGURE 2-18 People And Groups

6. From the Actions menu, click Remove Users From Group, as shown in Figure 2-19.

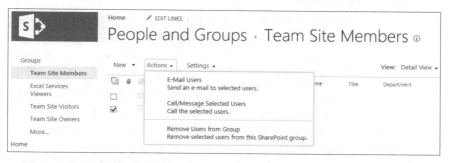

FIGURE 2-19 Remove Users From Group

7. When prompted about removing users from the group, as shown in Figure 2-20, click OK.

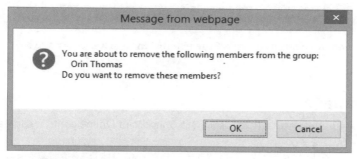

FIGURE 2-20 Confirmation message

There is no way, at the SharePoint Online tenancy level, to determine all of the sites to which an external user has been granted access. It is necessary to view the settings for individual sites to determine if a specific external user has been granted access to the site. There is also no method, at the SharePoint Online tenancy level, to determine which documents have been shared externally.

> **MORE INFO** **REVOKE USER ACCESS**
>
> You can learn more about revoking user access at *https://support.office.com/en-us/article/Share-sites-or-documents-with-people-outside-your-organization-80e49744-e30f-44db-8d51-16661b1d4232*.

EXAM TIP

Remember that the sharing settings configured at the SharePoint Online level will override the settings that can be configured at the site collection level.

Thought experiment

Removing external user access at Contoso

In this thought experiment, apply what you learned about this objective. You can find answers to these questions in the "Answers" section at the end of this chapter.

After performing an audit of how content was being shared from your organization's SharePoint Online tenancy, management has decided that it will no longer allow users to share content with users anonymously. In the future, all content shared with external users can only be shared if the user has a Microsoft or an Office 365 account. Management is also concerned about one external user, Kim, who has had content shared with her across multiple site collections. Kim has recently started working for a competitor and management wants to remove her current access to information in your organization's SharePoint Online site collections. With this information in mind, answer the following questions:

1. What's the quickest method of stopping anonymous users from accessing SharePoint Online content?

2. What steps need to be taken to remove the external user's access from site collections?

Objective summary

- External users are people with whom Office 365 SharePoint Online content can be shared.
- External users can authenticate with a Microsoft account, including an Office 365 account that is not part of the organization's tenancy.
- At the global level, you can configure an option for block sharing to external users, allow external users who have authenticated with Microsoft, or allow users who have authenticated with a Microsoft account and who have been provided with an anonymous link.
- Site owners and users who have Full Control permissions on a site are able to share sites with external users.
- Invitations sent to external users remain valid for seven days.
- Sharing settings configured at the SharePoint Online tenancy level determine the sharing options available at the site collection level. If sharing is blocked at the tenancy level, it is not available at the site collection level.
- Sharing settings configured at the site collection level determine the sharing options available at the document level.

Objective review

Answer the following questions to test your knowledge of the information in this objective. You can find the answers to these questions and explanations of why each answer choice is correct or incorrect in the "Answers" section at the end of this chapter.

1. How many days does an invitation to access shared content sent to an external user from an Office 365 SharePoint Site collection remain valid before it expires?

   A. 7 days

   B. 14 days

   C. 21 days

   D. 28 days

2. You want to block users sharing links and require all external users accessing shared content to authenticate using a Microsoft account. Which of the following steps can you take to accomplish this goal with a minimum amount of administrative effort?

   A. Disable sharing at the SharePoint Online tenancy level

   B. Restrict sharing to authenticated users at the SharePoint Online tenancy level

   C. Restrict sharing to authenticated users in each site collection

   D. Disable sharing in each site collection

3. You want to allow users in your organization's Office 365 tenancy to email links that will allow anonymous access to specific documents hosted in a specific site collection. Which of the following settings must be configured to allow this to occur? (Choose two. Each answer forms part of a complete solution.)

   A. Configure the Allow Both External Users Who Accept Sharing Invitations And Anonymous Guest Links option at the site collection level

   B. Configure the Allow External Users Who Accept Sharing Invitations And Sign In As Authenticated Users option at the site collection level

   C. Configure the Allow External Users Who Accept Sharing Invitations And Sign In As Authenticated Users option at the SharePoint Online tenancy level

   D. Configure the Allow Both External Users Who Accept Sharing Invitations And Anonymous Guest Links option at the SharePoint Online tenancy level

4. In most circumstances, you want to allow users in your organization to be able to send anonymous links to people outside your organization to documents hosted in site collections in your organization's Office 365 SharePoint Online tenancy. However, you want to ensure that anonymous links can't be used for documents hosted in a specific site collection. Documents in the site collection should be able to be shared with external users who have authenticated with a Microsoft account. With this in mind, which of the following settings should be configured to accomplish this goal? (Choose two. Each answer forms part of a complete solution.)

   A. Configure the Allow Both External Users Who Accept Sharing Invitations And Anonymous Guest Links option at the SharePoint Online tenancy level

B. Configure the Allow External Users Who Accept Sharing Invitations And Sign In As Authenticated Users option at the SharePoint Online tenancy level

C. Configure the Allow External Users Who Accept Sharing Invitations And Sign In As Authenticated Users option at the site collection level for the specific site collection where you want to block anonymous links

D. Configure the Allow Both External Users Who Accept Sharing Invitations And Anonymous Guest Links option at the site collection level for the specific site collection where you want to block anonymous links

5. After sensitive documents were leaked from your organization, you want to block all sharing of content hosted in SharePoint Online to people external to your organization. Which of the following steps could you take to accomplish this goal with a minimum amount of administrative effort?

A. Configure the Don't Allow Sharing Outside Your Organization option in the sharing settings of each site collection

B. Configure the Allow External Users Who Accept Sharing Invitations And Sign In As Authenticated Users at the SharePoint Online tenancy level

C. Configure the Allow Both External Users Who Accept Sharing Invitations And Anonymous Guest Links at the SharePoint Online tenancy level

D. Configure the Don't Allow Sharing Outside Your Organization option at the SharePoint Online tenancy level

Objective 2.2: Create SharePoint site collection

This objective deals with creating and managing SharePoint site collections. To master this objective, you'll need to understand how to configure a user as a site collection administrator, how to configure resource quotas, how to apply storage quotas, and other aspects of managing site collections within SharePoint Online.

This objective covers the following topics:
- Site collection administrators
- Resource quotas
- Configure public website
- Set storage quota for site collection
- Manage site collections

Understanding site collection administrators

Site collection administrators are users who have permission to manage SharePoint Online at the top of a specified site collection. A site collection administrator has permissions over all content in the site collection, including all subsites. Each site collection is a separate permissions root. For example, a site collection that has the URL *http://contoso347er.sharepoint.com/ sites/Research* does not have the same permissions as the site collection *http://contoso347er. sharepoint.com*.

A site collection has only one primary administrator, but can have multiple site collection administrators. A primary site collection administrator receives administrative email alerts for the site collection.

To configure site collection administrators for a site collection, perform the following steps:

1. Sign in to the Office 365 Admin Center with a user account that has SharePoint Online administrator privileges.

2. Under Admin, click SharePoint. This will open the SharePoint Admin Center.

3. Click Site Collections.

4. In the list of Site Collections, select the site for which you want to configure the site collection administrators. Figure 2-21 shows the site collection *https://contoso347er. sharepoint.com/sites/TeamSiteTemp* selected.

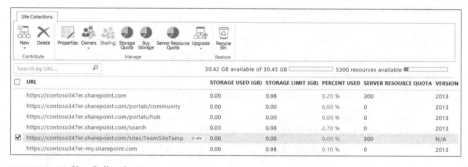

FIGURE 2-21 Site Collections

5. In the Site Collections section, click Owners and then click Manage Administrators as shown in Figure 2-22.

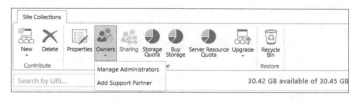

FIGURE 2-22 Manage Administrators

6. On the Manage Administrators dialog box, you can change the name of the Primary Site Collection Administrator, which is set when the site collection is created, and add the names of additional Site Collection Administrators. Figure 2-23 shows Don Funk set as the Primary Site Collection Administrator with Kim Akers and Dan Jump set as Site Collection Administrators.

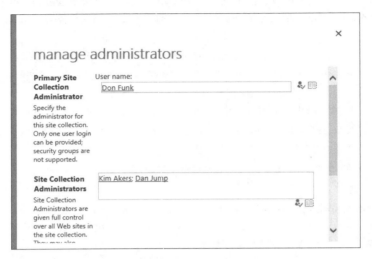

FIGURE 2-23 Manage Administrators

7. You can use the Check Names button to verify that the names entered are correct. When entering more than one name in the Site Collection Administrators text box, separate each name using a semicolon.

8. Click OK to assign the site collection administrator settings to the site collection.

> **MORE INFO SITE COLLECTION ADMINISTRATORS**
>
> You can learn more about site collection administrators at *https://support.office.com/en-au/article/Manage-administrators-for-a-site-collection-9a7e46f9-3fc4-4297-955a-82cb292a5be0*.

Understanding resource quotas

Server resources are a numerical way of representing server resources, including RAM and CPU utilization. Each SharePoint Online deployment is allocated a server resource figure based on the number of user licenses. This server resource figure is shared across all site collections. You can view the amount of resources available for a collection on the Site Collections page. Figure 2-24 shows a tenancy where 5,300 resources are available.

FIGURE 2-24 Resource quotas

Organizations that have customized site collections or sandboxed solutions can use resource quotas to ensure that resources, such as server CPU and RAM, aren't exhausted across the tenancy. If the number of resources used in a 24-hour period exceeds the resources available, SharePoint Online turns off the sandbox. When the sandbox is turned off, custom code will not run. The sandbox will be turned back on when the 24-hour period expires and the resource number is reset.

By applying resource quotas to specific collections, administrators can ensure that custom code running in specific site collections does not deplete all server resources assigned to the tenancy. Purchasing extra user licenses will increase the overall resource allocation to the tenancy.

To configure a resource quota for a specific site collection, perform the following steps:

1. Sign in to the Office 365 Admin Center with a user account that has SharePoint Online administrator privileges.

2. Under Admin, click SharePoint. This will open the SharePoint Admin Center.

3. Click Site Collections.

4. Select the site collection for which you want to configure the resource quota and then click Server Resource Quota. Figure 2-25 shows the site collection *https://contoso347er. sharepoint.com/sites/TeamSiteTemp* selected.

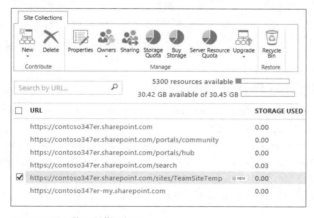

FIGURE 2-25 Site Collections

5. On the Set Server Resource Quota page, specify the number of server resources to be assigned to the collection. You can also configure an email to be sent to the primary site collection administrator when the resource utilization reaches a specific percentage of the assigned quota. Figure 2-26 shows a quota set to 300 and an email alert configured to be sent when the quota reached 95 percent.

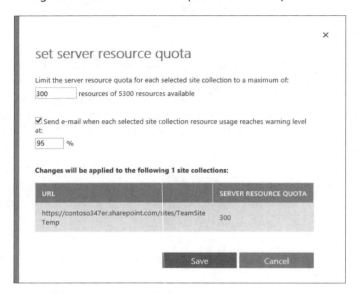

FIGURE 2-26 Server Resource Quota

6. Click Save to apply the new quota to the site collection.

> **MORE INFO RESOURCE QUOTAS**
>
> You can learn more about resource quotas at *https://support.office.com/en-us/article/ Manage-SharePoint-Online-server-resource-quotas-for-sandboxed-solutions-90e4e- aaa-899a-48d6-b850-f272366bf8cc.*

Using SharePoint Online Public Websites

SharePoint Online Public Websites were a feature that allowed organizations to create an online presence accessible to clients on the Internet without requiring authentication. As of March 2015, the SharePoint Online Public Website feature was not available to new Office 365 customers. Existing Office 365 customers will be able to use the SharePoint Online Public Website feature until March 2017. While this feature appears in the current 70-347 exam objectives, the feature becoming unavailable means that items related to it will be withdrawn from the exam.

Setting storage quota for site collection

Storage quotas determine how much storage space can be used. Office 365 tenancies are allocated an amount of storage space for SharePoint Online based on the number of users associated with the tenancy. The amount of storage space allocated to SharePoint Online uses the formula 10 GB plus 500 MB per user. For example, if an organization has 40 users associated with its Office 365 tenancy, the amount of storage space allocated to SharePoint Online is: 10 GB plus (500 MB * 40) equals 20 GB. It's possible for organizations to purchase additional storage on top of this initial allocation, as needed. Additional storage is allocated and on a GB per month basis. A site collection can be allocated a maximum of 1 TB of storage.

You can view the current amount of storage allocated to the tenancy by performing the following steps:

1. Sign in to the Office 365 Admin Center with a user account that has SharePoint Online administrator privileges.

2. Under Admin, click SharePoint. This will open the SharePoint Admin Center.

3. Click Site Collections. In the Site Collections area, you will be able to see the resources available as well as the remaining storage available. Figure 2-27 shows 30.42 GB available out of 30.45 GB.

FIGURE 2-27 Storage use

This storage allocation is available to all site collections associated with the tenant. It functions as a central storage pool from which all SharePoint Online storage can be allocated.

You can purchase additional storage for a tenancy by performing the following steps:

1. Sign in to the Office 365 Admin Center with a user account that has SharePoint Online administrator privileges.

2. Under Admin, click SharePoint. This will open the SharePoint Admin Center.

3. In the Site Collections area, shown in Figure 2-28, click Buy Storage.

FIGURE 2-28 Site Collections menu

4. You will need to re-sign in to Office 365 with an account with tenancy Administrator permissions or Billing Administrator permissions.

5. On the Manage Subscription page, select the subscription that you would like to add additional storage to and click the Add More link next to the text that indicates the number of current licenses.

6. In the section named Optional Add-Ons, enter the additional storage in GB that you want to add to the tenancy. It is not necessary to enter information in the user license field, though you can also use this section of the Manage Subscription page to add additional user licenses to a subscription.

7. Click Add licenses and then click Place Order.

There are two ways of allocating storage:

- **Automatically** You can choose to use the pooled storage model.
- **Manually** Allows you to manually configure storage allocations on a per-site collection basis.

> *MORE INFO* **ADD STORAGE TO SHAREPOINT ONLINE**
>
> You can learn more about adding extra storage to SharePoint online at *http://blogs.technet. com/b/lystavlen/archive/2012/07/11/how-to-add-extra-storage-to-sharepoint-online.aspx.*

Pooled storage model

The pooled storage model is a feature of SharePoint Online introduced in 2015. The pooled storage model allows SharePoint Online to manage storage automatically rather than storage management being a task performed manually by an administrator. The pooled storage model will be the default setting for new subscriptions created after late 2015.

If your organization has an existing Office 365 subscription, will need to enable the pooled storage model manually. When you do this, SharePoint Online removes the existing limits that you have configured for site collections and reset the limits to 1 TB.

To configure an Office 365 tenancy to use the pooled storage model for SharePoint Online, perform the following steps:

1. Sign in to the Office 365 Admin Center with a user account that has SharePoint Online administrator privileges.

2. Under Admin, click SharePoint. This will open the SharePoint Admin Center as shown in Figure 2-29.

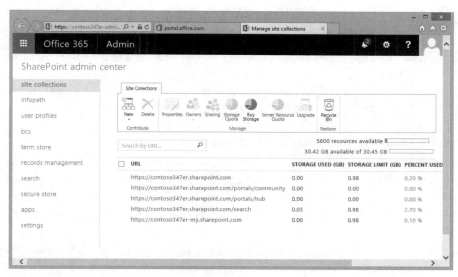

FIGURE 2-29 SharePoint Admin Center

3. In the SharePoint Admin Center, select Settings, as shown in Figure 2-30.

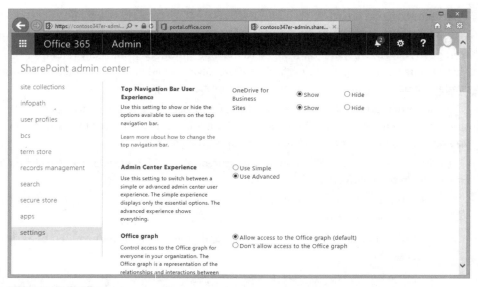

FIGURE 2-30 Settings

4. Under Site Collection Storage Management, select Auto and then click OK. Note that the pooled storage feature is being rolled out in 2015. The Site Collection Storage Management area might not be available through the settings section of all Office 365 subscriptions until the end of 2015.

Per-site collection storage management

The default option for Office 365 tenancies created before mid-2015 was that storage management occurred on a per-site collection basis. If you have switched to the pooled storage model and want to switch back, or have an Office 365 tenancy created after mid-2015, you can switch to per-site collection storage management by performing the following steps:

1. Sign in to the Office 365 Admin Center with a user account that has SharePoint Online administrator privileges.

2. Under Admin, click SharePoint. This will open the SharePoint Admin Center.

3. In the Settings section, in the Site Collection Management area, select Manual and then click OK. The Site Collection Storage Management area might not be available through the settings section of all Office 365 subscriptions until the end of 2015.

Setting site collection storage limits

You can configure storage limits on a per site-collection basis. To do this, perform the following steps:

1. Sign in to the Office 365 Admin Center with a user account that has SharePoint Online administrator privileges.

2. Under Admin, click SharePoint. This will open the SharePoint Admin Center.

3. Select the Site Collections area as shown in Figure 2-31.

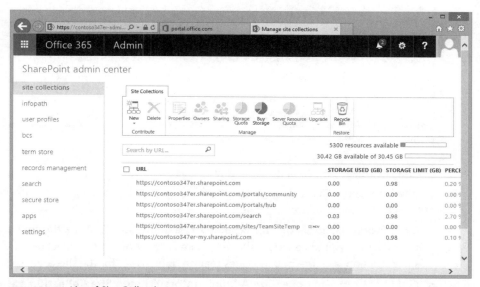

FIGURE 2-31 List of Site Collections

4. Select the site collection for which you want to configure the quota. Figure 2-32 shows the selection of the site collection with the URL *https://contoso347er.sharepoint.com/ sites/TeamSiteTemp*.

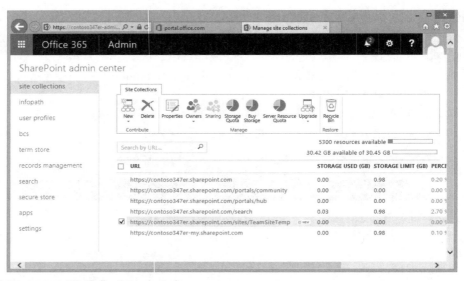

FIGURE 2-32 Site Collection selected

5. On the Site Collections toolbar, click Storage Quota.

6. On the Set Storage Quota dialog box, shown in Figure 2-33, configure the following options and then click Save:

- **Limit Storage Quota For Each Selected Site Collection To A Maximum Of** This option allows you to configure the maximum amount of storage allocated to each site collection. A figure of 0 indicates that no quota is set for the site collection.

- **Send Email To Site Collection Administrators When A Site Collection's Storage Reaches** Allows you to configure an email to be automatically sent after the storage allocated to the site collection reaches the specified percentage.

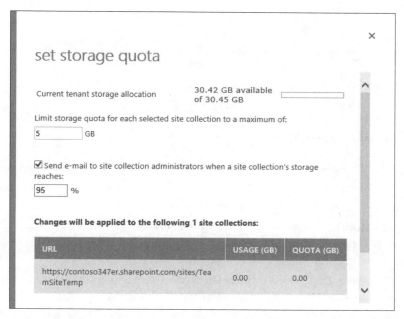

FIGURE 2-33 Storage Quota

MORE INFO **STORAGE QUOTAS FOR SITE COLLECTIONS**

You can learn more about storage quotas for site collections at *https://support.office. com/en-us/article/Manage-site-collection-storage-limits-77389c2c-8e7e-4b16-ab97-1c7103784b08.*

Managing site collections

A user with SharePoint Online Administrator permissions is able to create, delete, and restore deleted site collections.

Creating site collections

To create a site collection, perform the following steps:

1. Sign in to the Office 365 Admin Center with a user account that has SharePoint Online administrator privileges.

2. Under Admin, click SharePoint. This will open the SharePoint Admin Center.

3. In the site collections area, shown in Figure 2-34, click New and then click Private Site Collection.

FIGURE 2-34 Create Site Collection

4. On the New Site Collection page, shown in Figure 2-35, provide the following information and click OK:

- **Title**   The name of the site collection.

- **Website Address**   Allows you to specify the address of the website. Drop-down menus allow you to select the domain name and the URL path. The URL path can either have /sites/ or /teams/ after the domain name.

- **Template Selection**   Allows you to select which template to use for the site collection. Available templates are separated across the following categories: Collaboration, Enterprise, Publishing, and Custom. You also use this section to select a language from a drop-down list. Choosing the correct language at this stage of the process is critical because it is not possible to alter the language selection for the site collection after the collection is created. You can enable SharePoint's multiple language interface on a site collection, but the primary language will always be the one selected during site collection creation.

- **Time Zone**   Allows you to specify the time zone for the site collection.

- **Administrator**   Use this option to specify the administrator of the site collection. You can type the user name, or browse for a site collection administrator. You can alter the site collection administrator after the creation of the site collection.

- **Storage Quota**   Use this option to specify the storage quota in GB for the site collection up to a maximum value of 1 TB.

- **Server Resource Quota**   Use this option to specify the resources you want to allocate to this collection in terms of available resources. Resources are a combination of performance metrics related to the execution of code for sandboxed solutions.

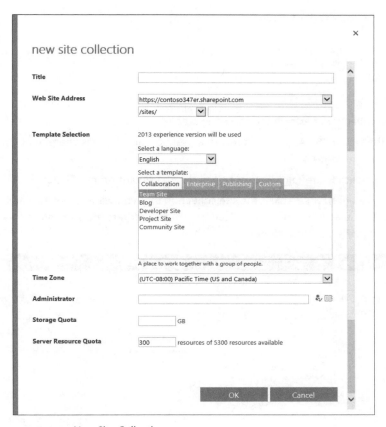

FIGURE 2-35 New Site Collection

Delete site collection

As part of ensuring that data stored on SharePoint Online is not retained past the point where no one is using it, you will occasionally need to delete site collections. For example, you might want to delete a site collection used for a specific project that has long since ended. Site collections that you delete are moved to the Recycle Bin. You will read more about the Recycle Bin later in this chapter.

Deleting a site collection deletes the site hierarchy hosted within the collection. It also deletes the following user and content data stored within the site collection, including:

- Documents and document libraries
- Lists and list data
- Site configuration settings
- Site and subsite role and security information

- Subsites of the top-level website
- Web parts
- Document workspaces
- Content types
- User associations

To delete a site collection, perform the following steps:

1. Sign in to the Office 365 Admin Center with a user account that has SharePoint Online administrator privileges.

2. Under Admin, click SharePoint. This will open the SharePoint Admin Center.

3. In the Site Collections area, select the site collection that you want to delete. Figure 2-36 shows the selection of the site collection with the address *https://contoso347er. sharepoint.com/sites/TeamSiteTemp*.

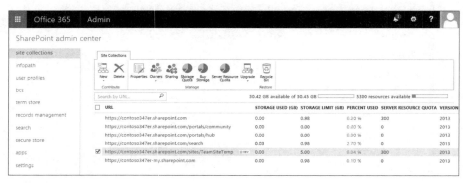

FIGURE 2-36 Site Collections

4. In the Site Collections area, shown in Figure 2-37, click Delete.

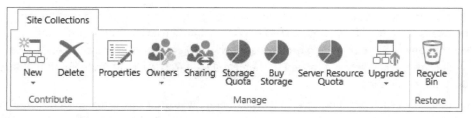

FIGURE 2-37 Delete Site Collections

5. On the Delete Site Collections page, shown in Figure 2-38, click Delete.

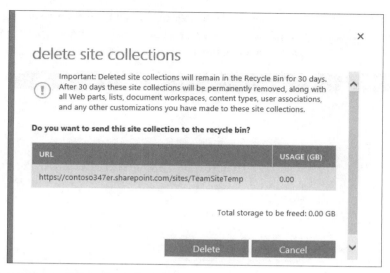

FIGURE 2-38 Delete Site Collections

> **MORE INFO** **CREATING AND DELETING SHAREPOINT ONLINE SITE COLLECTIONS**
>
> You can learn more about creating and deleting SharePoint Online site collections at *https://support.office.com/en-us/article/Create-or-delete-a-site-collection-3a3d-7ab9-5d21-41f1-b4bd-5200071dd539*.

Restore deleted site collection

When you delete a SharePoint Online site collection, it is moved to the Recycle Bin for 30 days before it is purged. If you need a site collection restored after this 30-day period has elapsed, you have an additional 14 days in which you can have Microsoft perform the restoration through a Service Request.

You can view the site collections in the Recycle Bin and the number of days remaining before being purged by performing the following steps:

1. Sign in to the Office 365 Admin Center with a user account that has SharePoint Online administrator privileges.

2. Under Admin, click SharePoint. This will open the SharePoint Admin Center.

3. In the Site Collections area, shown in Figure 2-39, click Recycle Bin.

FIGURE 2-39 Recycle Bin

4. In the Recycle Bin, you can see the list of site collections that have been deleted, and also when deleted, along with the number of days before being purged from the Recycle Bin. Figure 2-40 shows the Recycle Bin.

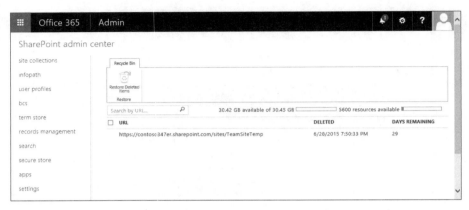

FIGURE 2-40 Recycle Bin contents

You can restore a deleted site collection under the following circumstances:

- The site collection has been in the Recycle Bin for less than 30 days.
- The usage quota for the SharePoint Online tenancy has not been exceeded.
- The storage quota for the SharePoint Online tenancy has not been exceeded.

Site collection URLs must be unique. This means that an active site collection cannot have the same URL as a deleted site collection that is still in the Recycle Bin. Should you need to create a new site with the same URL as a site in the Recycle Bin, the interface will prompt you to permanently delete the site collection. This will remove the site from the Recycle Bin.

To restore a deleted site collection, perform the following steps:

1. Sign in to the Office 365 Admin Center with a user account that has SharePoint Online administrator privileges.

2. Under Admin, click SharePoint. This will open the SharePoint Admin Center.

3. In the Site Collections area, shown in Figure 2-41, click Recycle Bin.

FIGURE 2-41 Recycle Bin

4. In the Recycle Bin area, select the site collection that you want to restore. Figure 2-42 shows the site collection *https://contoso347er.sharepoint.com/sites/TeamSiteTemp* selected. Click Restore Deleted Items.

FIGURE 2-42 Recover Site Collection

5. On the Restore Site Collections page, shown in Figure 2-43, click Restore.

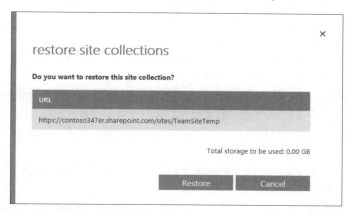

FIGURE 2-43 Restore Site Collections

> **MORE INFO RESTORE DELETED SITE COLLECTION**
>
> You can learn more about restoring deleted SharePoint Online site collections at *https://support.office.com/en-us/article/Restore-a-deleted-site-collection-91c18651-c017-47d1-9c27-3a22f325d6f1*.

Thought experiment
Managing site collections at Fabrikam

In this thought experiment, apply what you learned about this objective. You can find answers to these questions in the "Answers" section at the end of this chapter.

You have recently deleted a number of site collections from your organization's SharePoint Online tenancy. Several of these collections are still present in the Recycle Bin and others have been removed after exceeding the Recycle Bin retention period. With this information in mind, answer the following questions:

1. One of the site collections disappeared from the Recycle Bin yesterday. What steps could you take to recover it?

2. You want to create a new site collection with the URL of a recently deleted site collection. What steps must you take before you can perform this task?

Objective summary

- Site collection administrators are users who have permission to manage SharePoint Online at the top of a specified site collection.
- A site collection administrator has permissions over all content in the site collection, including all subsites.
- Server resources are a numerical way of representing server resources, including RAM and CPU utilization.
- Each SharePoint Online deployment is allocated a server resource figure based on the number of user licenses.
- If the number of resources used in a 24-hour period exceeds the resources available, the sandbox turns off and custom code will not run.
- SharePoint Online Public Websites is a functionality not available in new Office 365 subscriptions and only available in some existing subscriptions until March 2017.
- Office 365 tenancies are allocated an amount of storage space for SharePoint Online based on the number of users associated with the tenancy.
- You can assign storage quotas on a per-site collection basis to limit the amount of storage space consumed by individual site collections.
- When creating a site collection, you configure the name, URL, primary site collection administrator, template, storage quota, and server resource quota.
- A deleted site collection can be recovered from the Recycle Bin for 30 days.

Objective review

Answer the following questions to test your knowledge of the information in this objective. You can find the answers to these questions and explanations of why each answer choice is correct or incorrect in the "Answers" section at the end of this chapter.

1. An organization has 40 users associated with its Office 365 tenancy. You are planning allocation of SharePoint Online storage. How much storage space will be allocated to SharePoint Online by default given this number of users?

   A. 10 GB

   B. 20 GB

   C. 30 GB

   D. 40 GB

2. What is the maximum amount of storage that can be allocated to an individual SharePoint Online site collection?

   A. 100 GB

   B. 500 GB

   C. 1 TB

   D. 5 TB

3. You have allocated a 50 GB quota to a SharePoint Online site collection. You want to be notified when 48 GB of that quota has been consumed. Which of the following steps should you take to accomplish this goal?

   A. Set the quota to 48 GB

   B. Set the quota to 52 GB

   C. Set the quota warning email threshold to 48 percent

   D. Set the quota warning email threshold to 96 percent

4. Which of the following settings cannot be changed after the creation of a site collection?

   A. Site collection administrators

   B. Storage quota

   C. Server resource quota

   D. Primary language

5. How long do deleted site collections remain in the Recycle Bin before being purged?

   A. 15 days

   B. 30 days

   C. 60 days

   D. 90 days

6. In which of the following cases will you be unable to recover a site collection from the Recycle Bin? (Choose all that apply.)

   A. Usage quota for the SharePoint Online tenant has been exceeded

   B. Storage quota for SharePoint Online tenant has been exceeded

   C. Site collection was deleted more than 50 days ago

   D. Site collection was deleted less than 20 days ago

7. How many primary site collection administrators can be assigned to a site collection?

   A. 5

   B. 1

   C. 2

   D. 10

8. You want to ensure that the custom code running in a specific site collection doesn't consume all of the CPU and RAM resources allocated to your organization's SharePoint Online tenancy. Which of the following steps would you take to accomplish this goal?

   A. Configure a storage quota

   B. Configure a resource quota

   C. Configure site collection administrator

   D. Purchase additional user licenses

Objective 2.3: Plan a collaboration solution

This objective deals with using a variety of Office 365 tools for collaboration and coauthoring. To master this objective you'll need to understand the differences between Yammer and SharePoint newsfeeds, the settings related to coauthoring, the functionality of OneDrive For Business, the SharePoint App Store, and Enterprise eDiscovery.

This objective covers the following topics:

- Yammer versus newsfeeds
- Coauthoring
- Project Online
- Excel Services
- Visio Services
- OneDrive for Business
- App Store
- Enterprise eDiscovery

Using newsfeeds and Yammer

Newsfeeds and Yammer provide different methods for allowing users to share information throughout the organization.

Newsfeeds

Newsfeeds in SharePoint Online function as an organizational blog where members of the organization can post and reply to posts. A newsfeed exists at the SharePoint Online tenancy level. Newsfeeds also exist at the team site level. Figure 2-44 shows a post to the newsfeed in a SharePoint Online tenancy's team site.

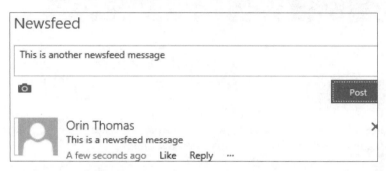

FIGURE 2-44 Newsfeeds

As is the case with other social networks, users can choose to like or reply to newsfeed posts. It is also possible to follow specific users. This allows for the newsfeed filter to be switched between those users a person is following and all users in the organization. People are also able to filter newsfeed posts so that only those posts that reference them are displayed.

In the event that you want to use a newsfeed to have a conversation with a small number of users rather than everyone in the organization, and you have permission to create new sites, you can do the following:

1. Create a new SharePoint Online site.

2. Share the site with the people who you want to have included in the conversation.

3. Use the site-specific newsfeed to have the conversation.

4. Ensure that users accessing the site select the Follow option, as shown in Figure 2-45, so that the users are subscribed to the newsfeed.

FIGURE 2-45 Follow option

Users can access all of the newsfeeds of sites that are followed through the newsfeed app. To access the newsfeed app, perform the following steps:

1. In the list of apps, shown in Figure 2-46, click Newsfeed.

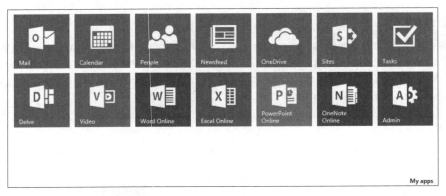

FIGURE 2-46 List of apps

2. The Newsfeed page will show you all existing posts on sites that you are following. Figure 2-47 shows a newsfeed where a user is following two sites.

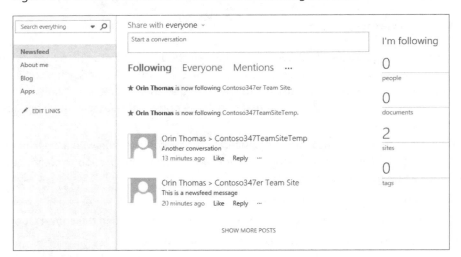

FIGURE 2-47 Newsfeed app

3. If you are following multiple sites, you are able to select which site you post to from the Newsfeed app by using the drop down menu, as shown in Figure 2-48.

FIGURE 2-48 Sharing options

> **MORE INFO** NEWSFEEDS
>
> You can learn more about SharePoint Online newsfeeds at *https://support.office.com/en-us/article/Post-something-to-a-small-group-of-people-229a1060-4420-45b1-bd94-81a0c3f8bc1a*.

Yammer

Yammer is a private social network that has features similar to many of the larger social networks. Yammer allows people in your organization to collaborate with one another. Only people with company email addresses are able to join a company Yammer network.

To use Yammer with SharePoint Online, you need to configure Yammer as the SharePoint social collaboration option. To configure Yammer as the SharePoint social collaboration option, perform the following steps:

1. Sign in to the Office 365 Admin Center with a user account that has SharePoint Online administrator privileges.

2. Under Admin, click SharePoint. This will open the SharePoint Admin Center.

3. Click Settings. Next to Enterprise Social Collaboration, click Use Yammer.com Service, as shown in Figure 2-49.

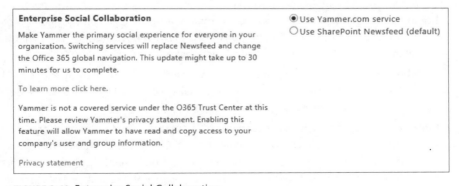

FIGURE 2-49 Enterprise Social Collaboration

4. Click Save.

Switching to Yammer doesn't disable Newsfeed functionality, though it does disable the ability to make posts to everyone in the organization. Newsfeeds associated with specific sites remain in place after you have enabled Yammer.

> **MORE INFO YAMMER VS. NEWSFEED**
>
> You can learn more about Yammer versus Newsfeed at *https://support.office.com/en-us/article/Pick-your-enterprise-social-experience-Yammer-or-Newsfeed--21954c85-4384-47d4-96c2-dfa1c9d56e66.*

Documenting coauthoring

The coauthoring feature of SharePoint Online allows multiple users to work on a document. This occurs in such a way that the changes made by one user do not interfere with the changes made by another. The ability to coauthor documents is enabled by default for documents stored in SharePoint Online.

Office 365 ProPlus provides coauthoring support for Word, PowerPoint, OneNote, and Visio. Coauthoring is also possible through the Word, PowerPoint, Excel, and OneNote Online web apps. The only restriction is that the Excel client application supports a Shared Workbook feature rather than direct coauthoring of workbooks stored in SharePoint Online.

When planning for document coauthoring in SharePoint Online, take the following into account:

- **Correct permissions**   Every user who will coauthor a document needs to have appropriate permissions to edit the document. One method of accomplishing this goal is to give all users who need to edit the document access to the SharePoint site where the document is stored. SharePoint permissions can also be used to limit which documents within a SharePoint site can be edited by particular users.

- **Versioning**   Versioning keeps track of documents and stores previous versions of a document. SharePoint Online supports major and minor versioning, with major versioning being the default value. Microsoft recommends that monitor versioning not be used for document libraries that are used with OneNote coauthoring, as it can interfere with OneNote's built-in versioning functionality.

- **Number of versions**   The number of versions kept doesn't directly impact coauthoring, but it will impact the amount of storage space consumed by versions. The default value for SharePoint Online is 500 versions.

- **Check out**   If a document is checked out by an author, the document is locked until the check out is released. This blocks coauthoring. Check out is disabled by default in SharePoint Online, but users can manually check out documents using the Advanced menu, as shown in Figure 2-50. You should warn users not to check out documents when engaging in the coauthoring process.

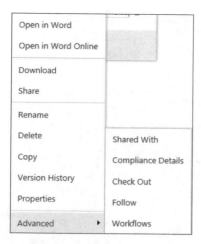

Open in Word

Open in Word Online

Download

Share

Rename

Delete | Shared With

Copy | Compliance Details

Version History | Check Out

Properties | Follow

Advanced ▶ | Workflows

FIGURE 2-50 Check Out

To configure versioning and check out settings in a SharePoint Online document library, perform the following steps:

1. In the SharePoint Site, click Documents and then click Library, as shown in Figure 2-51.

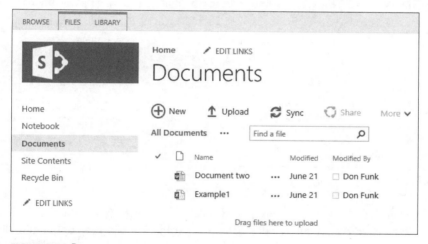

FIGURE 2-51 Documents

2. On the Library toolbar, shown in Figure 2-52, click Library Settings.

FIGURE 2-52 Library Settings

3. Under the General settings area, click Versioning Settings, as shown in Figure 2-53.

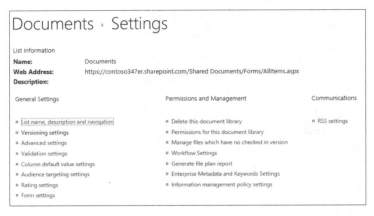

FIGURE 2-53 Library settings

4. Next to Document Version History, shown in Figure 2-54, choose whether you want to configure No versioning, Create Major Versions, or Create Major And Minor (Draft) Versions. You can also specify the number of major and minor versions to be kept. The default is to use major versions and to keep 500 major versions of a document.

FIGURE 2-54 Version History

5. In the Require Check Out section, shown in Figure 2-55, specify whether documents should be checked out before editing. Remember that enabling this option disables coauthoring.

FIGURE 2-55 Require Check Out

6. Click OK to apply the new settings.

Project Online

Project Online is a standalone web service that provides browser-based portfolio and project management tools. Project Online includes Project Web App. Depending on an organization's Office 365 subscription level, it might also include Project Pro for Office 365. Project Pro for Office 365 is a desktop application that runs on client computers.

Excel Services

When you open an Excel file hosted in a SharePoint Online tenancy in a browser, the file opens in Excel Online. When you perform the same task with an Excel file hosted in an on-premises SharePoint 2013 deployment, the file might be opened either in Excel Services or in Excel Web App if an Office Web Apps server is present.

Visio Services

Visio Services is included with SharePoint 2013 and Office 365. It allows Visio diagrams stored in SharePoint 2013 or SharePoint Online to be viewed in a browser without requiring a full Visio client or Visio Viewer. Visio Services works with the .VSDX Visio file format. Older Visio files in .VDW format will also be visible in a web browser through Visio Services.

Using OneDrive for Business

OneDrive for Business, formerly known as SkyDrive Pro, is a location that allows you to store, sync, and share work files. OneDrive for Business is separate from OneDrive, which was formerly known as SkyDrive. OneDrive for Business differs from OneDrive in the following ways:

- OneDrive is associated with a personal Microsoft account. People in your organization cannot access or manage OneDrive.

- OneDrive for Business is managed by an organization and is made available through an Office 365 subscription. This means that files stored in OneDrive for Business can be accessed by Office 365 administrators. OneDrive for Business allows Office 365 users to share files with each other for the purposes of collaboration. OneDrive for Business can also be used with an on-premises SharePoint deployment. As this is an Office 365-related exam, using OneDrive for Business is not covered.

Accessing OneDrive for Business

A user can access OneDrive for Business by performing the following steps:

1. Sign in to Office 365 with your user account.

2. On the list of apps, shown in Figure 2-56, click OneDrive.

FIGURE 2-56 App list

3. The OneDrive for Business site, which is a SharePoint Online personal site, will be opened. Documents can be uploaded to this site or created and added to this location. It is also possible to create a folder hierarchy in this location. Figure 2-57 shows a OneDrive for Business page with several documents and folders.

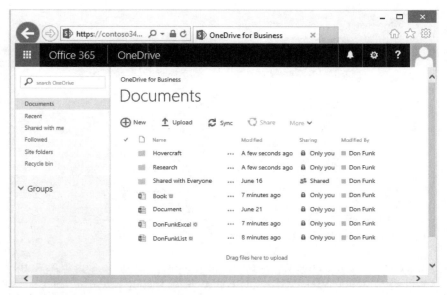

FIGURE 2-57 OneDrive For Business Documents

Collaborating with OneDrive for Business

Collaborating with someone using OneDrive for Business is very similar to collaborating using SharePoint Online. This makes sense considering OneDrive for Business stores data in Share-Point Online. The main difference is that the sharing done through SharePoint Online directly is usually managed by an administrator. The sharing done through OneDrive for Business is usually managed directly by an end user.

An end user can choose to share individual files or can create and share folders. As is the case with SharePoint Online, it's possible to share with people using a Microsoft account, or by sending an external link. Sharing settings are dependent on the sharing settings configured in the SharePoint Online tenancy.

■ If the Don't Allow Sharing Outside Your Organization option is selected at the tenancy level, users will only be able to share with other users in the tenancy. If the users attempt to share with external users, they will see the message shown in Figure 2-58, explaining that sharing with external users is not possible.

FIGURE 2-58 No sharing with external users

- If the Allow External Users Who Accept Sharing Invitations And Sign In As Authenticated Users option is selected at the tenancy level, sharing with external users will be possible as long as those users have a Microsoft account or an Office 365 account.

- If the Allow Both External Users Who Accept Sharing Invitations And Anonymous Guest Links option is selected at the tenancy level, it will be possible to share with external users with Office 365 or Microsoft accounts. It will also be possible to forward links to shared documents or folders to users so that they can access content without having to authenticate.

To share an individual document, perform the following steps:

1. Sign in to Office 365 with your user account.

2. On the list of apps, click OneDrive.

3. In the OneDrive for Business site, select the document that you want to share. Figure 2-59 shows the DonFunkExcel workbook selected.

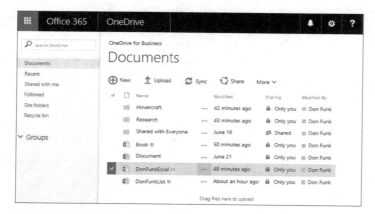

FIGURE 2-59 Select document

4. Click the Share icon. If the Allow Both External Users Who Accept Sharing Invitations And Anonymous Guest Links option is selected at the tenancy level, users will be able to share to external users and generate links. To share with external users, enter the user's email address and determine if the users have read-only or edit access. Figure 2-60 shows the user orin.thomas@outlook.com granted the edit permission.

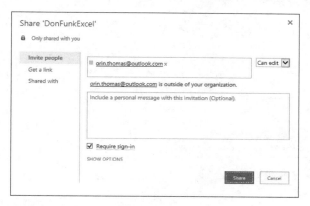

FIGURE 2-60 Share document

5. If you want to share the document with anonymous users, click the Get A Link section. On this page, you can click View Only or the Edit option, as shown in Figure 2-61.

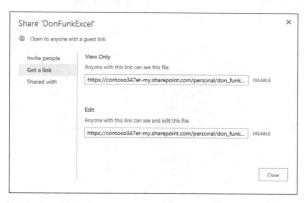

FIGURE 2-61 Anonymous sharing

You can view who a document is shared with on the document's Share page. Note that if you've invited someone to a document and they haven't accepted the invitation, their account will not be listed on the Shared With section of the Share page. Invitations remain valid for seven days.

To view who a document is shared with, perform the following steps:

1. Sign in to Office 365 with your user account.

2. On the list of apps, click OneDrive.

3. In the OneDrive for Business site, select the document of which you want to view the sharing properties. Any documents that are shared will have Shared in the Sharing column, as shown in Figure 2-62.

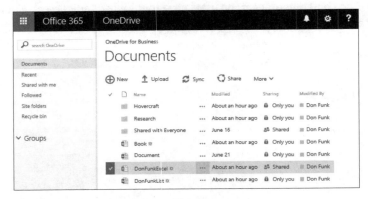

FIGURE 2-62 Document shown as Shared

4. On the toolbar, click Share.
5. The Shared With section will show with whom the document has been shared.
6. As Figure 2-63 shows, you can choose to remove someone's permission to access a document from this page.

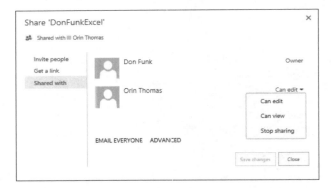

FIGURE 2-63 Who the document is shared with

You can share folders from OneDrive for Business. All of the content in a folder inherits the sharing settings of the parent folder. This makes sharing documents a matter of placing them in the appropriately configured folder.

To share a folder, perform the following steps:

1. Sign in to Office 365 with your user account.
2. On the list of apps, click OneDrive.

3. In the OneDrive for Business site, select the Folder you want to share. Figure 2-64 shows the Hovercraft folder selected.

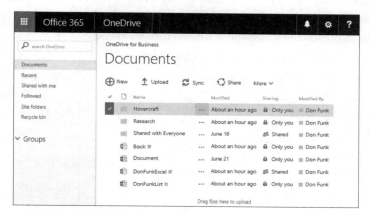

FIGURE 2-64 Share a folder

4. On the toolbar, click Share.

5. On the Invite People page, enter the email addresses of people who you want to invite to the folder and specify their permissions, either Read Only or Edit. Figure 2-65 shows sharing with an external user granted the Edit permission to items in the folder.

FIGURE 2-65 Share folder

You can't create links for anonymous users to folders. Anonymous links can only be created for documents.

Administering OneDrive for Business

Administrators are able to view files and folders stored in OneDrive for Business. To access a user's OneDrive for Business content, perform the following steps:

1. In the Admin area of the Office 365 Admin Center, click SharePoint.
2. In the SharePoint Admin Center, click User Profiles.
3. In the User Profiles setting, click Manage User Profiles, as shown in Figure 2-66.

FIGURE 2-66 User Profiles

4. In the Find User Profiles box, enter part of the account name. Figure 2-67 shows a search for the name Don.

FIGURE 2-67 Find Profiles

5. Select the user whose OneDrive for Business content you want to examine, and then click Manage Site Collection Owners, as shown in Figure 2-68.

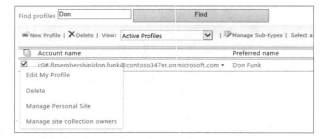

FIGURE 2-68 Manage Site Collection Owners

6. Add an administrator account to the list of Site Collection Administrators, and then click OK.

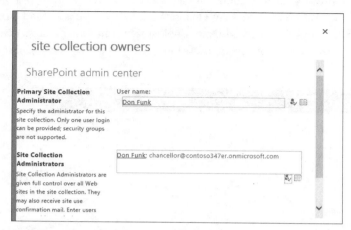

FIGURE 2-69 Add Site Collection Administrator

7. Select the user again, and this time select Manage Personal Site.

8. On the Site Settings page, click Documents.

9. The user's OneDrive for Business content will be displayed, as shown in Figure 2-70.

FIGURE 2-70 Administrator viewing documents

MORE INFO ONEDRIVE FOR BUSINESS

You can learn more about OneDrive for Business at *https://support.office.com/en-us/article/What-is-OneDrive-for-Business--187f90af-056f-47c0-9656-cc0ddca7fdc2.*

Understanding the App Store

The SharePoint App Store provides organizations with a collection of SharePoint apps that can be used with SharePoint 2013 and SharePoint Online. A SharePoint app is a stand-alone application that can add functionality to a SharePoint deployment. You can add apps to a SharePoint Online tenancy from the apps section of the SharePoint Admin Center, as shown in Figure 2-71.

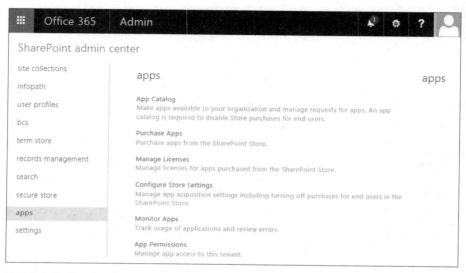

FIGURE 2-71 SharePoint Apps

From the Apps section of the SharePoint Admin Center, you can perform the following tasks:

- **App Catalog**   Allows you to make purchased apps available to people in your organization. You need an app catalog if you want to disable Store purchases for end users.

- **Purchase Apps**   Allows administrators to purchase apps from third-party developers, as well as Microsoft, from the SharePoint store.

- **Manage Licenses**   Allows you to manage licensing for apps purchased from the SharePoint Store.

- **Configure Store Settings**   Allows you to manage how apps are acquired by users from the SharePoint Store.

- **Monitor Apps**   Allows you to track how SharePoint apps are being used across the SharePoint Online tenancy.

- **App Permissions**   Allows you to manage how Apps interact with the SharePoint Online tenancy.

MORE INFO SHAREPOINT STORE APPS

You can learn more about SharePoint Store Apps at *https://support.office.com/en-us/article/Buy-an-app-from-the-SharePoint-Store-dd98e50e-d3db-4ecb-9bb7-82b189822d43*.

Understanding Enterprise eDiscovery

Enterprise eDiscovery is the process of locating content that will serve as evidence in litigation or an official investigation. SharePoint Online has a special site collection called the eDiscovery Center. This site collection allows you to create special SharePoint sites named cases that you can use to locate, hold, search, and export content from Exchange online, SharePoint Online, and OneDrive for Business.

Creating a case

To create an eDiscovery case, perform the following steps:

1. In the Admin area of the Office 365 Admin Center, click Compliance.

2. In the Compliance Center, click eDiscovery.

3. In the list of eDiscovery Cases, shown in Figure 2-72, click the Plus icon to create a new case.

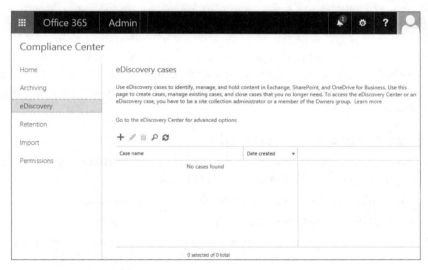

FIGURE 2-72 eDiscovery Cases

4. On the Site Contents, New SharePoint Site page, provide the following information, as shown in Figure 2-73, ensuring that you select the eDiscovery Case template:

    ▪ Title: Title for the eDiscovery case

    ▪ Description: Description for the case

    ▪ URL name: Address of the site related to the case

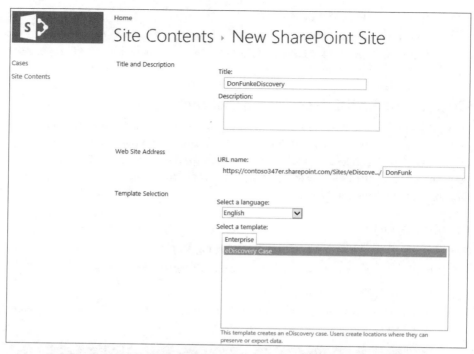

FIGURE 2-73 New SharePoint Site for eDiscovery case

5. You can specify whether the site will use the same permissions as the parent site or unique permissions. If you need to allow specific people access to one case, but not other eDiscovery cases stored within your SharePoint Online tenancy, choose unique permissions.

Add sources and place them on hold

Adding sources to an eDiscovery case allows information to be added to the case. To add sources to an eDiscovery case, perform the following steps:

1. In the Admin area of the Office 365 Admin Center, click Compliance.
2. In the Compliance Center, click eDiscovery.
3. In the list of eDiscovery Cases, shown in Figure 2-74, click the case that you want to add a source to and then click the pencil icon, which allows you to edit the case.

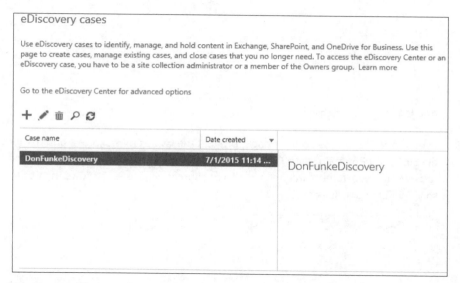

FIGURE 2-74 eDiscovery Cases

4. On the eDiscovery case page, shown in Figure 2-75, click New Item.

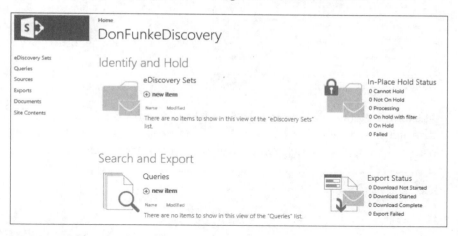

FIGURE 2-75 eDiscovery Case page

5. On the New: eDiscovery Set page, provide a name for the set and then click Add & Manage sources, as shown in Figure 2-76.

FIGURE 2-76 New: eDiscovery Set

6. On the Add & Manage Sources page, provide the names of mailboxes and the locations of SharePoint Sites and File Shares that are indexed by Search and click Save. All subsites and sub-folders will be included as sources. Figure 2-77 shows the Contoso347er Team Site selected.

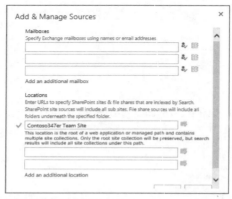

FIGURE 2-77 Add Sources

7. As shown in Figure 2-78, you can use the filter box to provide keywords; provide a start date and an end date; the name of an author; an email domain; and also enable in-place hold, stopping the deletion of objects that match the search criteria.

FIGURE 2-78 Add Filters

8. Click Save to save the eDiscovery Set.

EXAM TIP

Remember that document Check Out should be disabled if coauthoring is to take place with documents stored in SharePoint Online.

Thought experiment

SharePoint apps and Contoso's Office 365 deployment

In this thought experiment, apply what you learned about this objective. You can find answers to these questions in the "Answers" section at the end of this chapter.

Your organization has purchased several SharePoint apps to increase user productivity. You are in the process of training an assistant to manage how these apps are used. Which part of the apps section of the SharePoint Admin Center should be used to perform the following tasks?

1. Determine application usage and errors

2. View license utilization

3. Control which SharePoint apps interact with the tenant

Objective summary

- Newsfeeds in SharePoint Online function as an organizational blog where members of the organization can post and reply to posts.

- A newsfeed exists at the SharePoint Online tenancy level. Newsfeeds also exist at the team site level.

- Yammer is a private social network that has features similar to many of the larger social networks.

- To use Yammer with SharePoint Online, you need to configure Yammer as the SharePoint social collaboration option.

- Every user who will coauthor a document needs to have appropriate permissions to edit the document.

- If a document is checked out by an author, the document is locked until the check out is released, which blocks coauthoring.

- Project Online is a stand-alone web service that provides browser-based portfolio and project management tools.

- Excel Services is used when a file hosted in an on-premises SharePoint deployment is opened in a browser.

- Visio Services allows Visio diagrams stored SharePoint Online to be viewed in a browser without requiring a full Visio client or Visio Viewer.

- OneDrive for Business allows users to store, sync, and share work files.

- Whether users can share OneDrive for Business documents with external users depends on the settings in the SharePoint Online tenancy.

- eDiscovery allows you to configure search and hold for the purposes of litigation and investigation.

Objective review

Answer the following questions to test your knowledge of the information in this objective. You can find the answers to these questions and explanations of why each answer choice is correct or incorrect in the "Answers" section at the end of this chapter.

1. Which of the following can block collaboration when configured for a SharePoint Online document library?

   A. Disabling major versions

   B. Enabling major versions

   C. Disabling minor versions

   D. Enabling check out

2. You want to block users of OneDrive for Business from sharing documents with people external to the organization. Users should still be able to share documents with other users who have accounts in your organization's Office 365 tenant. Which of the following steps can you take to accomplish this goal with a minimum of administrative effort?

   A. Configure the Don't Allow Sharing Outside Your Organization option at the site collection level

   B. Configure the Allow External Users Who Accept Sharing Invitations And Sign In As Authenticated Users option at the site collection level

   C. Configure the Don't Allow Sharing Outside Your Organization option at the SharePoint Online tenancy level

   D. Configure the Allow External Users Who Accept Sharing Invitations And Sign In As Authenticated Users option at the site collection level

3. You want to block OneDrive for Business users from sending links that allow anonymous users to access documents stored in SharePoint Online. Users should still be able to share documents with external users that have Microsoft or Office 365 accounts. Which of the following steps could you take to accomplish this goal?

   A. Configure the Allow External Users Who Accept Sharing Invitations And Sign In As Authenticated Users option at the site collection level

   B. Configure the Don't Allow Sharing Outside Your Organization option at the SharePoint Online tenancy level

   C. Configure the Allow External Users Who Accept Sharing Invitations And Sign In As Authenticated Users option at the site collection level

   D. Configure the Don't Allow Sharing Outside Your Organization option at the site collection level

Answers

This section contains the solutions to the thought experiments and answers to the objective review questions in this chapter.

Objective 2.1: Thought experiment

1. Change the sharing settings at the SharePoint Online tenancy level.

2. It will be necessary to modify the sharing settings of each site collection to remove the external user's access.

Objective 2.1: Review

1. **Correct answer:** A

    A. **Correct:** An invitation to access shared content sent to an external user from an Office 365 SharePoint site collection remains valid for 7 days.

    B. **Incorrect:** An invitation to access shared content sent to an external user from an Office 365 SharePoint site collection remains valid for 7 rather than 14 days.

    C. **Incorrect:** An invitation to access shared content sent to an external user from an Office 365 SharePoint site collection remains valid for 7 rather than 21 days.

    D. **Incorrect:** An invitation to access shared content sent to an external user from an Office 365 SharePoint site collection remains valid for 7 rather than 28 days.

2. **Correct answer:** B

    A. **Incorrect:** This will block all sharing in all site collections in the tenancy.

    B. **Correct:** This will only allow sharing to be performed with authenticated users in all site collections.

    C. **Incorrect:** While this will accomplish the overall goal of requiring all external users to authenticate to access shared content, it will not do so with a minimum amount of administrative effort.

    D. **Incorrect:** This will block sharing of all content in each site collection.

3. **Correct answers:** A and D

    A. **Correct:** You must enable the ability to use anonymous guest links at both the tenancy level and the site collection level to allow anonymous access to documents hosted within that site collection.

    B. **Incorrect:** Configuring this option at the site collection level would block users from sending anonymous links.

    C. **Incorrect:** Configuring this option at the tenancy level will block the option for allowing anonymous links at the site collection level.

    D. **Correct:** You must enable the ability to use anonymous guest links at both the tenancy level and the site collection level to allow anonymous access to documents hosted within that site collection.

4. **Correct answers**: A and C

    A. **Correct:** To allow users to send anonymous links in other site collections, this option needs to be configured.

    B. **Incorrect:** This option will block anonymous links in other site collections.

    C. **Correct:** This option will block anonymous links for the specific site collection.

    D. **Incorrect:** This option will allow anonymous links for the specific site collection.

5. **Correct answer**: D

    A. **Incorrect:** While this will accomplish the goal, it will not do so with a minimum amount of administrative effort. Performing this task at the tenancy level will apply this setting across all site collections.

    B. **Incorrect:** This will allow sharing of content to people external to your organization who have Microsoft accounts.

    C. **Incorrect:** This will allow sharing of content to people external to your organization who have Microsoft accounts as well as to anonymous people.

    D. **Correct:** Configuring this setting at the SharePoint Online tenancy level will block sharing at the site collection and document levels.

Objective 2.2: Thought experiment

1. Microsoft support can recover site collections up to 14 days after being removed from the Recycle Bin.

2. You need to remove the site from the Recycle Bin, as site collection URLs must be unique.

Objective 2.2: Review

1. **Correct answer:** C

    A. **Incorrect:** The amount of storage space allocated uses the formula 10 GB plus 500 MB per user. This would mean that 30 GB, rather than 10 GB, will be available.

    B. **Incorrect:** The amount of storage space allocated uses the formula 10 GB plus 500 MB per user. This would mean that 30 GB, rather than 20 GB, will be available.

    C. **Correct:** The amount of storage space allocated uses the formula 10 GB plus 500 MB per user. This would mean that 30 GB will be available.

    D. **Incorrect:** The amount of storage space allocated uses the formula 10 GB plus 500 MB per user. This would mean that 30 GB, rather than 40 GB, will be available.

2. **Correct answer:** C

    A. **Incorrect:** The maximum amount of storage that can be allocated to an individual SharePoint Online site collection is 1 TB, not 100 GB.

    B. **Incorrect:** The maximum amount of storage that can be allocated to an individual SharePoint Online site collection is 1 TB, not 500 GB.

C. Correct: The maximum amount of storage that can be allocated to an individual SharePoint Online site collection is 1 TB.

D. Incorrect: The maximum amount of storage that can be allocated to an individual SharePoint Online site collection is 1 TB, not 5 TB.

3. Correct answer: D

A. Incorrect: You should configure the quota warning email threshold. Setting the quota to 48 GB will not notify you that 48 GB of a 50 GB quota has been consumed. It will simply limit the site collection storage to 48 GB.

B. Incorrect: You should configure the quota warning email threshold. Setting the quota to 52 GB will not notify you that 48 GB of a 50 GB quota has been consumed. It will simply limit the site collection storage to 52 GB.

C. Incorrect. Setting the email warning threshold to 48 percent will mean a notification will be sent when 24 GB of space is consumed, rather than 48 GB.

D. Correct: You should set the quota alert email threshold to 96 percent. The quota is already set to 50 GB, so this will send an email when 48 GB has been consumed.

4. Correct answer: D

A. Incorrect: You can alter which users are assigned site collection administrator privileges after site collection creation.

B. Incorrect: Storage Quota can be altered after site collection creation.

C. Incorrect: Server Resource Quota can be altered after site collection creation.

D. Correct: You cannot alter the primary language setting of a site collection after site collection creation.

5. Correct answer: B

A. Incorrect: Site collections remain in the Recycle Bin for 30 days, not 15 days.

B. Correct: Site collections remain in the Recycle Bin for 30 days.

C. Incorrect: Site collections remain in the Recycle Bin for 30 days, not 60 days.

D. Incorrect: While some older documentation might suggest that site collections remain in the Recycle Bin for 90 days, the figure listed in current documentation and in the actual SharePoint Online interface is 30 days.

6. Correct answers: A, B, and C

A. Correct: You cannot recover a site collection from the Recycle Bin if the resource quota has been exceeded.

B. Correct: You cannot recover a site collection from the Recycle Bin if the storage quota has been exceeded.

C. Correct: You will be unable to recover a site collection from the Recycle Bin that was deleted more than 50 days ago.

D. Incorrect: You will be able to recover a site collection that was deleted less than 20 days ago assuming that usage quotas and storage quotas have not been exceeded.

7. **Correct answer**: B

    A. **Incorrect**: Only 1 primary site collection administrator, rather than 5, can be assigned to a site collection.

    B. **Correct**: Only 1 primary site collection administrator can be assigned to a site collection.

    C. **Incorrect**: Only 1 primary site collection administrator, rather than 2, can be assigned to a site collection.

    D. **Incorrect**: Only 1 primary site collection administrator, rather than 10, can be assigned to a site collection.

8. **Correct answer**: B

    A. **Incorrect**: A storage quota restricts how much storage space a site collection can consume, not how much of the server resources in terms of RAM and CPU it can consume.

    B. **Correct**: A resource quota allows you to restrict how much RAM and CPU resources a specific site collection can consume.

    C. **Incorrect**: Assigning a user as a site collection administrator will not ensure that a specific site collection does not consume all of the RAM and CPU resources available to the tenancy.

    D. **Incorrect**: While purchasing additional user licenses will increase the overall server resource quota, it will not stop a specific site collection from consuming all those resources.

Objective 2.3: Thought experiment

1. You use the Monitor Apps section to determine application usage and review errors.
2. You use the Manage Licenses section to view SharePoint app license utilization.
3. You use the App Permissions section to configure which apps can access the SharePoint Online tenant.

Objective 2.3: Review

1. **Correct answer**: D

    A. **Incorrect**: Collaboration can function when the major versions versioning functionality is disabled.

    B. **Incorrect**: Collaboration can function when the major versions versioning functionality is enabled.

    C. **Incorrect**: Minor versioning allows previous versions of documents to be restored, but does not block collaboration.

    D. **Correct**: If users check out files when opened, other users will not be able to collaborate on that file until the file is closed.

2. **Correct answer**: C

   A. **Incorrect**: While this will function, it would take an extraordinary amount of effort to perform this task for each user's OneDrive for Business site collection.

   B. **Incorrect**: This would allow sharing with external users with Microsoft or Office 365 accounts. It would also require extraordinary effort to perform this task for each user's OneDrive for Business site collection.

   C. **Correct**: Configuring this option at the SharePoint Online tenancy level would accomplish your goal with a minimum of administrative effort.

   D. **Incorrect**: This would allow sharing with external users with Microsoft or Office 365 accounts.

3. **Correct answer**: A

   A. **Correct**: This would allow sharing with external users with Microsoft or Office 365 accounts.

   B. **Incorrect**: Configuring this option at the SharePoint Online tenancy level would block users from sharing documents with users that had Microsoft or Office 365 accounts.

   C. **Incorrect**: While this would work, it would also require extraordinary effort to perform this task for each user's OneDrive for Business site collection.

   D. **Incorrect**: This option would block sharing with external users. It would also take an extraordinary amount of effort to perform this task for each user's OneDrive for Business site collection.

CHAPTER 3

Configure Exchange Online and Skype for Business Online for end users

Exchange Online and Skype for Business Online are the primary communications tools available to Office 365 subscribers. Exchange Online includes many of the features of an on-premises Exchange 2013 deployment, and administrators of Exchange Online need to perform many of the same tasks, including managing email addresses, configuring mailbox permissions, managing resource and shared mailboxes, as well as configuring retention policies and archives. Similarly, many of the tasks that need to be performed by Skype for Business administrators, such as configuring presence settings and external communication options, need to be configured by Skype for Business Online.

Objectives in this chapter:

- Objective 3.1: Configure additional email addresses for users
- Objective 3.2: Create and manage external contacts, resources, and groups
- Objective 3.3: Configure personal archive policies
- Objective 3.4: Configure Skype for Business Online end-user communication settings

Objective 3.1: Configure additional email addresses for users

This objective deals with managing email addresses for Exchange Online mailboxes, including the SIP addresses used by Skype for Business Online.

> **This objective covers the following topics:**
> - Manage email addresses
> - Manage SIP addresses

Managing email addresses

The default address, also known as the primary address and as the reply-to address, is the address that users use to sign in to Office 365, and which recipients reply to when they receive an email message from a user. You can view the primary email address for a user in the Office 365 Admin Center on the User's Properties page, as shown in Figure 3-1.

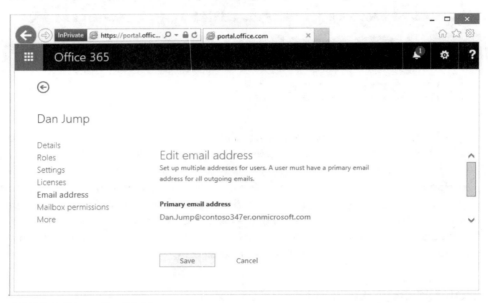

FIGURE 3-1 Primary Email Address

It's possible to change the primary email address after you have added an additional email address to an Office 365 user. It is important to note that changing the primary email address also changes the user name. For example, the Warning in Figure 3-2 indicates that by changing the primary email address associated with the Don Funk user account, the user name will also be changed. The email suffix for the primary address must be configured as an accepted domain for the Office 365 tenancy.

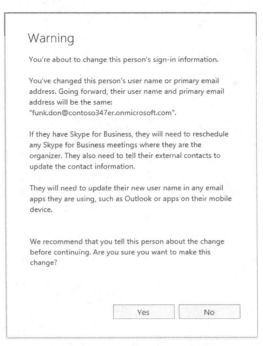

FIGURE 3-2 Primary name change warning

Additional email addresses

You can add additional email addresses to an Office 365 account's Exchange Online mailbox using a variety of methods. To add an additional email address to an Exchange Online mailbox using Exchange Admin Center, perform the following steps:

1. Sign in to the Office 365 Admin Center with a user account that has Tenant Administrator permissions.

2. In the Office 365 Admin Center, click Exchange under ADMIN, as shown in Figure 3-3.

FIGURE 3-3 Admin menu

3. In Exchange Admin Center, click Recipients and then click Mailboxes. Select the recipient to which you want to add an additional email address. Figure 3-4 shows the Don Funk mailbox selected.

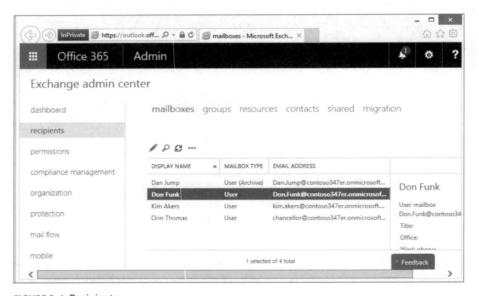

FIGURE 3-4 Recipients

4. Click the Edit (Pencil) icon.

5. On the User Mailbox Properties page, click Email Address, as shown in Figure 3-5.

FIGURE 3-5 Email addresses

6. Click the Plus (+) icon

7. On the New Email Address page, ensure that SMTP is selected, as shown in Figure 3-6, and then enter the new email address. You can also specify the new email address as the default reply-to address.

FIGURE 3-6 New Email Address

8. Click OK to save changes.

To add an additional email address to an Exchange Online mailbox using the Office 365 Admin Center, perform the following steps:

1. In the Office 365 Admin Center, select Active Users under Users.

2. Select the user for which you want to configure the primary email address. Figure 3-7 shows Kim Akers selected.

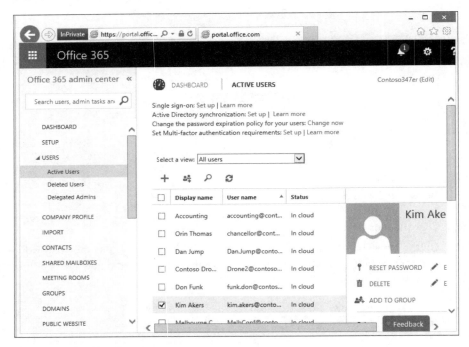

FIGURE 3-7 Kim Akers' user account

3. Click Edit and then click email address.

4. Under other email addresses, shown in Figure 3-8, click Add New.

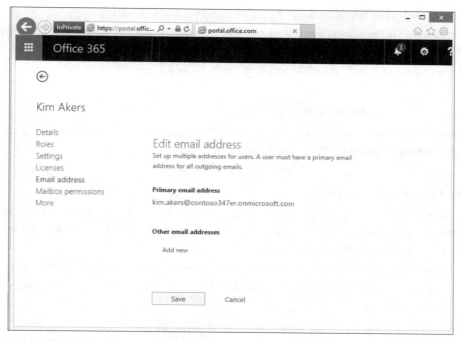

FIGURE 3-8 Edit Email Address

5. Enter the new email address and specify whether it should be configured as the new primary email address, as shown in Figure 3-9, and then click Save.

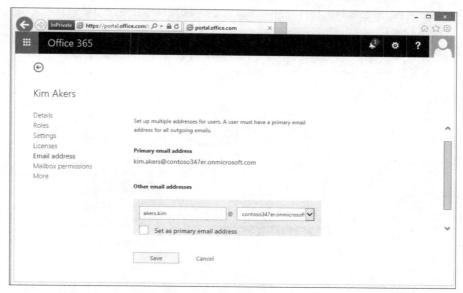

FIGURE 3-9 Other Email Addresses

You can use the Set-Mailbox cmdlet to add additional email addresses. For example, to add the email address funk.don@contoso347er.onmicrosoft.com to Don Funk's Exchange Online mailbox, issue the following command:

```
Set-Mailbox "Don Funk" -EmailAddresses @{Add=funk.don@contoso346er.onmicrosoft.com}
```

> **MORE INFO SECONDARY EMAIL ADDRESS**
>
> You can learn more about adding an email address to a mailbox at *https://technet.microsoft.com/en-us/library/bb123794(v=exchg.150).aspx*.

Manage reply-to address

When a user has more than one email address, you will need to specify which is the default address. This address is also known as the primary or reply-to email address. You can use multiple methods to set the reply-to address.

To use Exchange Admin Center to manage the reply-to address, perform the following steps:

1. Sign in to the Office 365 Admin Center with a user account that has Tenant Administrator permissions.

2. In the Office 365 Admin Center, click Exchange under ADMIN.

3. In Exchange Admin Center, click Recipients and then click Mailboxes. Select the recipient to which you want to configure the reply-to address.

4. Click the Edit (Pencil) icon. On the Mailbox Properties page, click email address.

5. On the email address page, the primary email address is designated with the acronym SMTP in capitals, with secondary email addresses having smtp in lowercase, as shown in Figure 3-10.

FIGURE 3-10 New Email Address

6. To set another email address as the primary, select the email address and click the Plus (+) icon.

7. On the Email Address page, select the Make This The Reply Address check box, as shown in Figure 3-11, click OK and then click Save.

FIGURE 3-11 Set Reply Address

To configure the primary email address using the Office 365 Admin Center, perform the following steps:

1. In the Office 365 Admin Center, select Active Users under Users.

2. Select the user for which you want to configure the primary email address. Figure 3-12 shows Don Funk selected.

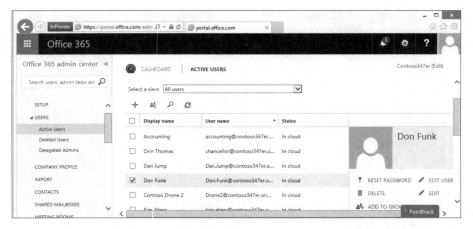

FIGURE 3-12 Don Funk selected

3. Click Edit.

4. On the User Properties page, click Email Address.

5. Under Other Email Addresses, shown in Figure 3-13, click Set As Primary to configure a new primary email address. You might need to mouse over the additional email address to get this option.

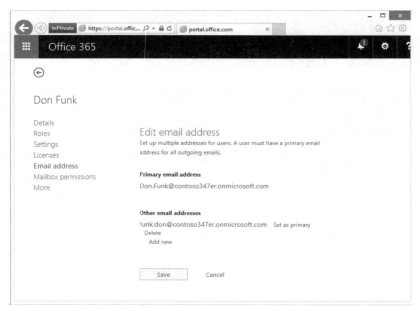

FIGURE 3-13 Edit Email Address

6. In the Warning dialog box, click OK.

Start fresh.

Stock your new home with

- fresh foods
- pantry staples
- cookware
- cleaning products
- ...and more!

Order online.

Publix offers Online Easy Ordering for store pickup. Visit **publix.com/order.**

- subs
- party platters
- sliced meats and cheeses
- cakes
- ...and more!

We prescribe convenience.

The Publix Pharmacy offers

- several medications for FREE*
- acceptance of 99% of all insurance plans
- services such as immunizations, screenings, and diabetes counseling

*Certain restrictions apply. Visit **publix.com/pharmacy** or your neighborhood Publix Pharmacy for details.

Get cooking.

Meal solutions from Publix Aprons Simple Meals:

- a one-stop area for featured recipes and ingredients
- daily recipe tastings
- more than 1,000 recipes online at **publix.com/aprons**

For locations, visit:

publix.com/store

A housewarming gift

from your neighborhood Publix Supermarket.

$5 OFF

YOUR PURCHASE OF $30 OR MORE

Limit one coupon per household per day. Excluding all alcohol, tobacco, lottery items, money services, postage stamps, gift cards, fuel, and prescriptions. Customer is responsible for all applicable taxes. Reproduction or transfer of this coupon constitutes fraud. Offer good through March 31, 2017 at all Publix locations.

Publix.
WHERE SHOPPING IS A PLEASURE®

LU# 17931

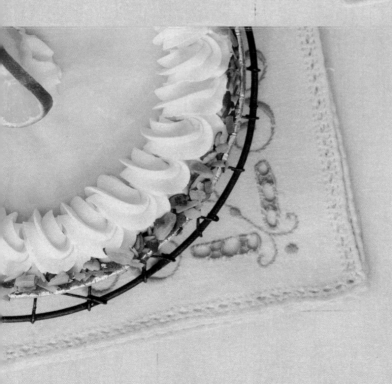

Welcome home!

See reverse for a great coupon offer from your neighborhood Publix Supermarket.

Publix.
WHERE SHOPPING IS A PLEASURE®

7. Review the email address settings to ensure that the correct email address is now set as the primary address, as shown in Figure 3-14.

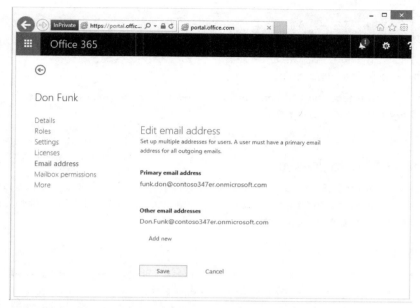

FIGURE 3-14 New Primary Email Address

MORE INFO **SET PRIMARY EMAIL ADDRESS**

You can learn more about configuring the primary email address at *https://support.office.com/en-us/article/Add-additional-email-addresses-to-a-user-in-Office-365-0b0bd900-68b1-4bf5-808b-5d240a7739f4.*

Bulk add for new domain

In some cases, it might be necessary to add email addresses to a large number of existing Office 365 accounts. You can do this using Windows PowerShell and a CSV file containing mailbox names and the new email addresses.

For example, you might have the file c:\import\NewEmailAddress.csv that contains the following contents:

```
Mailbox,NewEmailAddress
Dan Jump,danj@adatum347er.onmicrosoft.com
Don Funk,donf@adatum347er.onmicrosoft.com
Kim Akers,kima@adatum347er.onmicrosoft.com
Janet Schorr,janets@adatum347er.onmicrosoft.com
Jeffrey Zeng,jeffreyz@adatum347er.onmicrosoft.com
Spencer Low,spencerl@adatum347er.onmicrosoft.com
Toni Poe,tonip@adatum347er.onmicrosoft.com
```

You can use the following command to use the data in the CSV to add the email address to each appropriate mailbox.

```
Import-CSV "C:\import\NewEmailAddress.csv" | ForEach {Set-Mailbox $_.Mailbox
-EmailAddresses @{Add=$_.NewEmailAddress}}
```

> **MORE INFO** **BULK ADD EMAIL ADDRESSES**
>
> You can learn more about bulk adding email addresses at *https://technet.microsoft.com/
> en-us/library/bb123794(v=exchg.150).aspx.*

Managing SIP addresses

Session Initiation Protocol (SIP) addresses are used by Skype for Business to route incoming calls and send voicemail to an Office 365 user. Users are assigned SIP addresses automatically when you create their accounts using the Office 365 console.

Add a SIP address

When a user is created in Office 365, they will be assigned a SIP address. Should this address be removed, you can add another by performing the following steps:

To add a SIP address to an Exchange Online user, perform the following steps:

1. In the Office 365 Admin Center, click Exchange under ADMIN.

2. In Exchange Admin Center, click Recipients and then click Mailboxes. Select the recipient to which you want to add a SIP address, as shown in Figure 3-15.

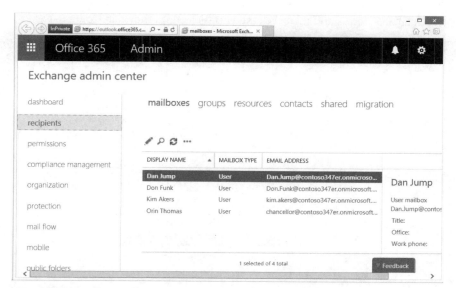

FIGURE 3-15 Dan Jump selected

3. On the toolbar, click the Edit icon, which is shown as a pencil. This will open the User's Properties dialog box, as shown in Figure 3-16.

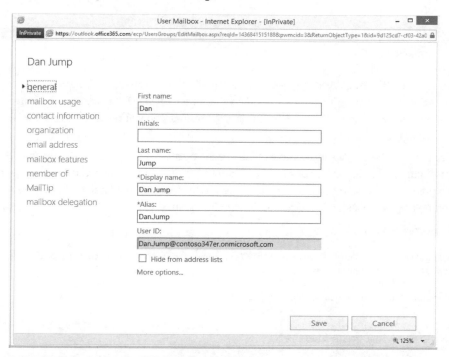

FIGURE 3-16 General page of User Mailbox properties

4. Click Email Address and then click the Plus (+) icon, as shown in Figure 3-17.

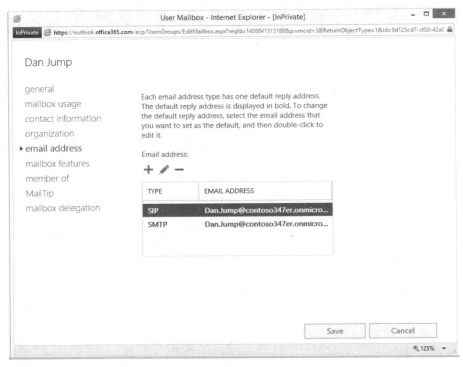

FIGURE 3-17 SIP address selected

5. On the New Email Address page, under email address type, select EUM. In the Address/Extension box, type the new SIP address, in the Dial Plan (Phone Context) box click Browse and select the SIP URI plan. Note that you will need to have a SIP URI plan configured to add a SIP address.

You can use the Set-Mailbox cmdlet to add a SIP address. For example, to add the SIP address djump@contoso347er.onmicrosoft.com to the Dan.Jump mailbox using the dial plan mydialplan.contoso347er.onmicrosoft.com, use the following PowerShell code when a PowerShell session is established to the Office 365 tenancy:

```
$mbx=Get-Mailbox Dan.Jump

$mbx.EmailAddress +="eum:djump@contoso347er.onmicrosoft.com;phone-context=mydialplan.
contoso347er.onmicrosoft.com"

Set-Mailbox Dan.Jump -EmailAddresses $mbx.EmailAddresses
```

> **MORE INFO** **ADD A SIP ADDRESS**
>
> You can learn more about adding a SIP address at *https://technet.microsoft.com/en-us/library/jj662760(v=exchg.150).aspx*.

Change a SIP address

To alter a SIP address, perform the following steps:

1. Sign in to the Office 365 Admin Center with a user account that has Tenant Administrator permissions.

2. In the Office 365 Admin Center, click Exchange under ADMIN.

3. In the list of recipients, select the recipient whose SIP address you want to modify. Figure 3-18 shows the Kim Akers recipient selected.

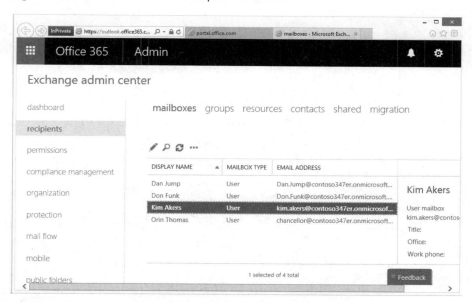

FIGURE 3-18 Kim Akers selected in Exchange Admin Center

4. On the toolbar, click the Edit icon, which is shown as a pencil. This will open the User's Properties dialog box, as shown in Figure 3-19.

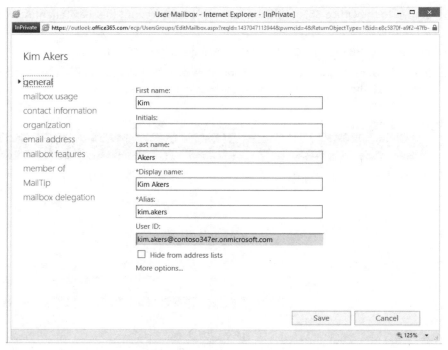

FIGURE 3-19 General page of Exchange Online mailbox properties

5. Click Email address and then select the current SIP address, as shown in Figure 3-20.

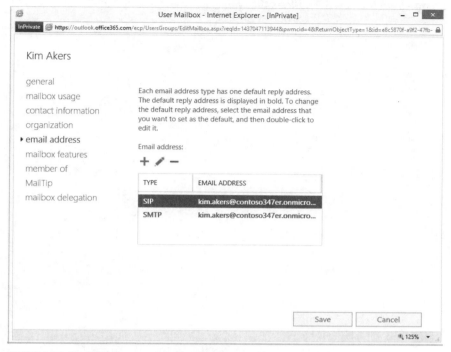

FIGURE 3-20 Email Address section of mailbox properties

6. Click the Edit icon. On the Email Address page, shown in Figure 3-21, change the SIP address to the new SIP address that you want to use and click OK.

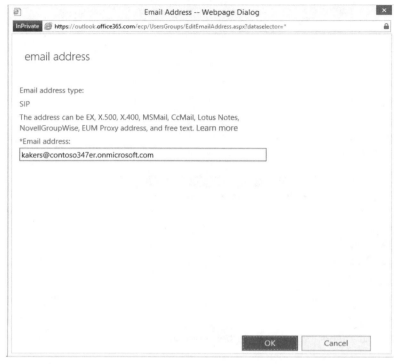

FIGURE 3-21 Modify SIP address

7. On the User Mailbox Properties page, click Save to save the change.

You can use the Set-Mailbox cmdlet to modify a SIP address. For example, to change the SIP address to kakers@contoso347er.onmicrosoft.com for the Kim.Akers mailbox using the dial plan mydialplan.contoso347er.onmicrosoft.com, use the following PowerShell code when a PowerShell session is established to the Office 365 tenancy:

```
$mbx=Get-Mailbox Kim.Akers

$mbx.EmailAddress.Item(1)="eum:kakers@contoso347er.onmicrosoft.com;phone-
context=MySIPDialPlan.contoso347er.onmicrosoft.com"

Set-Mailbox Kim.Akers –EmailAddresses $mbx.EmailAddresses
```

> **MORE INFO CHANGE A SIP ADDRESS**
>
> You can learn more about changing a SIP address at *https://technet.microsoft.com/en-us/library/dd335189(v=exchg.150).aspx.*

Remove a SIP address

You can remove a SIP address by performing the following steps:

1. Sign in to the Office 365 Admin Center with a user account that has Tenant Administrator permissions.

2. In the Office 365 Admin Center, click Exchange under ADMIN.

3. In the list of Recipients, select the recipient whose SIP address you want to modify and click the Edit (Pencil) icon.

4. In the email addresses section, shown in Figure 3-22, select the SIP address that you want to remove and then click the Minus (-) icon.

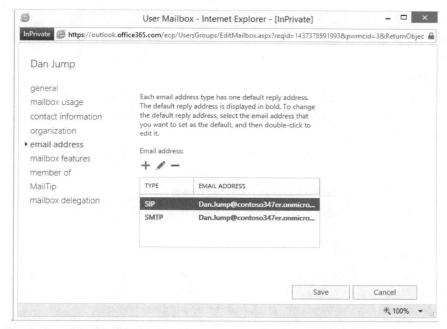

FIGURE 3-22 Remove SIP address

5. Click Save to remove the SIP address.

> **MORE INFO   REMOVE A SIP ADDRESS**
>
> You can learn more about removing a SIP address at *https://technet.microsoft.com/en-us/library/jj662761(v=exchg.150).aspx.*

EXAM TIP

Remember the PowerShell commands required to manipulate recipient email addresses.

Thought experiment

SIP address configuration at Tailspin Toys

In this thought experiment, apply what you learned about this objective. You can find answers to these questions in the "Answers" section at the end of this chapter.

You want to modify the SIP address configuration at Tailspin Toys. With this in mind, answer the following questions:

1. What must you have in place before you can add an additional SIP address?

2. Which Windows PowerShell cmdlet allows you to alter the SIP address of an Office 365 user?

Objective summary

- The default email address is also known as the primary email address and the reply-to address.
- You can add additional email addresses to an Office 365 Exchange Online mailbox.
- Once you add an additional email address to a mailbox, you can configure that as the primary email address.
- You can bulk add additional email addresses to existing Office 365 accounts using Windows PowerShell.
- SIP addresses are used to route Skype for Business calls.
- The default SIP address has the same format as the primary email address.

Objective review

Answer the following questions to test your knowledge of the information in this objective. You can find the answers to these questions and explanations of why each answer choice is correct or incorrect in the "Answers" section at the end of this chapter.

1. Which Windows PowerShell cmdlet would you use to add an additional email address to an Exchange Online email account?

   A. New-Mailbox

   B. Set-Mailbox

   C. Get-Mailbox

   D. Enable-mailbox

2. Which of the following represents the user's primary email address?

   A. SIP:Don.Funk@contoso347er.onmicrosoft.com

   B. SMTP:funk.don@contoso347er.onmicrosoft.com

   C. SIP:funk.don@contoso347er.onmicrosoft.com

   D. smtp:Don.Funk@contoso347er.onomicrosoft.com

3. Which two cmdlets would you use to bulk add new email addresses to existing Office 365 accounts if you had those email addresses in a list of comma separated values?

   A. Import-CSV

   B. Get-Mailbox

   C. Set-Mailbox

   D. Enable-Mailbox

Objective 3.2: Create and manage external contacts, resources, and groups

This objective deals with delegating permissions on mailboxes, the creation of shared and resource mailboxes, how to create external contacts, and how to create and manage Exchange Online distribution groups.

> **This objective covers the following topics:**
> - Delegate permissions
> - Create shared mailboxes
> - Manage resource mailboxes
> - Manage external contacts
> - Manage distribution groups

Delegating permissions

Through delegating permissions, you can allow one user to access another's mailbox, send email as that user, or send email on behalf of that user. For example, you can use the delegation functionality in Exchange Online to grant Dan the ability to access the content of Kim's mailbox, but to not allow Dan to send messages as Kim or on behalf of Kim. Or you can allow Kim to send messages as Dan, but to block Kim from accessing Dan's Exchange Online mailbox. The key to understanding permissions delegation is to understand the difference between the Send As, Send on Behalf, and Full Access permissions.

> **MORE INFO** **DELEGATING PERMISSIONS**
>
> You can learn more about managing recipient permissions at *https://technet.microsoft.com/en-us/library/JJ919240(v=EXCHG.150).aspx.*

Send As

The Send As permission allows the person delegated the permission to send messages as though they were sent by the mailbox owner. For example, if Don Funk is delegated the Send As permission to Kim Akers' Exchange Online mailbox, then Don will be able to send messages that appear to have been sent by Kim. If you delegate this permission to a group, the message will appear to be from the group. For example, if you delegate Don Funk the Sent As permission to the HelpDesk group, Don will be able to send message that appear to have been sent by the HelpDesk group.

To delegate the Send As permission for a mailbox, perform the following steps:

1. In the Office 365 Admin Center, click Exchange under ADMIN. This will open the Exchange Admin Center.

2. Click Recipients. In the list of mailboxes, select the Exchange Online mailbox to which you want to delegate the Send As permission. Figure 3-23 shows the Don Funk mailbox selected.

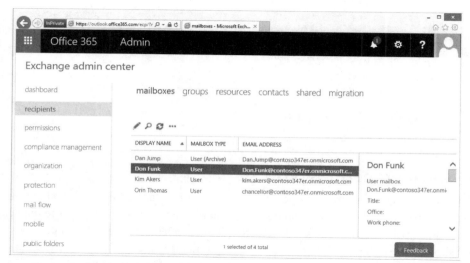

FIGURE 3-23 Don Funk selected

3. With the mailbox selected, click the Edit (Pencil) icon.

4. On the Mailbox Delegation tab, click the Plus (+) icon under Send As, as shown in Figure 3-24.

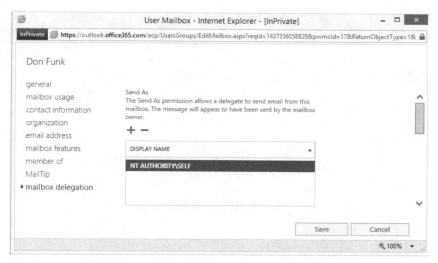

FIGURE 3-24 Mailbox Delegation

5. On the Select Send As dialog box, select the user to whom you want to delegate Send As permission. Figure 3-25 shows the Dan Jump user delegated the Send As permission. Click OK.

FIGURE 3-25 Select Send As user

6. Verify that the delegate is listed. Figure 3-26 shows Dan Jump delegated the Send As permission. Click Save to have the permission assigned.

FIGURE 3-26 Dan Jump with Send As permission

You can use the Add-RecipientPermission cmdlet to assign the Send As permission using Windows PowerShell. For example, to assign Dan Jump the Send As permission to the Don Funk mailbox, run the command:

```
Add-RecipientPermission –Identity "Don Funk" –Trustee "Dan Jump" –AccessRights SendAs
```

You can use the Remove-RecipientPermission cmdlet to remove the Send As permission using Windows PowerShell. For example, to remove the Send As permission from Dan Jump to the Don Funk mailbox, run the command:

```
Remove-RecipientPermission –Identity "Don Funk" –Trustee "Dan Jump" –AccessRights SendAs
```

Send on Behalf

The Send on Behalf permission allows the person delegated the permission to send messages on behalf of the mailbox owner. The from address of a message sent by the delegate will indicate that the message was sent by the person delegated the permission on behalf of the mailbox owner.

To delegate the Send on Behalf permission for a mailbox, perform the following steps:

1. In the Office 365 Admin Center, click Exchange under ADMIN. This will open the Exchange Admin Center.

2. Click Recipients. In the list of mailboxes, select the Exchange Online mailbox to which you want to delegate the Send As permission. Figure 3-27 shows the Kim Akers mailbox selected.

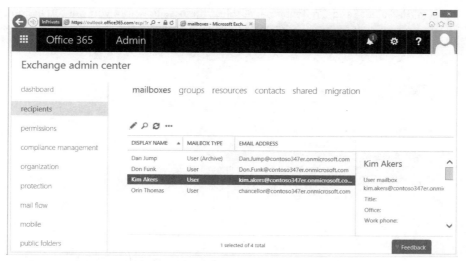

FIGURE 3-27 Kim Akers Recipient selected

3. With the mailbox selected, click the Edit (Pencil) icon.

4. On the Mailbox Delegation tab, click the Plus (+) icon under Send on Behalf, as shown in Figure 3-28.

FIGURE 3-28 Send On Behalf

5. On the Select Send On Behalf page, select the user to whom you want to assign the Send on Behalf permission, click Add and then click OK. Figure 3-29 shows Don Funk selected.

FIGURE 3-29 Select Send On Behalf

6. Verify that the correct user has been delegated the Send On Behalf permission, as shown in Figure 3-30, and then click Save.

FIGURE 3-30 Don Funk delegated Send On Behalf

You can use the Set-Mailbox cmdlet to assign the Send on Behalf permission. For example, to assign the Send on Behalf permission to the kim.akers@contoso347er.onmicrosoft.com mailbox to don.funk@contoso347er.onmicrosoft.com, issue the following command:

```
Set-Mailbox -Identity kim.akers@contoso347er.onmicrosoft.com -GrantSendOnBehalfTo
don.funk@contoso347er.onmicrosoft.com
```

You also use the Set-Mailbox cmdlet to remove the Send on Behalf permission. For example, to remove the Send on Behalf permission from Don Funk for the Kim Akers mailbox, issue the command:

```
Set-Mailbox -Identity kim.akers@contoeo347er.onmicrosoft.com -GrantSendOnBeahlfTo
@{Remove="don.funk@contoso347er.onmicrosoft.com}
```

Full Access

The Full Access permission allows the person delegated the permission the ability to open and access the contents of an Exchange Online mailbox. While the permission is named Full Access, being delegated the permission does not allow a delegate to send mail from the mailbox. The Send As or Send on Behalf permissions must be delegated for this to occur.

To delegate the Full Access permission for a mailbox, perform the following steps:

1. In the Office 365 Admin Center, click Exchange under ADMIN. This will open the Exchange Admin Center.

2. Click Recipients. In the list of mailboxes, select the Exchange Online mailbox to which you want to delegate the Send As permission. Figure 3-31 shows the Dan Jump mailbox selected.

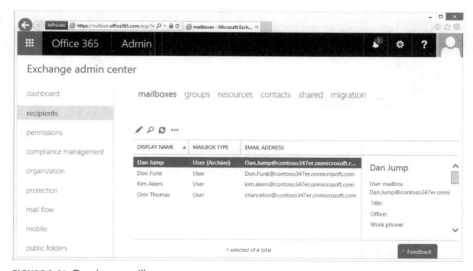

FIGURE 3-31 Dan Jump mailbox

3. With the mailbox selected, click the Edit (Pencil) icon.

4. In the Mailbox Delegation section, click the Plus (+) icon, next to Full Access, as shown in Figure 3-32.

FIGURE 3-32 Full Access

5. On the Select Full Access page, select the user to whom you want to assign full access, click Add and then click OK. Figure 3-33 shows the Kim Akers user being assigned full access.

FIGURE 3-33 Delegate Full Access

6. On the Mailbox Properties page, verify that the appropriate user is assigned access, as shown in Figure 3-34, and then click Save.

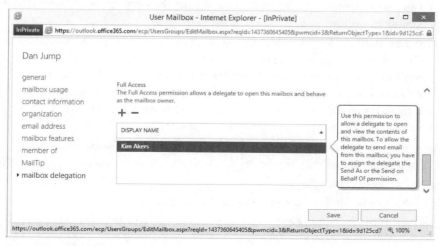

FIGURE 3-34 Kim Akers granted Full Access

You can use the Add-MailboxPermission cmdlet to assign the Full Access permission to a user mailbox. For example, to assign Kim Akers the Full Access permission on the Dan Jump mailbox, use the command:

```
Add-MailboxPermission -Identity "Dan Jump" -User "Kim Akers" -AccessRights FullAccess
-InheritanceType all
```

You use the Remove-MailboxPermission cmdlet to remove the Full Access permission on a user mailbox. For example, to remove the Full Access permission from Kim Akers on Dan Jump's mailbox, use the command:

```
Remove-MailboxPermission -Identity "Dan Jump" -User "Kim Akers" -AccessRights FullAccess
-InteritanceType All
```

Creating shared mailboxes

Shared mailboxes allow multiple users to view, respond to, and send email messages. Shared mailboxes also allow a group of users to have a common calendar. Users don't sign in to a shared mailbox, but are granted permissions on the shared mailbox. Shared mailboxes use the following permissions:

- **Full Access** Allows a user to act as an owner of the mailbox. User is able to create calendar items, read, view, and delete email messages and perform the same mailbox tasks as they can with their own Exchange Online mailbox. Users assigned the Full Access permission cannot send email from the shared mailbox unless assigned additional permissions.

- **Send As**   Allows the user to send email as the shared mailbox. For example, if you assign Kim Akers the Send As permission on the Accounting shared mailbox, Kim will be able to send email that appears to come from the email address assigned to the accounting mailbox.

- **Send on Behalf**   Allows a user to send email on behalf of the shared mailbox. Whereas Send As allows the user to impersonate the shared mailbox, the Send on Behalf permission provides an indication that the mail is sent on behalf of the shared mailbox. For example, if you assigned Kim Akers the Send on Behalf permission on the Accounting shared mailbox, and she sent an email from this mailbox, the email from her would be designated "Kim Akers on behalf of Accounting."

Shared mailboxes do not need to be assigned licenses until they exceed the storage quota of 50 GB. A shared mailbox that exceeds its 50 GB quota will be locked after a month if no license has been assigned.

To create a Shared Mailbox, perform the following steps:

1. In the Office 365 Admin Center, click Exchange under ADMIN. This will open the Exchange Admin Center.

2. Click Recipients and then click Shared.

3. On the toolbar shown in Figure 3-35, click the Plus (+) icon. This will open the New Shared Mailbox page.

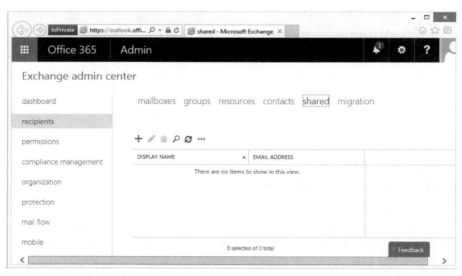

FIGURE 3-35 Shared Mailboxes

4. In the New Shared Mailbox dialog box, shown in Figure 3-36, provide the display name, the email address, and users who have permission to view and send email from the shared mailbox. Adding users here grants them both the Full Access and Send As permissions.

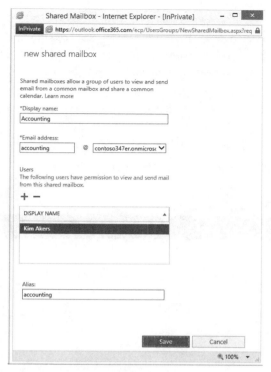

FIGURE 3-36 New Shared Mailbox

5. Click Save to create the shared mailbox.

You can create a New Shared Mailbox using the New-Mailbox Windows PowerShell cmdlet using the Shared parameter. For example, to create a New Shared Mailbox named Accounting, issue the command:

```
New-Mailbox –Shared –Name "Accounting" –DisplayName "Accounting" –Alias Accounting
```

> **MORE INFO SHARED MAILBOXES**
>
> You can learn more about shared mailboxes at *https://technet.microsoft.com/en-us/library/ jj966275(v=exchg.150).aspx.*

Managing resource mailboxes

Resource mailboxes represent organizational facilities and equipment. Users are able to book the facilities and equipment by including the resource mailbox in a meeting request. Users are also able to view existing bookings of facilities and equipment by viewing the resource mailbox's calendar. Exchange Online supports two types of resource mailboxes: room mailboxes and equipment mailboxes.

Equipment mailboxes

Equipment mailboxes are a type of resource mailbox that represents a piece of equipment such as a projector, camera, drone, or company hovercraft. Users reserve the equipment that corresponds to the mailbox by including it in a meeting request. To create an equipment mailbox, perform the following steps:

1. In the Office 365 Admin Center, click Exchange under ADMIN. This will open the Exchange Admin Center.

2. Click Recipients and then click Resources.

3. Click the Plus (+) icon and then click Equipment Mailbox, as shown in Figure 3-37.

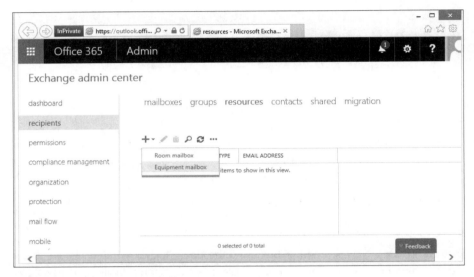

FIGURE 3-37 New Equipment Mailbox

4. On the new equipment mailbox page, shown in Figure 3-38, specify the following:
   - Equipment name
   - Email address

FIGURE 3-38 New Equipment Mailbox

5. Click Save to create the equipment mailbox.

Once the equipment mailbox is saved, you can edit the properties of the mailbox to configure additional options, including:

- **Booking Delegates** On the Booking Delegates page, you can configure whether booking requests are accepted automatically, or whether delegates can accept or decline booking requests. Figure 3-39 shows Don Funk configured as a delegate.

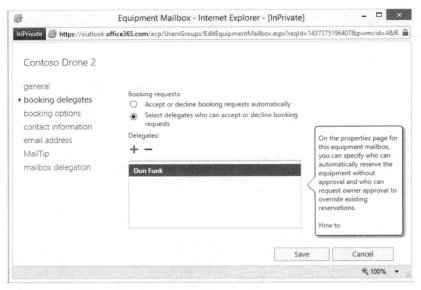

FIGURE 3-39 Booking Delegates

- **Booking Options** On the Booking Options page, shown in Figure 3-40, you can configure whether repeat bookings are allowed, whether bookings can only occur during working hours, how far in advance bookings can occur, and the maximum booking duration.

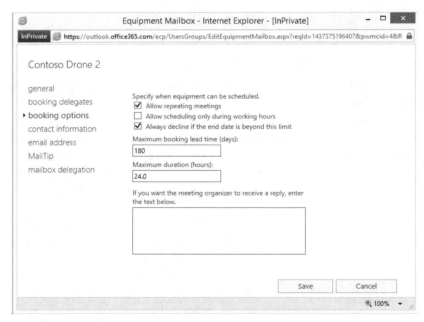

FIGURE 3-40 Booking Options

- **Contact Information**   Allows you to set contact information about the resource.
- **Email Address**   Allows you to configure email addresses for the resource.
- **MailTip**   Allows you to configure a MailTip for the resource
- **Mailbox Delegation**   Allows you to delegate permissions on the resource.

You can create an equipment mailbox using the New-Mailbox cmdlet and the Equipment parameter. For example, to create a new equipment mailbox named CompanyHovercraft, issue the command:

```
New-Mailbox -Name "CompanyHovercraft" -Equipment
```

> **MORE INFO** **EQUIPMENT MAILBOXES**
>
> You can learn more about equipment mailboxes at *https://technet.microsoft.com/en-us/library/jj215770(v=exchg.150).aspx.*

Room mailboxes

Room mailboxes allow users to book rooms for meetings and to view room availability. One of the differences between a room mailbox and an equipment mailbox is the ability to specify the room capacity. To create a room mailbox, perform the following steps:

1. In the Office 365 Admin Center, click Exchange under ADMIN. This will open the Exchange Admin Center.
2. Click Recipients and then click Resources.
3. Click the Plus (+) icon and then click Room Mailbox, as shown in Figure 3-41.

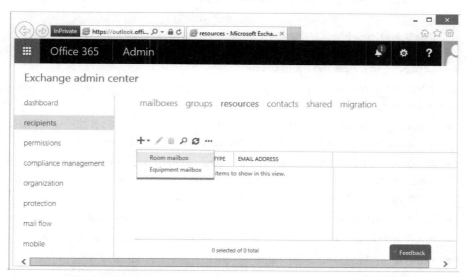

FIGURE 3-41 New Room Mailbox

4. On the New Room Mailbox page, shown in Figure 3-42, specify the following information:

- **Room Name** The name of the room as it will appear in the address list.
- **Email Address** The email address associated with the room.
- **Location** Room location (optional).
- **Phone** A phone number allocated to the room (optional).
- **Capacity** The room capacity (optional).

FIGURE 3-42 New Room Mailbox

5. Click Save to create the room mailbox.

Once the room mailbox is created, you can edit the mailbox to configure the following additional settings:

- **Booking Delegates** Allows you to configure whether the room can be booked automatically or whether bookings must be approved by a delegate.
- **Booking Options** Allows you to configure whether repeat meetings can be scheduled, whether meetings can only be scheduled during working hours, how far in advance bookings can be made, and the maximum booking duration.
- **Contact Information** Allows you to set contact information about the resource.
- **Email Address** Allows you to configure email addresses for the resource.
- **MailTip** Allows you to configure a MailTip for the resource.
- **Mailbox Delegation** Allows you to delegate permissions on the resource.

You can create a new room mailbox using the New-Mailbox Windows PowerShell cmdlet with the Room parameter. For example, to create a mailbox named Sydney Conference Room, use the following command:

```
New-Mailbox -Name SydConf -DisplayName "Sydney Conference Room" -Room
```

> **MORE INFO MANAGE ROOM MAILBOXES**
>
> You can learn more about managing room mailboxes at *https://technet.microsoft.com/en-us/library/JJ215781(v=EXCHG.150).aspx.*

Managing external contacts

External contacts allow you to add people with email addresses from outside your organization to your internal address books. For example, if you want to add the address of someone at Adatum Corporation to the Contoso address book, you could do so using an external contact.

To create an external contact, perform the following steps:

1. In the Office 365 Admin Center, click Exchange under ADMIN. This will open the Exchange Admin Center.

2. Click Recipients. Click Contacts. Click the Plus (+) icon and then click Mail Contact.

3. On the Mail Contact page, provide the following information:

   - First Name
   - Initial
   - Last Name
   - Display Name
   - Alias
   - External Email Address

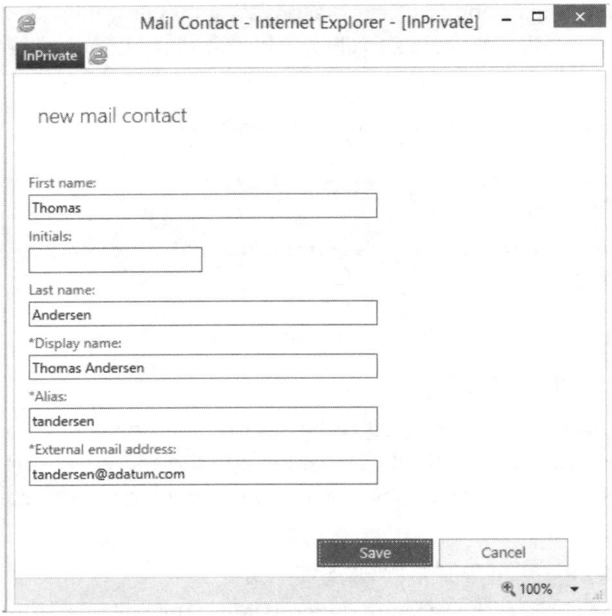

FIGURE 3-43 New Mail Contact

4. Click Save to save the contact.

You use the New-MailContact Windows PowerShell cmdlet to create a mail contact. For example, to create a mail contact for Thomas Andersen, issue the following command:

```
New-MailContact –Name "Thomas Andersen" –ExternalEmailAddress tandersen@adatum.com
```

You can add additional email addresses to a mail contact using the Set-MailContact Windows PowerShell cmdlet. For example, to add an addition email address to the Thomas Andersen contact for an email address in the tailspintoys.com email domain, issue the command:

```
Set-MailContact –Name "Thomas Andersen" –EmailAddresses
"SMTP:tandersen@adatum.com","smtp:tandersen@tailspintoys.com"
```

The uppercase SMTP defines the primary email address. There can only be one primary email address.

> **MORE INFO EXTERNAL CONTACTS**
>
> You can learn more about external contacts at *https://technet.microsoft.com/library/ aa998858(v=exchg.150).aspx.*

Managing distribution groups

Distribution groups allow users to send email messages to a single address and have those messages forwarded to all members of the distribution group. Exchange Online supports the following types of distribution group, as shown in Figure 3-44:

- **Distribution Group**   Also termed a distribution list, this type of group allows you to distribute messages to groups of users.
- **Security Group**   Also termed a mail-enabled security group, it allows you to distribute messages to groups of users, as well as allowing permissions to be configured for resources.
- **Dynamic Distribution Group**   A distribution list where the list of recipients is calculated each time a message is sent. Membership of the list is determined based on group settings and conditions.

FIGURE 3-44 Group types

MORE INFO DISTRIBUTION GROUP TYPES

You can learn more about Exchange Online Distribution Groups at *https://support.office.com/en-us/article/Create-edit-or-delete-a-security-group-55c96b32-e086-4c9e-948b-a018b44510cb #__groups_in_exchange.*

Distribution group

To create a distribution group that can be used to forward messages to users but cannot be used to assign security permissions, perform the following steps:

1. In the Office 365 Admin Center, click Exchange under ADMIN. This will open the Exchange Admin Center.
2. Click Recipients. Click Groups. Click the Plus (+) icon and then click Distribution Group.
3. On the New Distribution Group dialog box, provide the following information, as shown in Figure 3-45:

- **Display Name** The name of the security group as it appears in the address book.
- **Alias** The group alias.
- **Email Address** The prefix name. The group email address.
- **Owners** Users who have permission to manage the group.

FIGURE 3-45 New Distribution Group

- **Members** Allows you to specify members of the group.
- **Join settings** Specify whether approval is required to join the group. You can configure the group to be open, which means anyone can join; closed, which means group owners control membership; or owner approval, which allows people to request group membership subject to group owner approval. These options are shown in Figure 3-46.

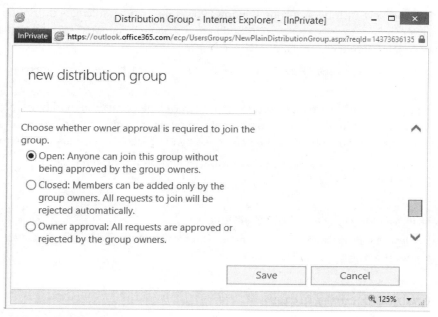

FIGURE 3-46 Joining settings

■ **Leave settings** Specify whether approval is required to leave the group. These options are shown in Figure 3-47.

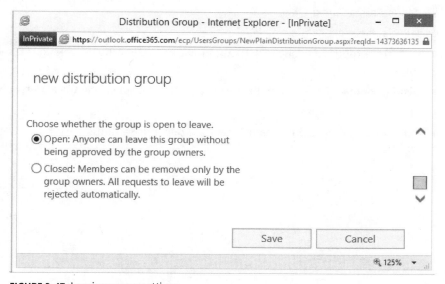

FIGURE 3-47 Leaving group settings

4. Click Save to create the distribution group.

You use the New-DistributionGroup Windows PowerShell cmdlet to create distribution groups. For example, to create a new distribution group named ExampleDistGroup that allows members to join, issue the command:

```
New-DistributionGroup –Name "ExampleDistGroup" –Alias ExampleDG –MemberJoinRestriction
Open
```

You can use the Set-DistributionGroup Windows PowerShell cmdlet to modify the properties of an existing distribution group. For example, to modify the distribution group Example-DistGroup so that new members must be approved by the group owner, issue the command:

```
Set-DistributionGroup –Identity "ExampleDistGroup" –MemberJoinRestriction
'ApprovalRequired'
```

> **MORE INFO** **MANAGE DISTRIBUTION GROUPS**
>
> You can learn more about managing Exchange Online distribution groups at *https://tech-net.microsoft.com/library/bb124513.aspx*.

Mail-enabled security group

Mail-enabled security groups are groups that allow you to send messages to multiple people and which can also be used to assign permissions. To create a mail-enabled security group, perform the following steps:

1. In the Office 365 Admin Center, click Exchange under ADMIN. This will open the Exchange Admin Center.
2. Click Recipients.
3. In the New Distribution Group dialog box, provide the following information, as shown in Figure 3-48:
   - **Display Name** The name of the security group as it appears in the address book.
   - **Alias** The group alias.
   - **Email Address** The prefix name and the group email address.

FIGURE 3-48 New Security Group

- **Owners** Users who have permission to manage the group.
- **Members** Allows you to specify members of the group. Owners and Members settings are shown in Figure 3-49.

FIGURE 3-49 New Security Group Owners and Members

- **Join settings** Specify whether approval is required to join the group. You can configure the group to be open, which means anyone can join; closed, which means group owners control membership; or owner approval, which allows people to request group membership subject to group owner approval.
- **Leave settings** Specify whether approval is required to leave the group.

4. Click Save to create the mail-enabled security group.

You use the New-DistributionGroup Windows PowerShell cmdlet with the Type parameter set to Security to create a mail-enabled security group. For example, to create a new security group named ExampleSecurityGroup, use the command:

```
New-DistributionGroup –Name "ExampleSecurityGroup" –Alias ExSecGroup –Type Security
```

You can use the Set-DistributionGroup Windows PowerShell cmdlet to modify the properties of a mail-enabled security group.

> **MORE INFO** **MAIL-ENABLED SECURITY GROUP**
>
> You can learn more about the mail-enabled security group at *https://technet.microsoft.com/library/bb123521.aspx*.

Dynamic distribution group

Dynamic distribution groups differ from distribution groups and mail-enabled security groups in that membership of the group is generated dynamically rather than including lists of users who have chosen to join or have been added to the group. You configure the membership by first specifying what types of recipients will be members, as shown in Figure 3-50, and then by adding rules. Recipient types that you can select include:

- Users With Exchange Mailboxes
- Mail Users With External Email Addresses
- Resource Mailboxes
- Mail Contacts With External Email Addresses
- Mail-Enabled Groups

FIGURE 3-50 New Dynamic Distribution Group

You can use the following attributes when creating a rule for a Dynamic Distribution Group:

- State or province
- Company
- Department
- Custom attributes 1 through 15

To create a rule, select the attribute and then specify the words or phrases that match the attribute. Figure 3-51 shows the word Accounting configured as the word that should be matched for a specific attribute.

FIGURE 3-51 Dynamic group filter

Figure 3-52 shows a distribution group where only users with Exchange Mailboxes whose Department attribute matches the word Accounting.

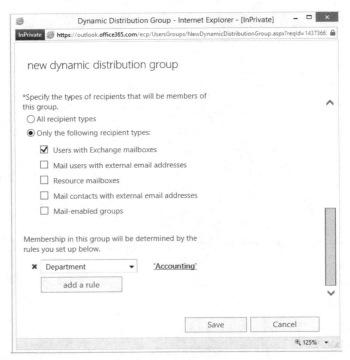

FIGURE 3-52 Users With Exchange Mailboxes in the Accounting Department

To create a Dynamic Distribution Group, perform the following steps:

1. In the Office 365 Admin Center, click Exchange under ADMIN. This will open the Exchange Admin Center.

2. Click Recipients. Click Groups. Click the Plus (+) icon, and then click Dynamic distribution group.

3. Provide the following information:

   - **Display Name** Name of the group that will be displayed.
   - **Alias** Group alias, which will also be the name used for the email address prefix.
   - **Owner** Allows you to specify a group owner. Group owners are able to change the properties of the dynamic distribution group and to perform moderation tasks on messages sent to the group. If not configured, the user that created the group will be set as the owner.
   - **Members** Specify the recipient types to be included.
   - **Membership Rules** Specify the rules that will filter the recipient types selected.

4. Click Save to save the group properties.

You can also use the New-DynamicDistributionGroup Windows PowerShell cmdlet to create dynamic distribution groups. For example, to create a new dynamic distribution group named AccountingDDG that includes only mailbox users from the Accounting department, issue the following command:

```
New-DynamicDistributionGroup -Name "AccountingDDG" -Alias "AccountingDDG"
-IncludedRecipients MailboxUsers -ConditionalDepartment "Accounting"
```

MORE INFO DYNAMIC DISTRIBUTION GROUPS

You can learn more about dynamic distribution groups at *https://technet.microsoft.com/library/bb123722.aspx*.

EXAM TIP

Remember the difference between Send As, Send on Behalf, and Full Access recipient permissions.

Thought experiment

Resource mailboxes and distribution lists at Contoso

In this thought experiment, apply what you learned about this objective. You can find answers to these questions in the "Answers" section at the end of this chapter.

You are the Office 365 administrator at Adatum. Adatum has recently purchased several Hololens devices that will be used by the research team to interact with several computer-aided design applications. You want to allow people to book these devices using Outlook. You also want to be able to send email messages to members of the research team, each of which has their department set to Research. The distribution group used for this purpose should not need to be maintained manually. With this information in mind, answer the following questions:

1. What type of resource mailboxes should you create for the Hololens devices?

2. What type of distribution list should you create for the research team?

Objective summary

- The Send As permission allows the person delegated the permission to send messages as though they were sent by the mailbox owner.
- The Send on Behalf permission allows the person delegated the permission to send messages on behalf of the mailbox owner.
- The Full Access permission allows the person delegated the permission the ability to open and access the contents of an Exchange Online mailbox.
- Being delegated the Full Access permission does not allow a delegate to send mail from the mailbox.
- Shared mailboxes allow multiple users to view, respond to, and send email messages. Shared mailboxes also allow a group of users to have a common calendar.
- Resource mailboxes represent organizational facilities and equipment.
- Exchange Online supports two types of resource mailbox, room mailboxes and equipment mailboxes.
- External contacts allow you to add people with email addresses from outside your organization to your internal address books.
- Distribution groups allow users to send email messages to a single address and have those messages forwarded to all members of the distribution group.
- Exchange Online supports distribution groups, mail-enabled security groups, and dynamic distribution groups.

Objective review

Answer the following questions to test your knowledge of the information in this objective. You can find the answers to these questions and explanations of why each answer choice is correct or incorrect in the "Answers" section at the end of this chapter.

1. Which of the following Windows PowerShell cmdlets would you use if you wanted to assign the Full Access permission to Kim Akers over Don Funk's Exchange Online mailbox?

   A. Add-RecipientPermission

   B. Set-Mailbox

   C. Remove-RecipientPermission

   D. Add-MailboxPermission

2. Which of the following Windows PowerShell cmdlets would you use if you wanted to assign the Send As permission to Don Funk for Kim Akers' Exchange Online mailbox?

   A. Add-MailboxPermission

   B. Add-RecipientPermission

   C. Set-Mailbox

   D. Remove-MailboxPermission

3. Which of the following Windows PowerShell cmdlets would you use to assign Don Funk the Send on Behalf permission on Kim Akers' Exchange Online mailbox?

   A. Set-Mailbox

   B. Add-MailboxPermission

   C. Add-RecipientPermission

   D. Remove-MailboxPermission

4. Which of the following Windows PowerShell cmdlets would you use to remove Kim Akers' Full Access permission on Don Funk's Exchange Online mailbox?

   A. Remove-MailboxPermission

   B. Remove-RecipientPermission

   C. Set-Mailbox

   D. Add-RecipientPermission

5. Which Windows PowerShell cmdlet would you use to remove the Send As permission assigned to Kim Akers from Don Funk's Exchange Online mailbox?

   A. Add-RecipientPermission

   B. Remove-MailboxPermission

   C. Set-Mailbox

   D. Remove-RecipientPermission

Objective 3.3: Configure personal archive policies

This objective deals with configuring personal archives, retention tags, and retention policies. These features control which information is kept and which information is discarded from Exchange Online mailboxes on a long-term basis.

> **This objective covers the following topics:**
> - Enable personal archive for mailboxes
> - Retention tags and retention policies

Enabling personal archive for mailboxes

Archive mailboxes, which are termed in-place archives in Exchange Online, allow for extra email storage. Once you enable an archive, messages that are in a user's Exchange Online mailbox that exceed two years of age will automatically be transferred to the archive by the default retention policy. Users are also able to manually move messages to the archive or they can create inbox rules that automatically move messages that match the rules to the archive. If an archive isn't enabled for a user, messages that exceed two years of age remain in the Exchange Online mailbox.

Archives also allow you to alleviate the need for personal store (PST) files on local computers. There are several advantages to using archives, including simplifying the process of managing retention and eDiscovery requests as all mail will be stored in a location accessible to administrators. For example, if you are in the process of responding to an eDiscovery request involving an executive's email, you need to be able to search all locations where that email is stored. If the executive stores email on their personal laptop computer in a PST file, you will need to search that file as well as the user's Exchange Online mailbox. Once you have configured an archive, you can use other tools to import the contents of any PST files into an Exchange Online mailbox and then block the utilization of PST files on client computers.

You can see which users have an archive enabled by noting the archive designation in the mailbox type column in the list of recipients. Figure 3-53 shows that the Dan Jump mailbox is configured with an archive.

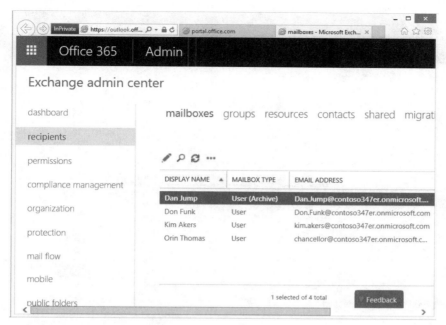

FIGURE 3-53 Dan Jump with Archive set

To enable the personal archive for an existing Exchange Online mailbox, perform the following steps:

1. In the Office 365 Admin Center, click Exchange under ADMIN. This will open the Exchange Admin Center.

2. In the Exchange Admin Center, click Recipients.

3. Click Mailboxes.

4. In the list of mailboxes, select the mailbox for which you want to enable the archive. Figure 3-54 shows the Dan Jump mailbox selected.

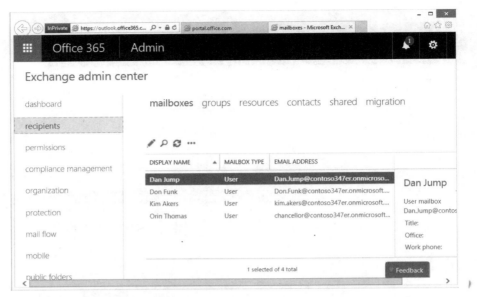

FIGURE 3-54 Dan Jump selected

5. Click the Edit (Pencil) icon.

6. Click Mailbox features. Under Archiving, shown in Figure 3-55, click Enable.

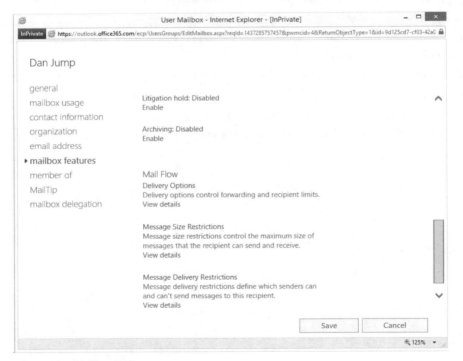

FIGURE 3-55 Mailbox Features

7. Once archiving is enabled, click View Details, as shown in Figure 3-56, to configure archive details.

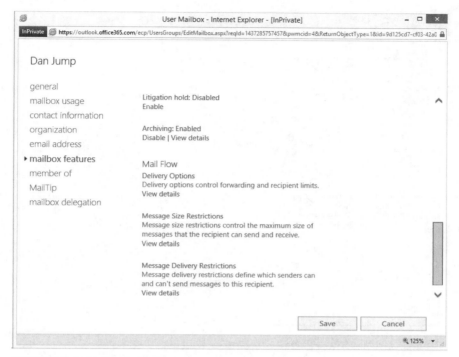

FIGURE 3-56 Archiving Enabled

8. On the Archive Mailbox dialog box, you can specify the name of the folder in the user's mailbox for the archive. Depending on the Exchange Online plan, you will be able to configure the Archive Quota and the warning threshold. Figure 3-57 shows the Archive Mailbox dialog with the name set to Archive. Click OK to save changes.

FIGURE 3-57 Archive Mailbox settings

9. Click Save on the User Mailbox dialog box to save settings.

You can use the Enable-mailbox Windows PowerShell cmdlet to enable an archive on a specific mailbox. For example, to enable an archive on Kim Akers mailbox, issue the following command:

```
Enable-mailbox "Kim Akers" -Archive
```

When you use this command, the mailbox will be assigned the name "Personal Archive - <display name>" by default. For example, for Kim Akers, the archive will be named "Personal Archive – Kim Akers."

To enable archives on all mailboxes that do not currently have archives enabled, run the following command:

```
Get-Mailbox -Filter {ArchiveStatus -Eq "None" -AND RecipientTypeDetails -eq
"UserMailbox"} | Enable-mailbox -Archive
```

> **MORE INFO ARCHIVES**
>
> You can learn more about archives at *https://technet.microsoft.com/en-us/library/ JJ984357(v=EXCHG.150).aspx.*

Understanding retention tags and retention policies

Messaging Records Management (MRM) allows organizations to manage how email messages are treated so that the legal risks associated with the long-term storage of messages and other communication is minimized. For example, when properly configured, MRM allows organizations to ensure that messages that they must keep for a certain period of time due to regulation or legal requirement are kept while other messages that are not subject to these restrictions are automatically removed if no longer required. Without MRM, you might have some users who delete email messages that should legally be stored and others that never delete anything, meaning that they are constantly at risk of exceeding their Exchange Online mailbox quota.

> **MORE INFO** **RETENTION TAGS AND RETENTION POLICIES**
>
> You can learn more about retention tags and retention policies at *https://technet.microsoft.com/en-us/library/dd297955(v=exchg.150).aspx*.

Create retention tags

Retention tags include a retention action and a retention period. A retention action specifies whether the tag deletes and allows recovery of a message, permanently deletes a message, or moves the message to the archive. The retention period defines the number of days that must pass before the tag is triggered.

To create a retention tag, perform the following steps:

1. In the Office 365 Admin Center, click Exchange under ADMIN. This will open the Exchange Admin Center.
2. In the Exchange Admin Center, click Compliance Management.
3. In Compliance Management, click Retention Tags, as shown in Figure 3-58.

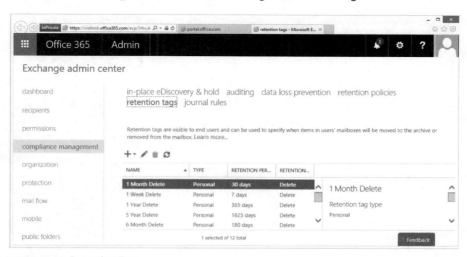

FIGURE 3-58 Retention Tags

4. On the toolbar, click the Plus (+) icon and select between the following options, as shown in Figure 3-59:

- Applied Automatically to Entire Mailbox
- Applied Automatically to a Default Folder
- Applied by Users to Items and Folders (personal)

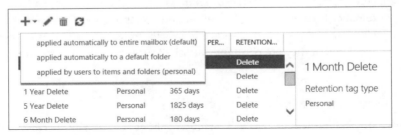

FIGURE 3-59 New Retention Tag

5. On the New Tag dialog box, shown in Figure 3-60, provide the following information:

- **Tag Name**   The name of the retention tag.
- **Retention Action**   Specify if the tag deletes and allows recovery, permanently deletes, or moves the message to the archive.
- **Retention Period**   The number of days that must pass before the tag is triggered.

FIGURE 3-60 New Tag for Entire Mailbox

You create retention tags using the New-RetentionPolicyTag Windows PowerShell cmdlet. For example, to create a retention tag of the default type named Research-Default that permanently deletes messages after 180 days, issue the following command:

```
New-RetentionPolicyTag "Research-Default" -Type All -RetentionEnabled $true
-AgeLimitForRetention 180 -RetentionAction PermanentlyDelete
```

MORE INFO **RETENTION TAGS**

You can learn more about creating retention tags in Windows PowerShell at *https://tech-net.microsoft.com/en-us/library/dd335226(v=exchg.150).aspx.*

Create custom retention policy

A retention policy is a collection of retention tags that can be applied to a mailbox. To create a new retention policy, perform the following steps:

1. In the Office 365 Admin Center, click Exchange under ADMIN. This will open the Exchange Admin Center.

2. In the Exchange Admin Center, click Compliance Management and click Retention Policies.

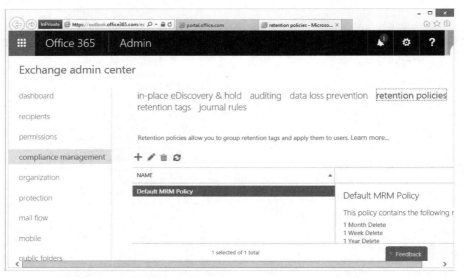

FIGURE 3-61 Default MRM Policy

3. On the toolbar, click the Plus (+) icon.

4. On the New Retention Policy page, shown in Figure 3-62, provide a name for the retention policy. Click the Plus (+) icon to add retention tags.

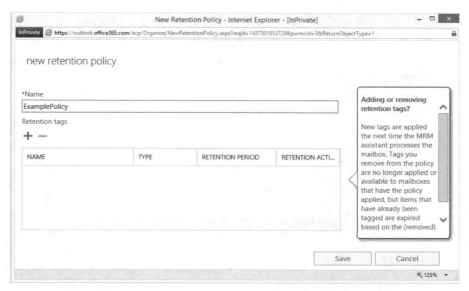

FIGURE 3-62 New Retention Policy

5. On the Select Retention Tags page, shown in Figure 3-63, select the tags that you want to add to the policy and click Add. Click OK to close the Select Retention Tags dialog box.

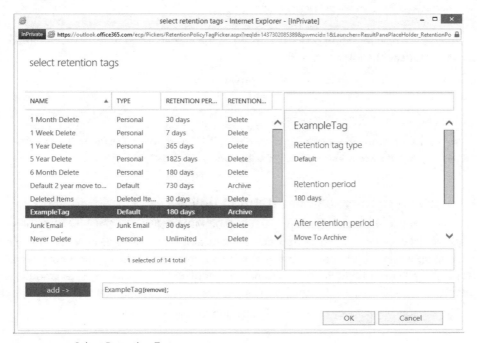

FIGURE 3-63 Select Retention Tags

6. In the New Retention Policy dialog box, shown in Figure 3-64, click Save to create the new retention policy.

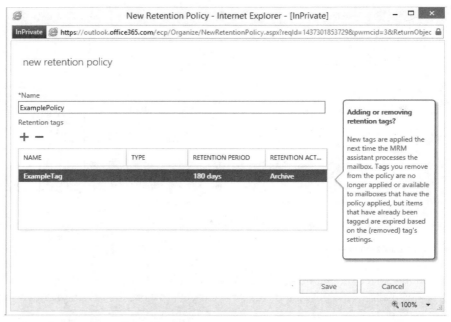

FIGURE 3-64 Example policy and tag

To create a new retention policy that includes the Research and Accounting retention policy tags, issue the following command:

```
New-RetentionPolicy "Contoso General" –RetentionPolicyTagLinks "Research","Accounting"
```

> **MORE INFO RETENTION POLICIES**
>
> You can learn more about creating retention policies using Windows PowerShell at *https://technet.microsoft.com/en-us/library/dd297970(v=exchg.150).aspx*.

Review and modify default retention policy

The name of the default retention policy is Default MRM Policy. The Default MRM Policy is always the default retention policy applied automatically to new users. Even if you create other retention policies, it is the default that is applied automatically. While you cannot change the fact that the Default MRM Policy is automatically applied to new users, you can modify which retention tags are contained in the policy, as well as modifying the retention tags themselves.

The Default MRM Policy contains the retention tags listed in Table 3-1:

Table 3-1: Retention tags in Default MRM Policy

NAME	TYPE	RETENTION PERIOD	ACTION
Default 2 years move to archive	Default Policy Tag (DPT)	730	Move to Archive
Recoverable Items 14 days move to archive	Recoverable Items folder	14	Move to Archive
Personal 1 year move to archive	Personal tag	365	Move to Archive
Personal 5 year move to archive	Personal tag	1825	Move to Archive
Personal never move to archive	Personal tag	Not applicable	Move to Archive
1 Week Delete	Personal tag	7	Delete and Allow Recovery
1 Month Delete	Personal tag	30	Delete and Allow Recovery
6 Month Delete	Personal tag	180	Delete and Allow Recovery
1 Year Delete	Personal tag	365	Delete and Allow Recovery
5 Year Delete	Personal tag	1825	Delete and Allow Recovery
Never Delete	Personal tag	Not applicable	Delete and Allow Recovery

To alter the default retention policy, perform the following steps:

1. In the Office 365 Admin Center, click Exchange under ADMIN. This will open the Exchange Admin Center.

2. In the Exchange Admin Center, click Compliance Management and click Retention policies.

3. In the list of retention policies, select the Default MRM Policy, as shown in Figure 3-65, and then click the Edit (Pencil) icon.

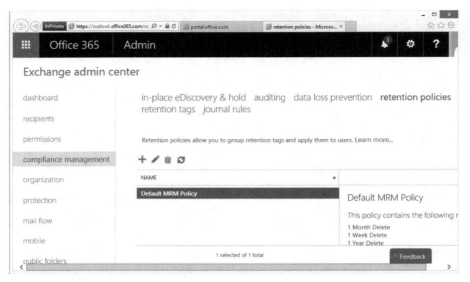

FIGURE 3-65 Default MRM Policy

4. On the Default MRM Policy page, shown in Figure 3-66, make the changes that you want to make to the policy by adding and removing retention tags.

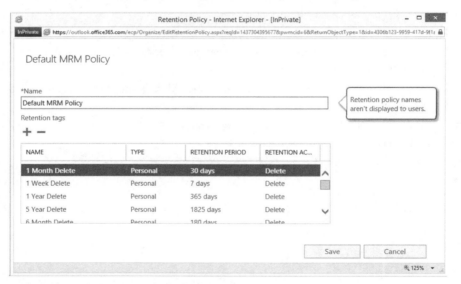

FIGURE 3-66 Retention Tags in Default MRM Policy

5. Click Save to save the modifications to the MRM policy.

You can use the Set-RetentionPolicy Windows PowerShell cmdlet to modify the default retention policy.

Apply retention policy to mailboxes

While the default retention policy is automatically applied to mailboxes and Exchange Online mailboxes can only have a single retention policy applied, it is possible to replace the default retention policy with a custom retention policy.

To apply a custom retention policy to a single mailbox, perform the following steps:

1.   In the Office 365 Admin Center, click Exchange under ADMIN. This will open the Exchange Admin Center.

2.   Click Recipients. In the list of mailboxes, select the Exchange Online mailbox to which you want to apply the retention policy. Figure 3-67 shows the Dan Jump mailbox selected.

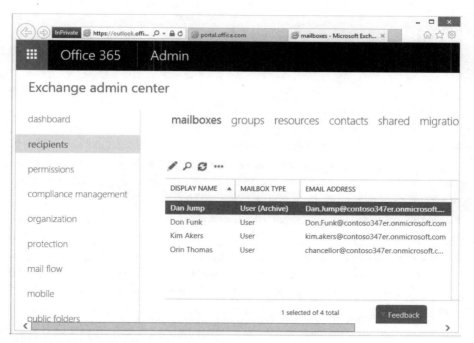

FIGURE 3-67 Dan Jump mailbox selected

3.   Click the Edit (Pencil) icon. This will bring up the Mailbox Properties page.

4.   Click Mailbox Features. Use the Retention Policy drop down list to select the retention policy that you want to apply to the mailbox. Figure 3-68 shows the ExamplePolicy retention policy applied to the mailbox.

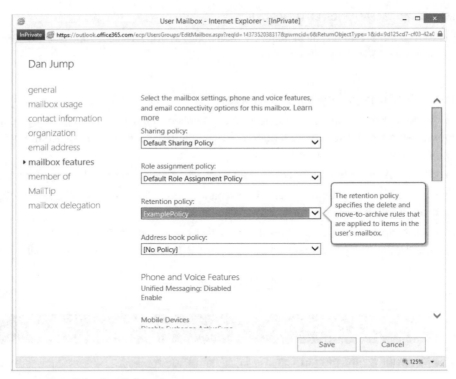

FIGURE 3-68 Retention Policy set

5. Click Save to apply the policy to the mailbox.

You don't have to apply retention policies on a per-mailbox basis. It is possible to apply the same retention policy to multiple Exchange Online mailboxes. To apply a custom retention policy to multiple mailboxes, perform the following steps:

1. In the Office 365 Admin Center, click Exchange under ADMIN. This will open the Exchange Admin Center.

2. Click Recipients. In the list of mailboxes, use the Shift or Ctrl keys to select the Exchange Online mailboxes to which you want to apply the retention policy. Figure 3-69 shows the Don Funk and Kim Akers mailboxes selected.

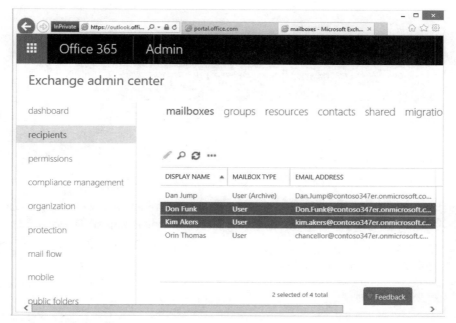

FIGURE 3-69 Multiple users selected

3. With the multiple mailboxes selected, click More Options, as shown in Figure 3-70.

FIGURE 3-70 More Options

4. Under Retention Policy, shown in Figure 3-71, click Update.

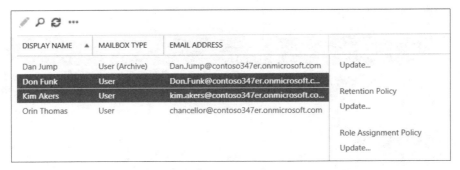

FIGURE 3-71 Update multiple users' retention policies

5. On the Bulk Assign Retention Policy page, select the retention policy that you want to assign to the selected mailboxes. Figure 3-72 shows the ExamplePolicy selected.

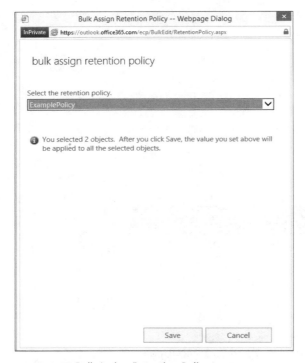

FIGURE 3-72 Bulk Assign Retention Policy

6. Click Save to apply the policy to the selected mailboxes.

You use the Set-Mailbox Windows PowerShell cmdlet to apply retention policies to mailboxes. For example, to apply the ExamplePolicy retention policy to Don Funk's mailbox, issue the command:

```
Set-Mailbox "Don Funk" -RetentionPolicy "ExamplePolicy"
```

MORE INFO APPLY RETENTION POLICY

You can learn more about applying retention policies at *https://technet.microsoft.com/en-us/library/Dd298052(v=EXCHG.150).aspx*.

EXAM TIP

Remember that unless you apply a different retention policy, the default retention policy will apply to all newly created Exchange Online mailboxes.

Thought experiment
MRM at Contoso

In this thought experiment, apply what you learned about this objective. You can find answers to these questions in the "Answers" section at the end of this chapter.

A large number of users at Contoso have very large inbox folders. These inbox folders have grown large because users are not deleting old messages. Unfortunately, some users are approaching their quota. With this in mind, answer the following questions:

1. What feature can you enable to allow users to keep old messages as long as they want?

2. What can you do to ensure that messages over 180 days are not stored in the user's inbox folder?

Objective summary

- In-place archives allow for extra email storage.
- Once you enable an archive, messages that are in a user's Exchange Online mailbox that exceed two years of age will automatically be transferred to the archive by the default retention policy.
- Users are able to manually move messages to the archive or can create inbox rules that automatically move messages that match the rules to the archive.
- Retention tags include a retention action and a retention period.
- Retention action specifies whether the tag deletes and allows recovery, permanently deletes, or moves the message to the archive.
- Retention period defines the number of days that must pass before the tag triggers.
- The Default MRM Policy is always the default retention policy applied automatically to new users.

Objective review

Answer the following questions to test your knowledge of the information in this objective. You can find the answers to these questions and explanations of why each answer choice is correct or incorrect in the "Answers" section at the end of this chapter.

1. Which of the following cmdlets can you use to enable an archive for an existing Exchange Online mailbox user?

    A. Enable-mailbox

    B. Set-Mailbox

    C. Get-Mailbox

    D. New-Mailbox

2. Which of the two following cmdlets would you use to enable archives for all Exchange Online mailbox users who do not currently have one enabled?

    A. Set-Mailbox

    B. Get-Mailbox

    C. Enable-mailbox

    D. New-Mailbox

3. Which of the following Windows PowerShell cmdlets would you use to create a new retention policy tag? (Choose Two.)

    A. Set-RetentionPolicyTag

    B. New-RetentionPolicyTag

    C. Set-RetentionPolicy

    D. New-RetentionPolicy

4. Which of the following Windows PowerShell cmdlets would you use to apply a retention policy to an Exchange Online mailbox?

    A. Set-Mailbox

    B. New-RetentionPolicy

    C. Set-RetentionPolicy

    D. Set-RetentionPolicyTag

5. An existing tag moves items to the archive after 365 days. You want to change this to 180 days. Which of the following Windows PowerShell cmdlets would you use to accomplish this goal?

    A. Set-RetentionPolicy

    B. Set-Mailbox

    C. New-RetentionPolicyTag

    D. Set-RetentionPolicyTag

6. You want to modify the list of policy tags in a retention policy that applies to several existing mailboxes. Which of the following Windows PowerShell cmdlets would you use to accomplish this goal?

   A. Set-RetentionPolicy

   B. Set-RetentionPolicyTag

   C. Set-Mailbox

   D. New-RetentionPolicy

Objective 3.4: Configure Skype for Business Online end-user communication settings

This objective deals with configuring end-user communication settings for Skype for Business Online. To master this objective, you'll need to understand how to configure user settings, including presence, external communication, whether meetings are recorded, and disabling features that cannot be recorded to ensure that compliance obligations are met.

> **This objective covers the following topics:**
> - Configure presence
> - Configure per user external communication
> - Configure user settings

Configuring presence

Presence settings determine who is able to see when a user is available, in a meeting, or out of office in Skype for Business Online. You can configure the following options:

- **Automatically Display Presence Information**   When you choose this option, any user that does not belong to the External or Blocked privacy group can view the user's presence information.

- **Display Presence Information Only To A User's Contacts**   When you choose this option, presence information is visible only to people in the user's Contacts list who are not in the External or Blocked privacy group.

To configure presence settings for Skype for Business Online, perform the following steps:

1. In the Office 365 Admin Center, click Skype for Business under ADMIN.

2. In the Skype for Business Admin Center, click Organization.

3. Under Presence Privacy Mode, shown in Figure 3-73, select the appropriate privacy mode.

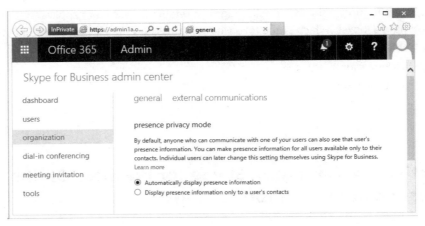

FIGURE 3-73 Presence Privacy Mode

MORE INFO **CONFIGURE PRESENCE IN SKYPE FOR BUSINESS ONLINE**

You can learn more about configuring presence for Skype for Business Online at *https://support.office.com/en-us/article/Configure-presence-in-Skype-for-Business-Online-ce59ac0b-8115-4c6b-8174-e3aef982d3cb*.

Configuring external communication

External communication settings allow you to configure whether users can add Skype or Skype of Business users external to your organization to their list of business contacts. You can configure these settings across the tenancy or on a per-user basis.

When configuring external communications settings across the tenancy, you can choose between the following options:

- **Off Completely**   This blocks access to users from outside the tenancy.
- **On Except For Blocked Domains**   This allows communications with users except those who come from blocked domains.
- **On Only For Allowed Domains**   This allows communications with users who are from the list of allowed domains.

Separate from this, you can also allow connectivity with Skype users and other public IM service providers. This option is disabled if you select the Off Completely option. To configure external communications settings across the tenancy, perform the following steps:

1. In the Office 365 Admin Center, click Skype for Business under ADMIN.
2. In the Skype for Business Admin Center, click Organization.
3. Click External Communications.

4. On the External Access page, select the External Access option and whether you want to allow communication with Skype users and other public IM providers. These options are shown in Figure 3-74.

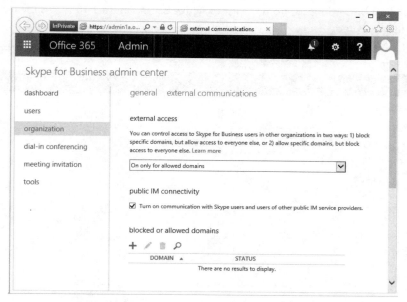

FIGURE 3-74 External Access

5. To add a blocked or allowed domain, click the Plus (+) icon.

6. On the Add A Domain page, shown in Figure 3-75, enter the domain name and click Add. If the setting is configured for blocked domains, the added domain will be blocked. If the setting is configured for allowed domains, the added domain will be allowed.

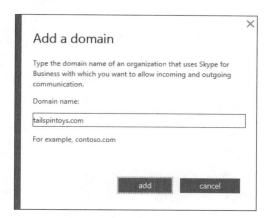

FIGURE 3-75 Add A Domain

To configure external communication settings on a per-user basis, perform the following steps:

1. In the Office 365 Admin Center, select the user that you want to configure external communication settings for from the list of Active Users. Figure 3-76 shows the Dan Jump user selected.

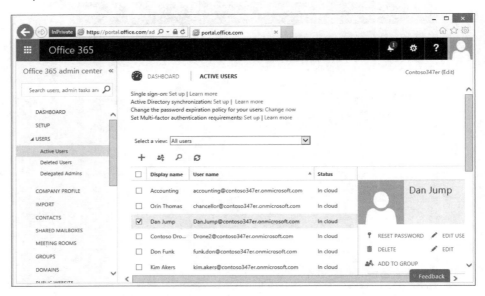

FIGURE 3-76 Dan Jump selected

2. When the user is selected, click Edit.

3. On the User Properties page, shown in Figure 3-77, click More.

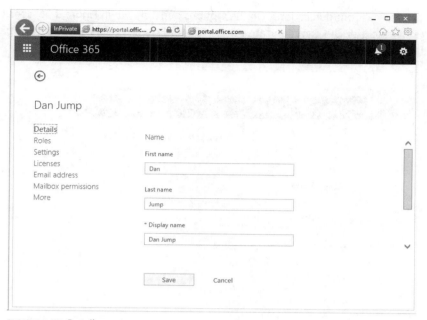

FIGURE 3-77 Details page

4. Under Skype for Business, click Edit Skype for Business Properties, as shown in Figure 3-78.

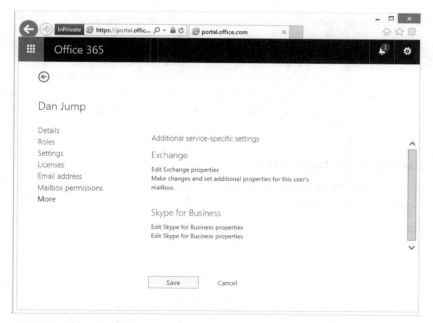

FIGURE 3-78 More options

5. Click External Communications. On the Options page, shown in Figure 3-79, specify whether the user can communicate with Skype for Business Users outside the organization and/or users on public IM networks.

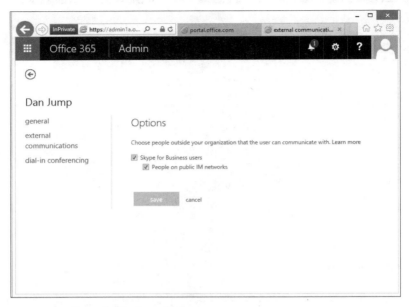

FIGURE 3-79 Skype For Business Options

6. Click Save to save changes.

> **MORE INFO** **CONFIGURING EXTERNAL COMMUNICATIONS**
>
> You can learn more about configuring external communications at *https://support.office. com/en-us/article/Let-Skype-for-Business-Online-users-communicate-with-external-Skype- for-Business-or-Skype-contacts-b414873a-0059-4cd5-aea1-e5d0857dbc94*.

Configuring user options

You can configure which features you want a user to have access to in the General setting of the Options page shown in Figure 3-80.

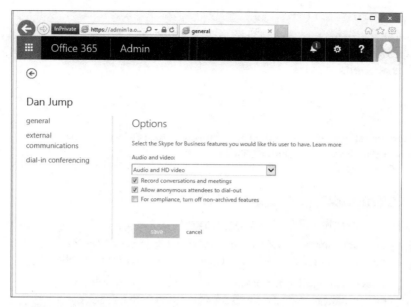

FIGURE 3-80 Skype For Business Options

You can configure the following Audio and video settings:

- **None**   Blocks use of audio and video when using Skype for Business.
- **Online**   Text-based messaging is available.
- **Audio Only**   Allows use of audio and text based messaging, but not video.
- **Audio And Video**   Allows use of audio, standard-definition video, and text based messaging.
- **Audio And HD Video**   Allows use of audio, high-definition video- and text-based messaging.

You can configure the following additional options:

- **Record Conversations And Meetings**   When the Record Conversations And Meetings option is selected, conversations and meetings are recorded. This allows conversations and meetings to be reviewed at a later point in time.
- **Allow Anonymous Attendees To Dial-Out**   When the Allow Anonymous Attendees To Dial-Out option is selected, it is possible for anonymous attendees to connect to meeting audio by having the conferencing service call them. If this option is not enabled, anonymous attendees must call in to the conferencing service.
- **For Compliance, Turn Off Non-Archived Features**   When you enable this option, features that are not recorded when an in-place hold is enacted are unavailable. This includes file transfers through instant messaging, shared OneNote pages, and annotations made to PowerPoint presentations conducted across Skype for Business.

MORE INFO **CONFIGURE USER SETTINGS**

You can learn more about configuring user settings for Skype for Business Online at *https://support.office.com/en-US/article/Configure-settings-for-individual-users-77B26EAC-8228-4161-BA9F-733B187BD836*.

EXAM TIP

Remember what functionality is disabled if the For Compliance, Turn Off Non-Archived Features option is enabled in Skype for Business Online.

Thought experiment

Skype for Business Online Presence Configuration

In this thought experiment, apply what you learned about this objective. You can find answers to these questions in the "Answers" section at the end of this chapter.

You are in the process of configuring the presence settings for Skype for Business Online at Fabrikam. You want to only allow presence information to be seen by users who are in a person's contact list. With this information in mind, answer the following questions:

1. Which presence option should you configure for users at Fabrikam?

2. When this setting is configured, which users who are in the user's contacts list will be unable to view presence information?

Objective summary

- Presence settings determine who is able to see when a user is available, in a meeting, or out of office in Skype for Business Online.
- You can allow presence information to be displayed to any user not in the external or blocked privacy group or choose to have presence information only displayed to a user's contacts.
- External communication settings allow you to configure whether users can add Skype for Business or Skype users external to your organization to their list of business contacts.
- You can configure audio and video and conversation recording settings on a per-user basis.
- You can configure whether Skype for Business Online non-archived features are disabled to meet compliance requirements.

Objective review

Answer the following questions to test your knowledge of the information in this objective. You can find the answers to these questions and explanations of why each answer choice is correct or incorrect in the "Answers" section at the end of this chapter.

1. Which of the following are disabled in Skype for Business Online if you enable the For Compliance, Turn Off Non-Archived Features? (Choose all that apply.)

   A. File transfers through instant messaging

   B. Audio and HD Video

   C. Shared OneNote pages

   D. Annotations to shared PowerPoint presentations

2. Which of the following settings would you configure if you wanted to block Skype for Business users from communicating with people outside your organization?

   A. On except for blocked domains

   B. Off completely

   C. On only for allowed domains

   D. Turn on communication with Skype users and users of other public IM providers

3. Which of the following settings would you configure if you only wanted to block Skype for Business users from communicating with those rapscallions at Tailspin Toys?

   A. Off completely

   B. On except for blocked domains

   C. On only for allowed domains

   D. Turn on communication with Skype users and users of other public IM providers

4. Which of the following settings would you configure if you wanted to only allow Skype for Business users to communicate with users from Contoso, Adatum, and Fabrikam?

   A. Turn on communication with Skype users and users of other public IM providers

   B. On only for allowed domains

   C. On except for blocked domains

   D. Off completely

Answers

This section contains the solutions to the thought experiments and answers to the objective review questions in this chapter.

Objective 3.1: Thought experiment

1. You will need to have a SIP URI plan configured to add a SIP address.
2. You use the Set-Mailbox cmdlet to alter the SIP address of an Office 365 user.

Objective 3.1: Review

1. **Correct answer:** B
   A. **Incorrect**: You use the New-Mailbox cmdlet to create a new mailbox rather than altering an existing mailbox.
   B. **Correct**: You use the Set-Mailbox cmdlet to add an additional email address to an Exchange Online email account.
   C. **Incorrect**: You use the Get-Mailbox cmdlet to view existing mailboxes, not make modifications to them.
   D. **Incorrect**: You use the Enable-Mailbox cmdlet to enable a mailbox, not make address modifications to mailboxes.

2. **Correct answer:** B
   A. **Incorrect**: The SIP designator indicates that this address is used for Skype rather than email messaging.
   B. **Correct**: The primary email address is indicated by SMTP in caps.
   C. **Incorrect:** The SIP designator indicates that this address is used for Skype rather than email messaging.
   D. **Incorrect:** The lowercase smtp indicates that this is a secondary, rather than primary, email address.

3. **Correct answers:** A and C
   A. **Correct:** You use the Import-CSV cmdlet with the Set-Mailbox cmdlet to bulk update email addresses for existing users.
   B. **Incorrect:** You do not use the Get-Mailbox cmdlet as this cmdlet allows you to view the properties of a mailbox rather than set them.
   C. **Correct**: You use the Import-CSV cmdlet with the Set-Mailbox cmdlet to bulk update email addresses for existing users.
   D. **Incorrect:** You do not use the Enable-Mailbox cmdlet as this cmdlet allows you to enable a mailbox, not update the email address properties of a mailbox.

Objective 3.2: Thought experiment

1. You should create equipment mailboxes for the Hololens devices.

2. You should create a dynamic distribution list for the research team. This will use the Research department setting on each account when calculating group membership.

Objective 3.2: Review

1. **Correct answer:** D

   A. **Incorrect**: This cmdlet allows you to assign the Send As permission.

   B. **Incorrect:** Use Set-Mailbox cmdlet with the GrantSendOnBehalfTo parameter to assign the Send On Behalf permission.

   C. **Incorrect**: This cmdlet allows you to remove the Send As permission.

   D. **Correct**: Use the Add-MailboxPermission cmdlet to assign the Full Access permission.

2. **Correct answer:** B

   A. **Incorrect**: You use the Add-MailboxPermission cmdlet to assign the Full Access permission.

   B. **Correct**: This cmdlet allows you to assign the Send As permission.

   C. **Incorrect**: You use Set-Mailbox cmdlet with the GrantSendOnBehalfTo parameter to assign the Send On Behalf permission.

   D. **Incorrect**: You use the Remove-MailboxPermission cmdlet to remove the Full Access permission.

3. **Correct answer:** A

   A. **Correct**: You use Set-Mailbox cmdlet with the GrantSendOnBehalfTo parameter to assign the Send On Behalf permission.

   B. **Incorrect:** You use the Add-MailboxPermission cmdlet to assign the Full Access permission.

   C. **Incorrect:** This cmdlet allows you to assign the Send As permission.

   D. **Incorrect:** You use the Remove-MailboxPermission cmdlet to remove the Full Access permission.

4. **Correct answer:** A

   A. **Correct:** You use the Remove-MailboxPermission cmdlet to remove the Full Access permission.

   B. **Incorrect**: This cmdlet allows you to remove the Send As permission.

   C. **Incorrect**: You use Set-Mailbox cmdlet with the GrantSendOnBehalfTo parameter to assign the Send On Behalf permission.

    D.   **Incorrect:** This cmdlet allows you to assign the Send As permission.

  5.   **Correct answer:** D

    A.   **Incorrect:** This cmdlet allows you to assign the Send As permission.

    B.   **Incorrect**: You use the Remove-MailboxPermission cmdlet to remove the Full Access permission.

    C.   **Incorrect**: You use Set-Mailbox cmdlet with the GrantSendOnBehalfTo parameter to assign the Send On Behalf permission.

    D.   **Correct**: This cmdlet allows you to remove the Send As permission.

Objective 3.3: Thought experiment

  1.   You can enable the archive to allow users to keep messages as long as they want.

  2.   You can configure retention tags and retention policies to deal with messages that are over 180 days old.

Objective 3.3: Review

  1.   **Correct answer:** A

    A.   **Correct**: You use the Enable-Mailbox cmdlet to enable an archive for an Exchange Online mailbox user.

    B.   **Incorrect:** You cannot use the Set-Mailbox cmdlet to enable an archive for an Exchange Online mailbox user.

    C.   **Incorrect**: The Get-Mailbox cmdlet gets the properties of a mailbox, you cannot use it to enable an archive.

    D.   **Incorrect**: The New-Mailbox cmdlet allows you to create a new mailbox, but does not allow you to enable an archive for an existing user.

  2.   **Correct answers:** B and C

    A.   **Incorrect**: You cannot use the Set-Mailbox cmdlet to enable an archive for an Exchange Online mailbox user.

    B.   **Correct:** You use Get-Mailbox to locate all Exchange Online mailbox users without an archive enabled and you pipe the result into the Enable-Mailbox cmdlet to enable the archive.

    C.   **Correct**: You use Get-Mailbox to locate all Exchange Online mailbox users without an archive enabled and you pipe the result into the Enable-Mailbox cmdlet to enable the archive.

    D.   **Incorrect**: The New-Mailbox cmdlet allows you to create a new mailbox, but does not allow you to enable an archive for an existing user.

  3.   **Correct answer:** B

A. **Incorrect**: You use this cmdlet to modify an existing retention policy tag.

B. **Correct:** You use this cmdlet to create a new retention policy tag.

C. **Incorrect:** You use this cmdlet to alter the retention policy tags contained in a retention policy.

D. **Incorrect**: You use this cmdlet to create a new retention policy.

4. **Correct answer:** A

A. **Correct**: You use this cmdlet to apply a retention policy to a mailbox.

B. **Incorrect**: You use this cmdlet to create a new retention policy.

C. **Incorrect:** You use this cmdlet to alter the retention policy tags contained in a retention policy.

D. **Incorrect**: You use this cmdlet to modify an existing retention policy tag.

5. **Correct answer:** D

A. **Incorrect:** You use this cmdlet to alter the retention policy tags contained in a retention policy.

B. **Incorrect:** You use this cmdlet to apply a retention policy to a mailbox.

C. **Incorrect**: You use this cmdlet to create a new retention policy tag.

D. **Correct**: You use this cmdlet to modify an existing retention policy tag, such as changing the retention period.

6. **Correct answer:** A

A. **Correct**: You use this cmdlet to alter the retention policy tags contained in a retention policy.

B. **Incorrect**: You use this cmdlet to modify an existing retention policy tag.

C. **Incorrect**: You use this cmdlet to apply a retention policy to a mailbox.

D. **Incorrect**: You use this cmdlet to create a new retention policy.

Objective 3.4: Thought experiment

1. You would configure the Display presence information only to a user's contacts option.

2. Any users in the External or Blocked privacy group will be unable to view presence information.

Objective 3.4: Review

1. **Correct answers:** A, C, and D

   A. **Correct**: File transfers through instant messaging are disabled if you enable the For Compliance, Turn Off Non-Archived Features option.

   B. **Incorrect**: Audio and HD video are not disabled if you enable the For Compliance, Turn Off Non-Archived Features option.

   C. **Correct**: Shared OneNote pages are disabled if you enable the For Compliance, Turn Off Non-Archived Features option.

   D. **Correct:** Annotations to shared PowerPoint presentations are disabled if you enable the For Compliance, Turn Off Non-Archived Features option.

2. **Correct answer:** B

   A. **Incorrect**: This option allows communication with all domains except the blocked ones.

   B. **Correct**: This option disables external communication using Skype for Business entirely.

   C. **Incorrect**: This option allows communication only with allowed domains.

   D. **Incorrect**: This option allows communication with Skype users and other public IM providers.

3. **Correct answer:** B

   A. **Incorrect**: This option disables external communication using Skype for Business entirely.

   B. **Correct**: This option allows communication with all domains except the blocked ones.

   C. **Incorrect:** This option allows communication only with allowed domains.

   D. **Incorrect**: This option allows communication with Skype users and other public IM providers.

4. **Correct answer:** B

   A. **Incorrect**: This option allows communication with Skype users and other public IM providers.

   B. **Correct**: This option allows communication only with allowed domains.

   C. **Incorrect**: This option allows communication with all domains except the blocked ones.

   D. **Incorrect**: This option disables external communication using Skype for Business entirely.

CHAPTER 4

Plan for Exchange Online and Skype for Business Online

For many organizations, the default settings for Exchange Online and Skype for Business Online within an Office 365 tenancy don't require much attention or modification. This is because the default configuration of these services does what the tenants need them to do. For other users, it is necessary to tune the settings on these services to better meet organizational requirements. In this chapter, you'll read about configuring anti-spam and anti-malware policies, determining an appropriate mailbox migration strategy, performing compliance operations, and managing settings at a tenancy level for Skype for Business Online.

Objectives in this chapter:

- Objective 4.1: Manage anti-malware and anti-spam policies
- Objective 4.2: Recommend a mailbox migration strategy
- Objective 4.3: Plan for Exchange Online
- Objective 4.4: Manage Skype for Business global external communications settings

Objective 4.1: Manage anti-malware and anti-spam policies

This objective deals with the Exchange Online anti-malware and anti-spam functionality. You manage this functionality through the configuration of anti-malware and spam filter policies. These policies determine what action Exchange Online will take with spam and malware as it passes through the service.

> **This objective covers the following topics:**
> - Anti-malware policies
> - Spam filter policies
> - Outbound spam policy
> - Quarantine

Anti-malware policies

Anti-malware policies allow you to block incoming malware from reaching user inboxes. Anti-malware policies also allow you to stop your own users from inadvertently sending malware to other people in your organization or others on the Internet. Anti-malware policies are part of an in-depth defense strategy. Users in your organization are far less likely to be infected by malware transmitted through email messages if malware is being purged by Exchange Online, as well as by an anti-malware solution installed on the client computer.

> **MORE INFO ANTI-MALWARE POLICIES**
>
> You can learn more about anti-malware policies at *https://technet.microsoft.com/en-us/library/jj200745(v=exchg.150).aspx.*

Malware detection response

The malware detection response settings determine what happens when malware is detected in a message attachment on inbound and outbound messages. You can configure the following options, as shown in Figure 4-1:

- **Delete Entire Message**   This is the default option. The entire message, both the message text and any attachments, will be deleted.
- **Delete All Attachments And Use Default Alert Text**   This option deletes all message attachments, not just ones detected as the host of an infection. The following default text alert is placed into a file that replaces the attachments: "Malware Was Detected In One Or More Attachments Included With This Email. All Attachments Have Been Deleted." When this option is selected, the intended recipient still receives the original message body.
- **Delete All Attachments And Use Custom Alert Text**   This option also deletes all message attachments, not just those with detected infections. Custom text is placed into a file that replaces the removed attachments. When this option is selected, the intended recipient still receives the original message body.

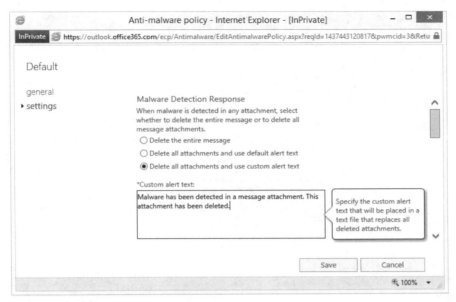

FIGURE 4-1 Malware Detection Response

If the message body is found to contain malware, then the entire message, including all attachments, is deleted. This will occur no matter which option is selected.

Anti-malware notifications

Notifications allow you to configure whether the sender of the message in which malware is detected will be notified and whether administrators will be notified. Notifications are only sent when the entire message is deleted. The notification language is dependent on the location of the message being processed. You can choose the following options, shown in Figure 4-2:

- **Notify Internal Senders** Sends a message to a sender from within your organization who sends a message in which malware is detected.
- **Notify External Senders** Sends a message to a sender external to your organization who sends a message to someone inside your organization in which malware is detected.
- **Notify Administrators About Undelivered Messages From Internal Senders** Allows you to have an administrator send a message about messages from internal senders in which malware is detected. You need to provide the administrator email address.
- **Notify Administrators About Undelivered Messages From External Senders** Allows you to have an administrator send a message about messages from external senders in which malware is detected. You need to provide the administrator email address.

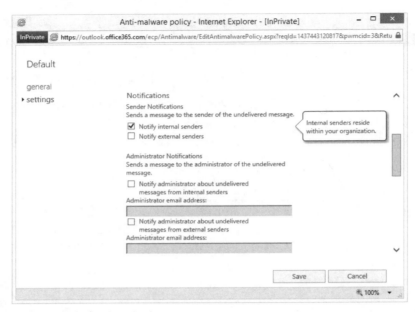

FIGURE 4-2 Notifications Settings

The default notification text is as follows, "This message was created automatically by mail delivery software. Your email message was not delivered to the intended recipients because malware was detected." If you don't want to use the default notification text, you can create your own custom notification text by configuring the following settings, shown in Figure 4-3. These settings are only available if the relevant notifications are configured.

- **From Name**   The name that the email message will appear to be from.
- **From Address**   The email address the message will appear to originate from.
- **Messages From Internal Senders**   The subject and the message sent to internal senders who have messages deleted by the anti-malware policy.
- **Messages From External Senders**   The subject and the message sent to external senders who have messages deleted by the anti-malware policy.

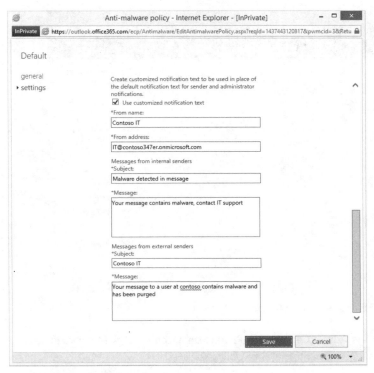

FIGURE 4-3 Customized notifications

Review default anti-malware policy

To review the default anti-malware policy, perform the following steps:

1. In the Office 365 Admin Center, click Exchange under ADMIN. The location of the Exchange link is shown in Figure 4-4.

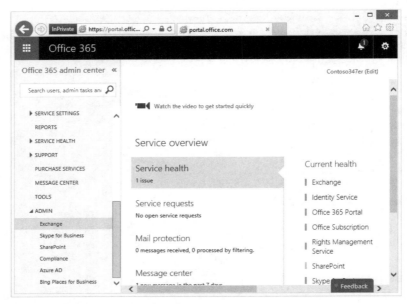

FIGURE 4-4 Exchange section of Office 365 Admin Center

2. In the Exchange Admin Center, click Protection and then click Malware Filter. Figure 4-5 shows the Default anti-malware policy selected.

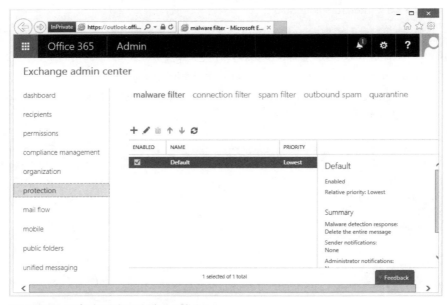

FIGURE 4-5 Default Malware Filter policies

3. With the Default policy selected, click the Edit (Pencil) icon on the toolbar. This will open the Anti-Malware Policy Properties page. The General section, shown in Figure 4-6, shows the policy Name and Description.

FIGURE 4-6 Default Policy

4. On the Settings page, you can configure the following settings:
   - Malware Detection Response
   - Notifications
   - Administrator Notifications
   - Customize Notifications

Create an anti-malware policy

You can create different anti-malware policies and then apply them to different groups of mail users. For example, you might want to have an anti-malware policy for one group of users that provides notifications to the user if malware is detected and a message is purged, and another policy that sends notifications to an administrator if malware is detected and the message purged.

When creating a new custom anti-malware policy, you need to configure the Applied To setting. This setting takes the form of an If statement with a condition and exceptions. As Figure 4-7 shows, the If conditions can include:

- **The Recipient Is**   Use this to specify a specific recipient.
- **The Recipient Domain Is**   Use this to specify the recipient's mail domain.
- **The Recipient Is A Member Of**   Use this to specify a recipient group.

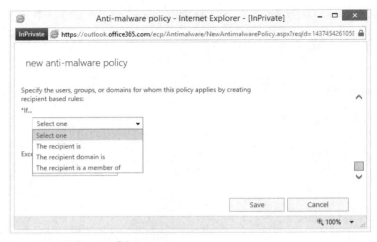

FIGURE 4-7 Select condition

The exceptions are the same and include:

- **The Recipient Is**   Use this to specify a specific recipient.
- **The Recipient Domain Is**   Use this to specify the recipient's mail domain.
- **The Recipient Is A Member Of**   Use this to specify a recipient group.

You can create as many conditions as you want, as long as those conditions are unique. For example, Figure 4-8 shows a set of conditions that will apply if the recipient is a member of the Accounting group, the recipient domain is contoso347er.onmicrosoft.com, but not if the recipient is Dan Jump or Don Funk.

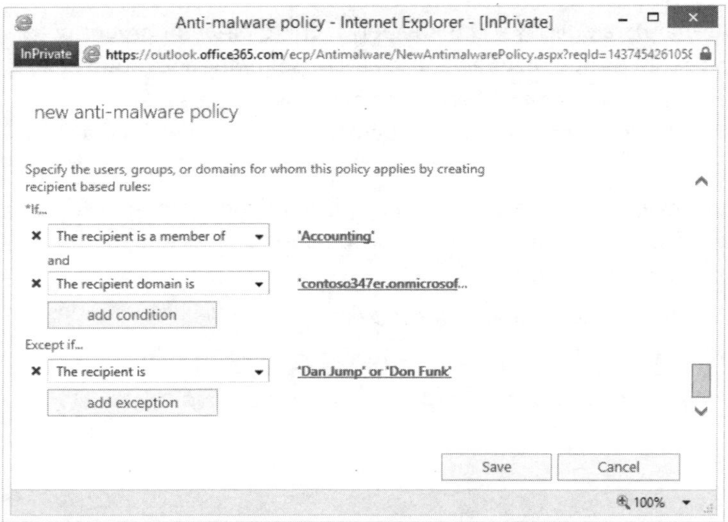

FIGURE 4-8 Policy conditions

To create a new anti-malware policy, perform the following steps:

1. In the Office 365 Admin Center, click Exchange under ADMIN.

2. In Exchange Admin Center, click Protection and then click Malware Filter.

3. Click the Plus (+) icon. This will open the New Anti-Malware Policy page, shown in Figure 4-9. Provide the following information:

   - Policy Name
   - Policy Description
   - Malware Detection Response
   - Notification Settings
   - Applies To Settings

FIGURE 4-9 New anti-malware policy

When you have multiple policies, you can use the Malware Filter list to determine which apply and in which order they apply. The policy with the number closest to zero applies first. If the conditions of a message don't match the first policy, it moves to the next policy until it encounters the Default policy. If any malware filter policies are configured, as shown in Figure 4-10, then ExampleAntiMalwarePolicy will be applied first, then ExamplePolicy2, and then finally the Default policy. You can use the arrows to change the priority assigned to each policy.

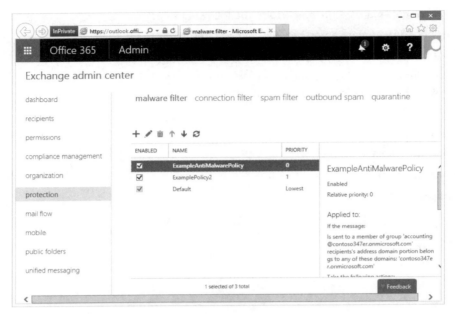

FIGURE 4-10 Policy priorities

Windows PowerShell anti-malware policy cmdlets

There are a number of Windows PowerShell cmdlets that you can use to manage filter policies and malware filter rules. Filter rules determine the conditions under which a malware filter policy applies. For example, you might have one malware filter policy that applies to recipients in one recipient domain and another malware filter policy that applies to recipients in another recipient domain. The Windows PowerShell anti-malware policy cmdlets are as follows:

- **Get-MalwareFilterPolicy** This cmdlet allows you to view malware filter policy settings.
- **Set-MalwareFilterPolicy** This cmdlet allows you to modify malware filter policy settings.
- **New-MalwareFilterPolicy** Allows you to create a new custom malware filter policy. This includes configuring an action, either blocking a message, replacing attachments with the default alert or with a custom alert, or configuring notification settings.
- **Remove-MalwareFilterPolicy** This cmdlet allows you to remove a custom filter policy.
- **New-MalwareFilterRule** Use this cmdlet to create a new filter rule that can be applied to a custom policy. For example, you could use this cmdlet to apply a specific malware filter policy named ContosoExamplePolicy when the email recipient is in the contoso.com domain.

- **Set-MalwareFilterRule**   Use this cmdlet to edit an existing malware filter rule. For example, to change a rule so that it applies a specific policy to recipients in more than one email domain.
- **Enable-MalwareFilterRule**   Use this cmdlet to turn on a malware filter rule.
- **Disable-MalwareFilterRule**   Allows you to turn off a malware filter rule.

Connection filter policies

Connection filter policies let you always allow email from trusted senders and always block email from known spammers. Exchange Online only supports the default connection filter policy. You configure connection filters by configuring an IP Allow list and an IP block list, as shown in Figure 4-11.

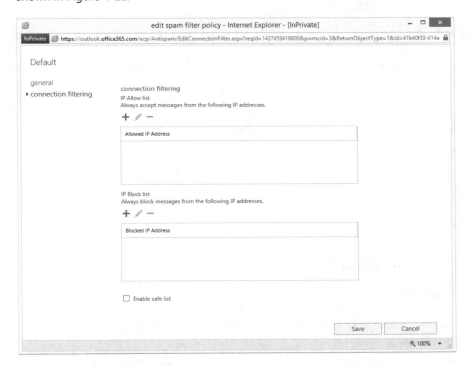

FIGURE 4-11 Connection Filtering

When configuring connection filters, you can also enable the Safe List checkbox. When you enable this checkbox, your connection filter will allow messages from a list of third-party sources of trusted senders to which Microsoft subscribes.

When adding an IP address list, you can either specify the IP address directly, or use CIDR notation in the form xxx.xxx.xxx.xxx/yy, where yy is a number between 24 and 32. You can specify a maximum of 1,273 separate entries, where an entry is either a single IP address or a

CIDR range. IPv6 addresses are supported for TLS encrypted messages. You enter allowed IP addresses on the Allowed IP Address WebPage Dialog box, shown in Figure 4-12.

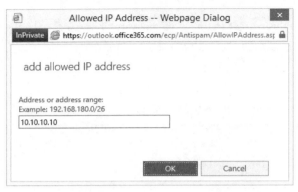

FIGURE 4-12 Allowed IP address

You enter blocked IP address ranges on the Blocked IP Address Webpage Dialog box, as shown in Figure 4-13.

FIGURE 4-13 Add Blocked IP Address

If an IP address is added to both the allow list and the block list, then email from that IP address will be allowed.

To edit the default connection filter policy, perform the following steps:

1. In the Office 365 Admin Center, click Exchange under ADMIN.

2. In Exchange Admin Center, click Protection and then click Connection Filter.

3. With the Default policy selected, as shown in Figure 4-14, click the Edit (Pencil) icon.

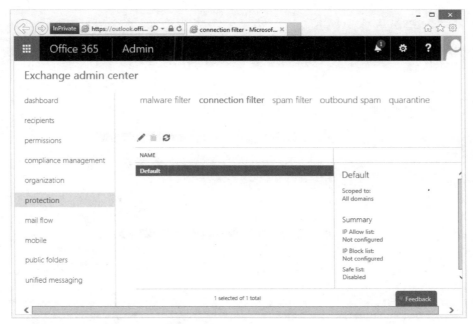

FIGURE 4-14 Default Connection Filter policy

4. Click the Connection Filtering tab to access the IP Allow list, the IP Block list, and the Enable Safe List option, as shown in Figure 4-15.

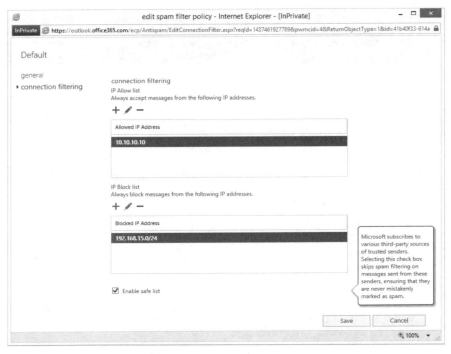

FIGURE 4-15 IP Allow and Block lists

You can use the following Windows PowerShell cmdlets to managed the connection filter policy:

- **Get-HostedConnectionFilterPolicy**   Use this cmdlet when you want to review the default policy settings.

- **Set-HostedConnectionFilterPolicy**   Use this cmdlet to configure the connection filter policy settings. This cmdlet includes the IPAllowLIst and IPBlockList parameters.

> **MORE INFO CONNECTION FILTER POLICIES**
>
> You can learn more about connection filter policies at *https://technet.microsoft.com/en-us/library/jj200718(v=exchg.150).aspx.*

Spam filter policies

Spam filter policies allow you to configure how incoming messages are categorized, including which characteristics a message might have that means you want if flagged as spam. The default policy applies to all users in the company. You can also configure custom policies that apply to specific users, groups, and domains within the organization.

You configure spam filter policies on the Spam Filter tab of the Protection section in Exchange Admin Center, as shown in Figure 4-16. You can have multiple policies as long as each policy has a different set of conditions. The highest priority policy that has conditions that match a message will apply. When there are multiple custom policies, you can adjust their priority using the arrow buttons in the Exchange Admin Center.

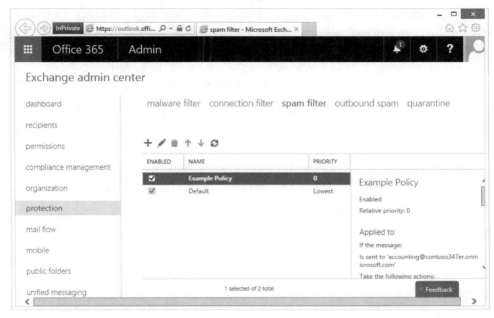

FIGURE 4-16 Policy priority

> **MORE INFO** **SPAM FILTER POLICIES**
>
> You can learn more about spam filter policies at *https://technet.microsoft.com/en-us/library/jj200684(v=exchg.150).aspx*.

Spam and bulk actions

When configuring the default policy or creating a custom policy, you need to configure which actions to take for messages that are likely to be spam and messages that are almost certainly spam.

You can choose from the following options for messages that are likely to be spam and for messages that are almost certainly spam:

- **Move Message To Junk Email Folder**   This is the default, with messages moved to each user's junk email folder.
- **Quarantine Message**   When this setting is chosen, messages are moved to a quarantine folder for up to 15 days before being deleted. Being moved to quarantine allows someone to review the message so that they can determine whether or not it

is actually spam. For example, you might choose to quarantine message that are likely to be spam and delete messages that are almost certainly spam.

- **Delete Message**   When this setting is chosen, the message and any attachments are simply deleted.

You can also configure whether bulk email is marked as spam and the threshold that should be applied to bulk email. Setting the threshold as 1 will have almost all bulk email treated as spam and a setting of 9 will allow almost all bulk email to be delivered. A setting of 7 is the default. The Spam and Bulk Actions tab of a spam filter policy is shown in Figure 4-17.

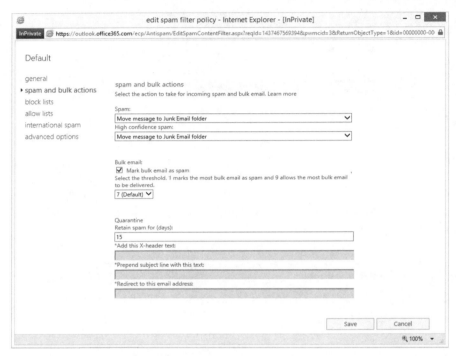

FIGURE 4-17 Spam And Bulk Actions

Spam filter block lists

The block lists setting of a spam filter policy, shown in Figure 4-18, allows you to block email messages from specific email addresses or specific email domains. When a message comes from a blocked sender or a blocked domain, it is subject to the high confidence spam action configured in the Spam and Bulk Actions section of the policy.

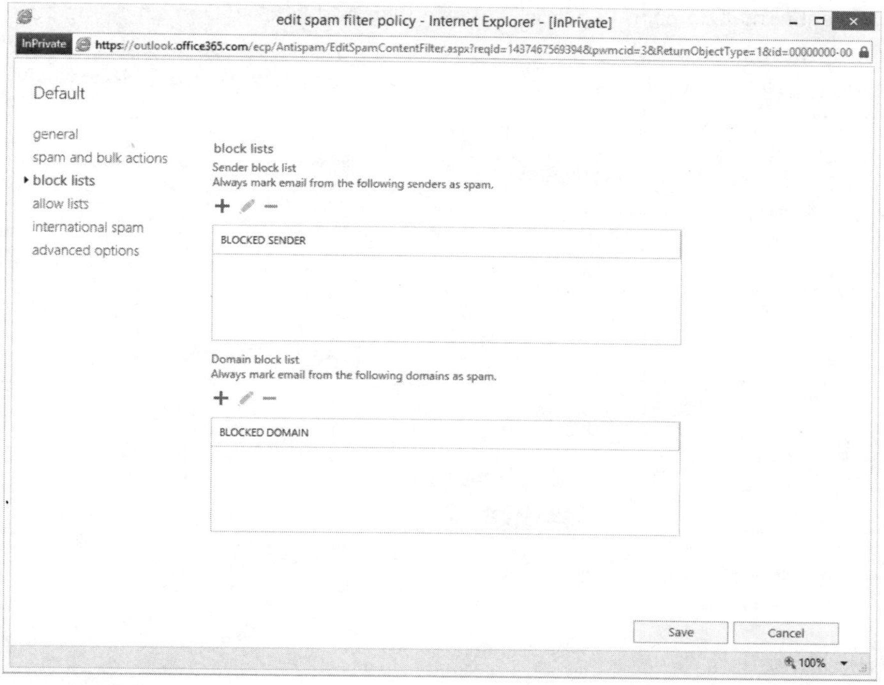

FIGURE 4-18 Block Lists

If you want to block all messages from a specific email address, you can add that email address to the blocked sender list. Figure 4-19 shows the email address don.funk@adatum.com being added to this list. The owner of the email address added to the list will not be notified that their email messages are being categorized as spam.

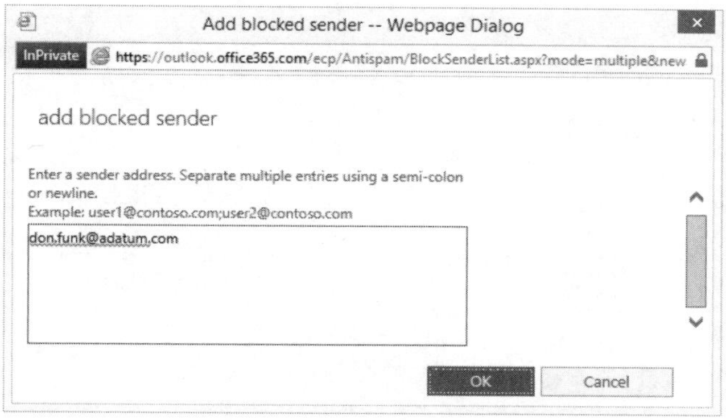

FIGURE 4-19 Blocked Sender

You can add entire mail domains to a Block List using the Add Blocked Domain dialog box. You should be as specific as possible when adding domains. If you add a top level domain, such as .com or .org to this list, all email messages that come from .com or .org addresses will be marked as spam.

FIGURE 4-20 Blocked Domain

Spam filter allow lists

Spam filter allow lists provide you with a way of ensuring that email messages from specific users or from specific domains will always be delivered to users in your organization. When configuring Allow Lists in a spam filter policy, you configure the Sender Allow List for specific email addresses and the Domain Allow List for specific email domains. The Allow Lists section of the spam filter policy is shown in Figure 4-21.

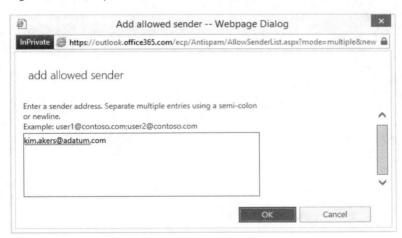

FIGURE 4-21 Allow Lists

You add users to the Allow List using the Add Allowed Sender dialog box, as shown in Figure 4-22. To separate email address entries, use a semicolon.

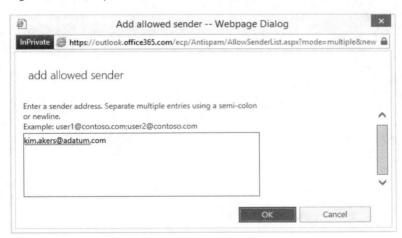

FIGURE 4-22 Allowed Sender

You Add Allowed Domains on the Add Allowed Domain dialog box, shown in Figure 4-23. You should be as specific as possible and not add generic top-level domains such as .com or .org because this will allow email from all .com and .org domains.

FIGURE 4-23 Allowed Domain

International spam

The International Spam settings, shown in Figure 4-24, allow you to filter messages based on the message language and the country or region from which the message is sent.

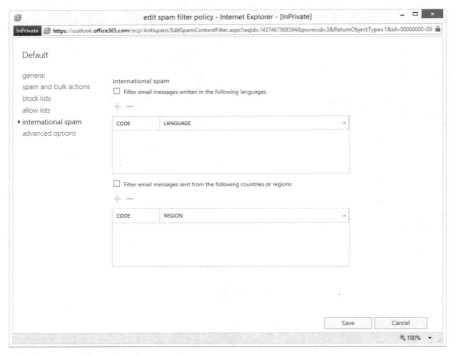

FIGURE 4-24 International Spam

When blocking message content on the basis of language, you enable the Filter email messages written in the following languages option and then specify the languages you want to filter on the Select Language dialog box, as shown in Figure 4-25.

FIGURE 4-25 Select language

To block messages from specific regions, enable the Filter email messages sent from the following countries or regions option and then specify the countries or regions that you want to filter out on the Select Region dialog box, as shown in Figure 4-26.

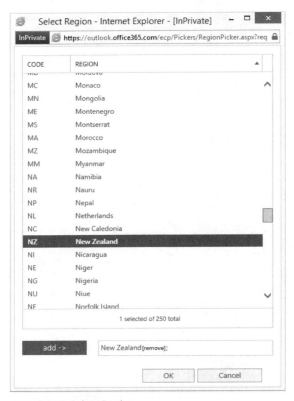

FIGURE 4-26 Select Region

Advanced policy options

Advanced policy options, shown in Figure 4-27, allow you to toggle specific options that either increase the spam score, making it more likely that Exchange Online will recognize the message as spam, or simply mark the message as spam directly.

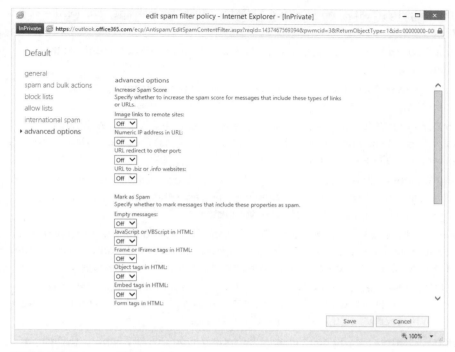

FIGURE 4-27 Advanced Options

You can configure the policy to increase the spam score if the message includes the following types of links or URLs:

- **Image Links To Remote Sites**   Triggered if the message contains HTML content with an IMG tag linked to an image on a remote site.

- **Numeric IP Address In URL**   Triggered if the message has an URL with a numeric IP address.

- **URL Redirect To Other Port**   Triggered if the message contains a hyperlink that redirects to a port other than port 80, port 8080, or port 443.

- **URL To .Biz Or .Info Websites**   Triggered if the message contains a URL that includes the .biz or .info suffix.

You can configure the policy to mark a message as spam under the following conditions:

- **Empty Messages**   Triggered if the body and subject line are both empty and there is no attachment.

- **JavaScript Or VBScript In HTML**   Triggered if either JavaScript or VBScript is present in the HTML included in the message.

- **Frame Or IFrame Tags In HTML**   Triggered if the HTML code in the message includes the Frame or IFrame tags.

- **Object Tags In HTML** Triggered if the HTML code in the message contains the <Object> tag.

- **Embed Tags In HTML** Triggered if the HTML code in the message contains the <Embed> tag.

- **Form Tags In HTML** Triggered if the HTML code in the message contains the <Form> tag.

- **Web Bugs In HTML** Triggered if the message contains a web bug. Web bugs are small, usually one pixel by one pixel graphic images that are used to determine whether an email message has been read.

- **Apply Sensitive Word List** Triggered if a word on the sensitive word list is present in the message. These words are associated with messages that are likely to be offensive. Administrators cannot edit the sensitive word list.

- **SPR Record: Hard Fail** Triggered if the message fails a Sender Protection Framework (SPF) check. This means that the message was received from an IP address not listed in the SPF record. Used by organizations concerned about phishing messages.

- **Conditional Sender ID Filtering: Hard Fail** Triggered if the message fails a conditional sender ID check, which combines an SPF check with a Sender ID check to protect against messages where the sender header is forged.

- **NDR Backscatter** If you don't enable this setting, Non Delivery Reports (NDRs) go through spam filtering.

MORE INFO **ADVANCED SPAM FILTERING OPTIONS**

You can learn more about advanced spam filtering options at *https://technet.microsoft.com/en-us/library/jj200750(v=exchg.150).aspx*.

Spam confidence levels

When a new message passes through the Exchange Online spam filtering algorithms, it is assigned a spam score. This spam score maps to a Spam Confidence Level (SCL) rating and is stamped in an X-Header for the message. Exchange Online performs actions on messages based on the SCL rating.

TABLE 4-1: SCL ratings

SCL RATING	MEANING	ACTION
-1	Message coming from a sender, recipient, or IP address listed as trusted	Delivered to recipient
0,1	Message unlikely to be spam	Delivered to recipient
5,6	Message likely to be spam	Determined by filter policy setting for spam
7,8,9	Message very likely to be spam	Determined by filter policy setting for high confidence spam

You can have Exchange manually set an SCL rating for a message using a transport rule, but transport rules are not addressed by the 70-347 exam.

MORE INFO **SPAM CONFIDENCE LEVELS**

You can learn more about spam confidence levels at *https://technet.microsoft.com/en-us/library/JJ200686(v=EXCHG.150).aspx*.

Applying spam filter policies

When creating a new custom spam filter policy, you need to configure the Applied To setting. This setting determines which recipients the policy applies. This setting takes the form of an If statement with a condition and exceptions. As is the case with anti-malware policies, the If conditions can include:

- The Recipient Is
- The Recipient Domain Is
- The Recipient Is A Member Of

The exceptions are the same and include:

- The Recipient Is
- The Recipient Domain Is
- The Recipient Is A Member Of

You can create as many conditions as you want, as long as those conditions are unique. For example, Figure 4-28 shows a set of condition that will apply if the recipient domain is contoso347er.onmicrosoft.com, the recipient is a member of the Accounting group, and the recipient is not Don Funk.

FIGURE 4-28 Applied To

Spam filter Windows PowerShell cmdlets

You can use the following PowerShell commands to configure spam filter policies:

- **Get-HostedContentFilterPolicy** This allows you to view existing spam filter settings.
- **Set-HostedContentFilterPolicy** Use this cmdlet to edit spam filter settings, including the recipients to which the spam filter policy applies.
- **New-HostedContentFilterPolicy** Use this cmdlet to create a new custom spam filter policy.
- **Remove-HostedContentFilterPolicy** This cmdlet allows you to remove a custom spam filter policy.

Outbound spam policy

The Outbound Spam policy blocks users inside the organization from sending spam to recipients outside the organization. If an outbound message is suspected to be spam, it is sent through the higher risk delivery pool. Using the higher risk delivery pool reduces the likelihood that the IP address of the normal outbound delivery pool will be added to a Block List by real-time providers.

By configuring the default Outbound Spam policy, you can specify whether:

- A copy of all suspicious messages is forwarded to one or more email addresses for review.

- A notification is sent to one or more email addresses when a sender is blocked for sending outbound spam.

You can configure the default outbound spam policy by performing the following steps:

1. In the Office 365 Admin Center, click Exchange under ADMIN.
2. In Exchange Admin Center, click Protection and then click Outbound Spam.
3. Ensure that the Default policy is selected, as shown in Figure 4-29, and then click the Edit (Pencil) icon.

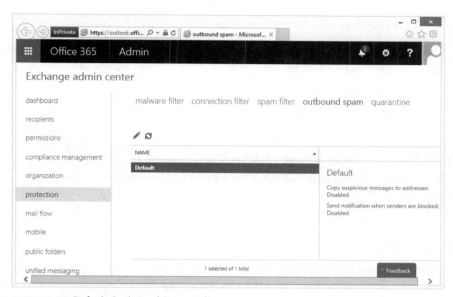

FIGURE 4-29 Default Outbound Spam policy

4. On the Outbound Spam Preferences page, shown in Figure 4-30, configure whether a copy of all suspicious messages is forwarded to one or more email addresses for review, and whether a notification is sent to one or more email addresses when a sender is blocked for sending outbound spam.

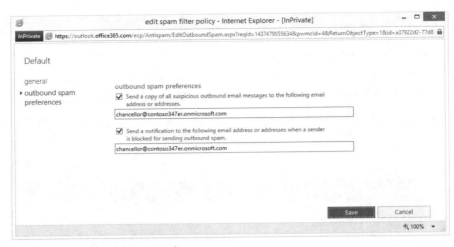

FIGURE 4-30 Outbound Spam Preferences

> **MORE INFO OUTBOUND SPAM POLICY**
>
> You can learn more about the outbound spam policy at *https://technet.microsoft.com/en-us/library/jj200737(v=exchg.150).aspx*.

Quarantine

Content filtering can be configured to send messages to Quarantine rather than to a recipient's junk email folder, or to simply delete them. Messages sent to Quarantine can be viewed in the Quarantine section of the Exchange Admin Center, as shown in Figure 4-31. Messages in Quarantine will remain there until released by an administrator or until they are automatically deleted when the Quarantine period expires. The maximum Quarantine period for messages recognized as spam is 15 days.

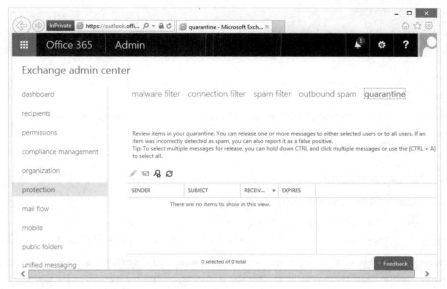

FIGURE 4-31 Quarantine

Administrators can use the Quarantine section of the Exchange Admin Center to search for quarantined messages and to release messages to their intended recipients. When releasing a message, an administrator can choose between the following options:

- **Release The Message Without Reporting It As A False Positive**   When you select this option, you can choose to release the message to some or all of the message's original recipients.

- **Release The Message And Report It As A False Positive**   If you choose this option, the message is released to all recipients. The message is also reported to the Microsoft Spam Analysis team, which might use the false positive result to adjust content filter rules across Exchange Online.

You can use the following Windows PowerShell cmdlets to manage quarantine:

- **Get-QuarantineMessage**   Allows you to search for messages in quarantine. For example use the following command to find all messages from the adatum.com email domain:

```
Get-QuarantineMessage | ? {$_.Senderaddress –like "*@adatum.com"}
```

- **Release-QuarantineMessage**   Allows you to release a message from quarantine. Use the ReleaseToAll parameter to allow the message.

EXAM TIP

Remember the Windows PowerShell cmdlets used to manage anti-malware policies and spam settings.

Thought experiment
Default spam filter configuration

In this thought experiment, apply what you learned about this objective. You can find answers to these questions in the "Answers" section at the end of this chapter.

You are in the process of planning the alteration of the default spam filter used for your organization's Office 365 tenancy. Currently, messages that have an SCL of 7 are being placed in a user's junk email folders. Many of these messages are turning out to be legitimate, so for the next six months you want to have them moved to quarantine instead, where they can be examined by members of your team to check if they are being classified appropriately.

Recently, for reasons that aren't entirely clear, several email accounts at your organization are being sent email from addresses in New Zealand. The contents of these emails are entirely in the Esperanto language. A variety of different IP addresses are used to send the emails, so filtering based on IP addresses hasn't been entirely successful. You have been asked to ensure that all messages of this nature are classified as spam.

Finally, as you will need to now have your team manage quarantine, you need to brush up on your Windows PowerShell skills when it comes to performing this task.

With all of this in mind, answer the following questions:

1. What steps do you need to take to modify the default spam filter policy to ensure that messages with an SCL of 7 are placed in quarantine?

2. What steps do you need to take to modify the default spam filter policy to ensure that all messages in the Esperanto language that originate from New Zealand are marked as spam?

3. Which Windows PowerShell cmdlet and parameter should be used to release a message to all recipients if that message is currently in quarantine?

Objective summary

- The malware detection response settings are Delete Entire Message, Delete All Attachments And Use Default Alert Text, and Delete All Attachments And Use Custom Alert Text.

- You can configure the following notification options when malware is detected: Notify Internal Senders, Notify External Senders, Notify Sdministrators About Undelivered Messages From Internal Senders, and Notify Administrators About Undelivered Messages From External Senders.

- You can create different anti-malware policies and then apply them to different groups of mail users.

- When creating a new custom anti-malware policy, you need to configure the Applied To setting. This setting takes the form of an If statement with a condition and exceptions.

- Spam filter block lists and allow lists allow you to filter on the basis of email address and sender domain.

- Spam filter international settings allow you to filter based on language and country or region of origin.

- Outbound spam policy allows you to configure how spam originating from within your organization is managed.

- Use the cmdlets with the MalwareFilterPolicy page to view, modify, create, and remove malware filter policies.

- Use the cmdlets with the MalwareFilterRule page to view, modify, create, and disable malware filter rules.

- Use the cmdlets with the HostedConnectionFilterPolicy page to manage connection filter policies.

- Use the cmdlets with the HostedContentFilterPolicy page to view and edit spam filter settings.

- Use the Get and Release-QuarantineMessage cmdlets to search for and release messages from quarantine.

Objective review

Answer the following questions to test your knowledge of the information in this objective. You can find the answers to these questions and explanations of why each answer choice is correct or incorrect in the "Answers" section at the end of the chapter.

1. You need to review the specifics of a particular malware filter policy. Which of the following Windows PowerShell cmdlets do you use to accomplish this task?

   A. Set-MalwareFilterPolicy

   B. Get-MalwareFilterPolicy

   C. Set-MalwareFilterRule

   D. Get-MalwareFilterRule

2. You need to temporarily suspend a malware filter rule. Which of the following Windows PowerShell cmdlets do you use to accomplish this goal?

   A. Remove-MalwareFilterPolicy

   B. Remove-MalwareFilterRule

   C. Remove-HostedContentFilterPolicy

   D. Disable-MalwareFilterRule

3. You need to delete a custom spam filter policy. Which of the following Windows PowerShell cmdlets do you use to accomplish this goal?

   A. Remove-HostedContentFilterPolicy

   B. Disable-MalwareFilterRule

   C. Remove-MalwareFilterRule

   D. Remove-MalwareFilterPolicy

4. Which of the following Windows PowerShell cmdlets do you use to view the existing spam filter settings?

   A. New-HostedContentFilterPolicy

   B. Get-MalwareFilterRule

   C. Get-HostedContentFilterPolicy

   D. Get-MalwareFilterPolicy

5. You want to create a new custom malware filtering policy for users in the Research group. Which of the following Windows PowerShell cmdlets do you use to accomplish this goal?

   A. New-HostedContentFilterPolicy

   B. New-MalwareFilterPolicy

   C. Enable-MalwareFilterRule

   D. Set-MalwareFilterPolicy

6. Which of the following Windows PowerShell cmdlets do you use to turn on a disabled malware filter rule?

   A. Set-MalwareFilterRule

   B. Enable-MalwareFilterRule

   C. New-HostedContentFilterPolicy

   D. New-MalwareFilterRule

7. You need to delete an existing malware filter rule. Which of the following Windows PowerShell cmdlets do you use to perform this task?

   A. Remove-MalwareFilterRule

   B. Remove-HostedContentFilterPolicy

   C. Remove-MalwareFilterPolicy

   D. Disable-MalwareFilterRule

8. Which of the following Windows PowerShell cmdlets do you use to create a new custom spam filter policy?

   A. New-MalwareFilterPolicy

   B. New-MalwareFilterRule

   C. Set-HostedConnectionFilterPolicy

   D. New-HostedContentFilterPolicy

9. Which of the following Windows PowerShell cmdlets do you use to configure IP allow lists and IP block lists in an existing connection filter policy?

   A. Set-HostedConnectionFilterPolicy

   B. Get-HostedContentFilterPolicy

   C. Set-MalwareFilterPolicy

   D. Set-MalwareFilterRule

10. You need to edit an existing malware filter rule. Which of the following Windows PowerShell cmdlets do you use to accomplish this task?

   A. Set-MalwareFilterPolicy

   B. Set-MalwareFilterRule

   C. Set-HostedConnectionFilterPolicy

   D. Get-MalwareFilterPolicy

Objective 4.2: Recommend a mailbox migration strategy

This objective deals with migrating mailboxes from an on-premises messaging solution, which in most cases will be Microsoft Exchange, to Exchange Online. To master this objective, you'll need to understand the different migration options and the conditions why you would choose one migration method over another.

> **This objective covers the following topics:**
> - Remote move migration
> - Staged migration
> - Cutover migration
> - IMAP migration
> - Migration comparison

Remote move migration method

You use a remote move migration when you have an Exchange hybrid deployment. A hybrid deployment is where you have coexistence between an on-premises Exchange deployment and an Exchange Online deployment. You have to use a hybrid deployment and use the remote move migration method when you need to migrate more than 2,000 Exchange Server 2010 or Exchange Server 2013 mailboxes to Exchange Online.

With a hybrid deployment, you get the following advantages:

- User accounts are managed through your on-premises tools.
- Directory synchronization connects your on-premises Exchange organization with Exchange Online.
- Users are able to use single-sign on to access their mailbox whether the mailbox is hosted in the on-premises Exchange organization or Exchange Online.
- Email is routed securely between the on-premises Exchange deployment and Exchange Online.
- Free/busy calendar sharing between users with mailboxes hosted in the on-premises Exchange organization and mailboxes hosted in Exchange Online.

Prior to performing a remote move migration, you need to ensure the following prerequisites are met:

- A hybrid deployment has already been configured between your on-premises Exchange organization and Exchange Online.
- You need to have been assigned the appropriate permissions. For mailbox moves in a hybrid deployment, this means that you need to have an account that is a member of the Organization Management or the Recipient Management role groups.

- You need to have deployed the Mailbox Replication Proxy Service (MRSProxy) on all on-premises Exchange 2013 Client Access servers.

Once these prerequisites have been met, you can move mailboxes from your on-premises Exchange deployment to Exchange Online by performing the following steps:

1. **Create Migration Endpoint**   Migration endpoints host connection settings for an on-premises Exchange server running the MRS proxy service.

2. **Enable MRSProxy Service**   The MRSProxy service is hosted on on-premises Client Access servers. This service can be enabled using Exchange Administration Console by selecting the Client Access server, editing the properties of the EWS virtual directory, and ensuring that the MRS Proxy enabled checkbox is selected.

3. **Move Mailboxes**   You can move mailboxes using the Office 365 tab in EAC on the on-premises Exchange server by creating a new migration batch in Exchange Admin Console, as shown in Figure 4-32, or by using Windows PowerShell. When moving mailboxes, you move some of the mailboxes at a time in groups, which are termed batches.

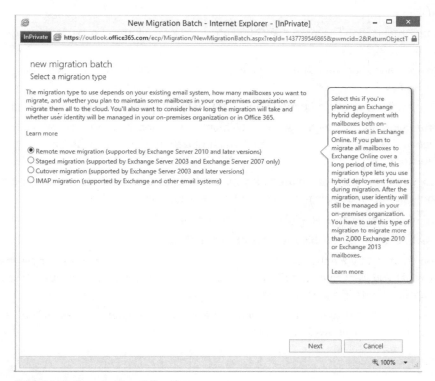

FIGURE 4-32 Remote Move Migration

4. **Remove Completed Migration Batches**   Once migration of a batch is complete, remove the migration batch using Exchange Administration Center or Windows PowerShell.

5. **Re-enable Offline Access for Outlook Web App**   If users have been migrated from Exchange Server 2013 to Office 365, it will be necessary to reset the offline access setting in their browser.

> *MORE INFO* **REMOTE MOVE MIGRATION**
>
> You can learn more about remote move migrations at *https://technet.microsoft.com/en-us/library/jj863291(v=exchg.150).aspx#remotemove.*

Staged migration method

In a staged migration, you Migrate mailboxes from your on-premises Exchange organization to Office 365 in groups, termed batches. You would select a staged migration in the following circumstances:

- Your organization has more than 2,000 on-premises mailboxes hosted in Exchange 2007.
- Your organization intends to completely move its messaging infrastructure to Office 365.
- Your available migration period is in the timeframe of several weeks to several months.
- After migration completes, you will still manage user accounts using on-premises management tools and have account synchronization performed with Azure Active Directory.
- The primary domain name used for your on-premises Exchange organization must be configured as a domain associated with the tenancy in Office 365.

Staged migration involves the following general steps:

1. Create empty mail-enabled security groups in Office 365.

2. You create a CSV file that includes a row for every user who has an on-premises mailbox that you want to migrate. This is not every user in the organization, just those that you will migrate in a particular batch.

3. Create a staged migration batch using Exchange Admin Center, as shown in Figure 4-33, or using Windows PowerShell.

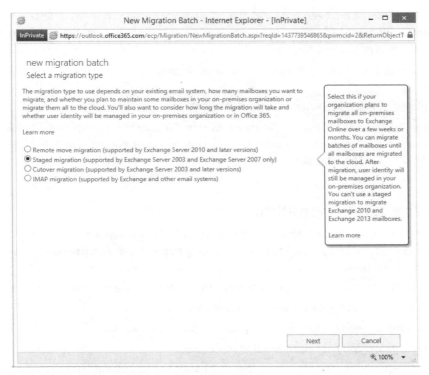

FIGURE 4-33 Staged Migration

4. Trigger the migration batch. Once the migration batch is triggered, Exchange Online will perform the following steps:

   - Verify that directory synchronization is enabled and functioning. Directory synchronization migrates distribution groups, contacts, and mail enabled users.

   - Verifies that a mail-enabled user exists in Office 365 for every user listed in the batch CSV file.

   - Converts the Office 365 mail-enabled user to an Exchange Online mailbox for each user in the migration batch.

   - Configures mail forwarding for the on-premises mailbox.

5. Once these steps have been completed, Exchange Online sends you a status report informing you of which mailboxes have migrated successfully and which mailboxes have not migrated successfully. Successfully migrated users can start using Exchange Online mailboxes.

6. Once migration is successful, you convert the mailboxes of successfully migrated on-premises users to mail-enabled users in the on-premises Exchange deployment.

7. You configure a new batch of users to migrate and delete the current migration batch.

8. Once all users have been migrated, the administrator assigns licenses to Office 365 users, configures MX records to point to Exchange Online, and creates an Autodiscover record that points to Office 365.

9. Decommission the on-premises Exchange deployment.

> **MORE INFO STAGED MIGRATION METHOD**
>
> You can learn more about staged migrations at *https://support.office.com/en-us/article/ What-you-need-to-know-about-a-staged-email-migration-to-Office-365-7e2c82be- 5f3d-4e36-bc6b-e5b4d411e207*.

Cutover migration method

In a cutover migration, all mailboxes in an on-premises Exchange deployment are migrated to Office 365 in a single migration batch. Cutover migrations migrate global mail contacts as well as distribution groups. Cutover migrations are suitable when:

- You intend all mailboxes to be hosted in Office 365 when the migration completes.
- You intend to manage user accounts using Office 365 tools.
- You want to perform the migration period in less than a week.
- Your organization has less than 2,000 mailboxes.
- Your on-premises messaging solution is Exchange Server 2007 or later. Exchange Server 2003 reached the end of extended support in April 2014.
- The primary domain name used for your on-premises Exchange organization must be configured as a domain associated with the tenancy in Office 365.

You can perform a cutover migration using the Exchange Admin Center, as shown in Figure 4-34, or by using Windows PowerShell.

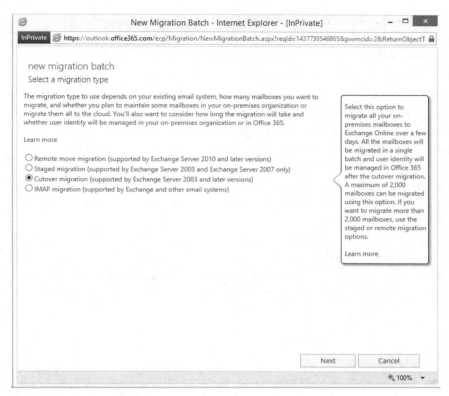

FIGURE 4-34 Cutover Migration

The cutover migration method involves the following general steps:

1. An administrator creates empty mail-enabled security groups in Office 365.

2. An administrator connects Office 365 to the on-premises Exchange deployment. This is also termed creating a migration endpoint.

3. An administrator creates and starts a cutover migration batch using Exchange Admin Center or Windows PowerShell.

4. Once the migration batch is triggered, Exchange Online performs the following steps:

    ■ The address book of the on-premises Exchange deployment is queried to identify mailboxes, distribution groups, and contacts.

    ■ New Exchange Online mailboxes are provisioned.

    ■ Distribution groups and contacts are created within Exchange Online.

    ■ Mailbox data, including email messages, contacts, and calendar items, are migrated from each on-premises mailbox to the corresponding Exchange Online mailbox.

5. Exchange Online forwards the administrator a report providing statistics including the number of successful and failed migrations. The migration report includes automati-

cally generated passwords for each new Exchange Online mailbox. Users will be forced to change passwords the first time they sign in to Office 365.

6. Incremental synchronization occurs every 24 hours, updating Exchange Online with any new items created in the on-premises mailboxes.

7. Once migration issues have been resolved, the administrator changes the MX records to point to Exchange Online.

8. Once mail flow to Exchange Online has been successfully established, the administrator deletes the cutover migration batch. This terminates synchronization between the on-premises mailboxes and Office 365.

9. Administrator performs post migration tasks, including assigning Office 365 licenses, creating an Autodiscover DNS record, and decommissioning on-premises Exchange servers.

MORE INFO CUTOVER MIGRATION

You can learn more about cutover migrations at *https://support.office.com/en-us/article/ What-you-need-to-know-about-a-cutover-email-migration-to-Office-365-961978ef-f434- 472d-a811-1801733869da.*

IMAP migration

IMAP migrations use the IMAP protocol to move the contents of on-premises user mailboxes to Exchange Online. IMAP migrations are suitable where the on-premises mail server is not running Exchange Server, but is instead running an alternate mail server solution.

IMAP migration is supported for the following on-premises messaging solutions:

- Courier-IMAP
- Cyrus
- Dovecot
- UW-IMAP

IMAP migrations involve the following general steps:

1. A tenant administrator creates Office 365 user accounts and assigns them Exchange Online user licenses. This provisions the user accounts with Exchange Online mailboxes.

2. The tenant administrator creates a CSV file. This CSV file includes a row for each on-premises user who will be migrated to Exchange Online using IMAP. This CSV file will need to include the passwords used by each on-premises IMAP mailbox user. It is recommended that you reset user passwords for on-premises IMAP mailbox users to simplify this process.

3. The administrator creates and then triggers an IMAP migration batch. This can be done using the Migration dashboard, as shown in Figure 4-35, or through Windows PowerShell.

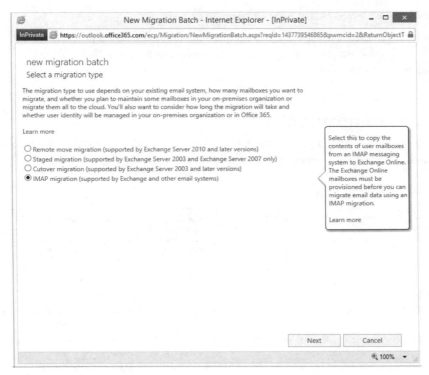

FIGURE 4-35 IMAP Migration

4. Once the migration batch is initiated, the following occurs:

   - Exchange Online creates a migration request for each user in the CSV file.
   - Each migration request includes the credentials for the user in the on-premises IMAP messaging system.
   - Messages from each user's IMAP mailbox are copied to the corresponding Exchange Online mailbox until all data is migrated.

5. Exchange Online provides a status email to the administrator informing them of the status of the migration. This email contains statistics about the number of mailboxes successfully migrated, how many could not be migrated, and any error reports.

6. Exchange Online and the IMAP messaging system are synchronized every 24 hours to move any new messages from the on-premises environment to Exchange Online.

7. Once all migration issues have been resolved, the administrator updates MX records to point to Exchange Online. Once mail is flowing to Exchange Online, the administrator deletes the migration batches.

Migration comparison

Table 4-2 lists the difference between the different methods you can use to migrate from an on-premises messaging environment to Exchange Online.

TABLE 4-2: Migration type comparison

On-premises messaging environment	Number of mailboxes	Will user accounts be managed on-premises	Migration method
Exchange 2007 to Exchange 2013	Less than 2,000	No	Cutover migration
Exchange 2007	Less than 2,000	No	Staged migration
Exchange 2007	More than 2,000	Yes	Staged migration or remote move migration in hybrid deployment
Exchange 2010 or Exchange 2013	More than 2,000	Yes	Remote move migration in hybrid deployment
Non-Exchange on-premises messaging system	No maximum	Yes	IMAP migration

Remember the conditions under which you would choose a specific migration type.

> **Thought experiment**
>
> **IMAP migration process**
>
> In this thought experiment, apply what you learned about this objective. You can find answers to these questions in the "Answers" section at the end of this chapter.
>
> You are in the process of planning an IMAP migration from a third-party on-premises messaging system that hosts 200 mailboxes to Office 365. You are reviewing the migration process. With this in mind, answer the following questions:
>
> 1. What is the first step in an IMAP migration?
>
> 2. What step should an administrator take after all IMAP mailboxes that will be migrated are successfully synchronized to corresponding Office 365 mailboxes and are successfully performing periodic synchronization every 24 hours?
>
> 3. When should the tenant administrator delete the IMAP migration batches?

Objective summary

- Cutover migration is suitable if your on-premises environment has Exchange Server 2007 or later, less than 200 mailboxes, and you will perform cloud-based account management.

- Staged migration is suitable if you have an on-premises deployment of Exchange 2007 deployment with any number of user accounts. Staged migration can be used with on-premises or cloud-based user account management.

- Remove move migrations are appropriate if you have more than 2,000 user accounts, have Exchange 2007 or later, and intend to manage migrated users using cloud tools.

- IMAP migration is appropriate if you have non-Exchange on-premises messaging solutions.

Objective review

Answer the following questions to test your knowledge of the information in this objective. You can find the answers to these questions and explanations of why each answer choice is correct or incorrect in the "Answers" section at the end of the chapter.

1. Your organization has 5,000 mailboxes in an Exchange Server 2010 deployment. Which of the following migration methods is appropriate given this scenario?

   A. Cutover migration

   B. Staged migration

   C. Remote move migration in hybrid deployment

   D. IMAP migration

2. You have a non-Exchange-based on-premises messaging solution that allows users to access their mailboxes using the IMAP protocol. You want to migrate all on-premises mailboxes to Office 365. Which of the following migration methods is appropriate given this information?

    A. Remote move migration in hybrid deployment

    B. IMAP migration

    C. Staged migration

    D. Cutover migration

3. You have an Exchange 2007 on-premises deployment with 4,000 user accounts. You want to manage user accounts using on-premises tools when the migration to Office 365 of these accounts is complete. Which of the following migration methods should you use?

    A. IMAP migration

    B. Remote move migration in hybrid deployment

    C. Staged migration

    D. Cutover migration

4. Your organization has an on-premises deployment of Exchange Server 2013 with 400 mailboxes. You want to migrate these mailboxes to Office 365. When the migration is complete, you intend to perform all user account management tasks using the Office 365 online tools. Given this information, which of the following is the most appropriate migration strategy?

    A. Staged migration

    B. Remote move migration in hybrid deployment

    C. IMAP migration

    D. Cutover migration

Objective 4.3: Plan for Exchange Online

This objective deals with planning how to implement a variety of features in Exchange Online. This includes understanding what client prerequisites are required to ensure that users are able to access archive mailboxes, configuring in-place hold and litigation hold, allowing and blocking access to OWA, and allowing and blocking access to ActiveSync.

This objective covers the following topics:

- Plan client requirements for archive
- In-place hold and litigation hold
- Configure OWA access
- Configure ActiveSync

Plan client requirements for archive

In Chapter 3, "Configure Exchange Online and Skype for Business Online for end users," you read about archive mailboxes. Users can access archive mailboxes on a computer running Outlook or Outlook Web App through a browser, but are unable to access the archive mailbox when using Outlook on a mobile device or accessing Outlook Web App through a browser on a mobile device. Archive mailboxes can be used with the following versions of Outlook:

- Outlook 2016
- Outlook 2013
- Outlook 2010
- Outlook 2007

The archive mailbox appears in Outlook as a folder, as shown in Figure 4-36.

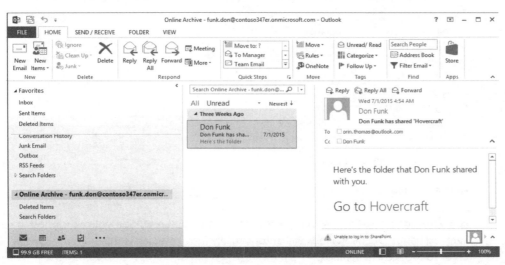

FIGURE 4-36 Move to archive mailbox

There are several methods that users can use to transfer items to the archive mailbox. These include:

- **Move Messages Manually**   Users of clients that support archive mailboxes can manually move messages to the archive mailbox. This process is labor-intensive. Figure 4-37 shows moving an item to an archive mailbox.

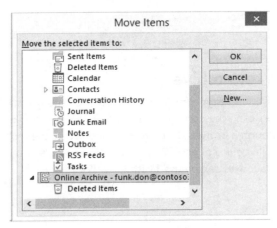

FIGURE 4-37 Move to archive mailbox

- **Use Inbox Rules to Move Messages**   Messages can be moved to the archive mailbox using inbox rules. This requires the user to configure the inbox rule.

FIGURE 4-38 Create Rule

- **Have Retention Policies Move Messages**   The default retention policy assigned to each Exchange Online mailbox will automatically move messages that are two years or older to the archive mailbox.
- **Importing Messages From PST Files**   Users are able to manually import data from PST files on their local computers into the archive mailbox. Having the data stored centrally in Office 365, rather than on a specific computer, is also beneficial for users who want to ensure that the message data in the PST file is backed up and available on other computers.

Users can import PST files into their archive mailbox by performing the following steps:

1. In Outlook, select the Archive folder.
2. Click File, then click Open & Export.
3. On the Open page, shown in Figure 4-39, click Import/Export.

FIGURE 4-39 Import/Export

4. On the Import And Export Wizard, click Import From Another Program Or File, as shown in Figure 4-40, and then click Next.

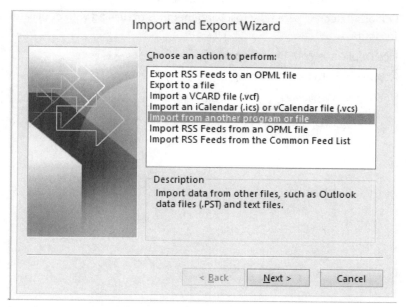

FIGURE 4-40 Import From Another Program Or File

5. On the Import A File page, select Outlook Data File (.pst), as shown in Figure 4-41, and click Next.

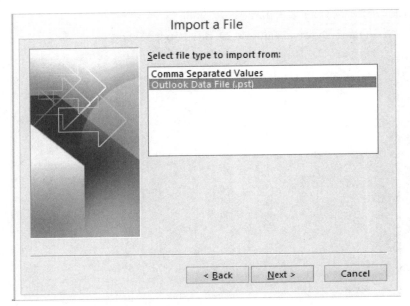

FIGURE 4-41 Import Outlook Data File

6. Select the PST file that you will import.

7. Under Options, select between the following methods of dealing with duplicates, as shown in Figure 4-42.

   ■ Replace Duplicates With Items Imported.

   ■ Allow Duplicates To Be Created.

   ■ Do Not Import Duplicates.

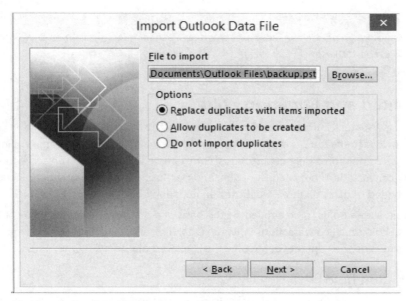

FIGURE 4-42 Duplicate Options

8. Click Next. On the Import Outlook Data File page, ensure that the option to Import items into the same folder is set to Online Archive, as shown in Figure 4-43.

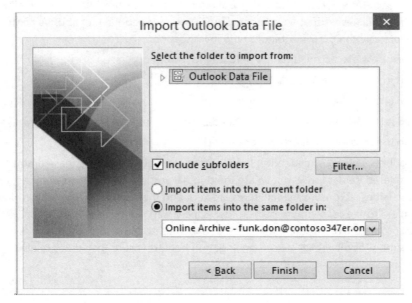

FIGURE 4-43 Import to archive

9. Click Finish.

In-place hold and litigation hold

Litigation hold is a feature introduced in Exchange Server 2010 that allows preservation of data for eDiscovery. The feature is available in Exchange Server 2013 and Exchange Online. You apply litigation hold on a per-mailbox basis. For example, if you want to preserve the contents of all conversations between Don, Kim, and Dan, using the litigation hold functionality, you would need to place all three mailboxes on litigation hold.

In-place hold allows holds to be applied on the basis of a query. For example, you could put an in-place hold on all conversations between Don, Kim, and Dan, but the hold would not apply to items outside the contents defined by the in-place hold query.

Enable litigation hold

Litigation hold, also termed legal hold, is used when one or more users at an organization is subject to an internal investigation, legal discovery, or other procedure that requires the organization to preserve the stage of their Exchange Online mailbox. Litigation hold is necessary to avoid tampering with evidence. For example, if a person has sent abusive email messages from the email account associated with their Exchange Online mailbox, placing the mailbox on litigation hold will ensure that any potential email messages containing abusive content will not be deleted by the person subject to the investigation.

When a mailbox is placed on litigation hold, the following occurs:

- Content in the archive mailbox is preserved.
- Original and modified versions of items are preserved.
- Deleted items are preserved for a specified period or until the hold is removed.
- Items in the recoverable items are preserved.

When a mailbox is placed on litigation hold, its storage requirements increase dramatically. Not only are deleted items stored, but so are the original versions of modified items as well as the modified versions. To ensure that all items are kept and the mailbox remains functional, the quota applied to the recoverable items folder is increased from 30 GB to 100 GB. Even though the quota on the recoverable items folder is increased, Microsoft recommends that administrators monitor mailboxes placed on litigation hold to ensure that issues related to the exhaustion of applied quotas do not arise.

When you place a mailbox on litigation hold you can specify the duration of the hold. The person requesting the litigation hold should specify whether the litigation hold will be of a specific duration or indefinite. You should also ensure that documentation requesting the implementation of the hold is in order as litigation hold is usually requested by a company's human resources or legal department. To leave the mailbox on litigation hold indefinitely, leave the litigation hold duration field empty, as shown in Figure 4-44.

FIGURE 4-44 Litigation Hold

It is important to note that a litigation hold can take up to 60 minutes to be enforced. This Warning is shown in Figure 4-45. You will need to take this period into account in scenarios where you need to immediately preserve the contents of a mailbox and you suspect that the person subject to the litigation hold might attempt to scrub evidence. You should talk to your organization's human resources department about putting policies in place that provide enough time for a litigation hold to be enacted before the person subject to that hold is informed that this has occurred.

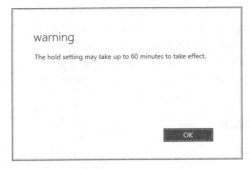

FIGURE 4-45 60-minute Warning

To put an Exchange Online mailbox on litigation hold, perform the following steps:

1. In the Recipients section of Exchange Admin Center, select the Mailboxes area and then select the mailbox of the user for whom you want to configure a litigation hold. Figure 4-46 shows the Dan Jump mailbox selected.

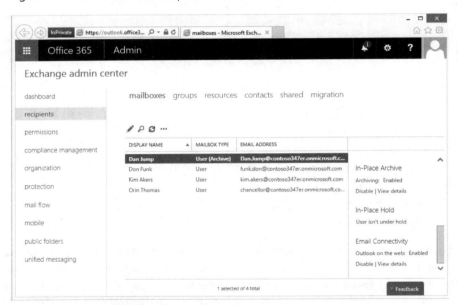

FIGURE 4-46 List of Mailboxes

2. Click the Edit (Pencil) icon to access the Mailbox Properties page.

3. On the Mailbox Properties page, shown in Figure 4-47, click Mailbox Features.

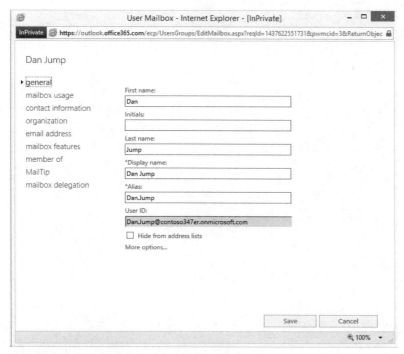

FIGURE 4-47 General mailbox properties

4. Under Litigation Hold: Disabled, shown in Figure 4-48, click Enable.

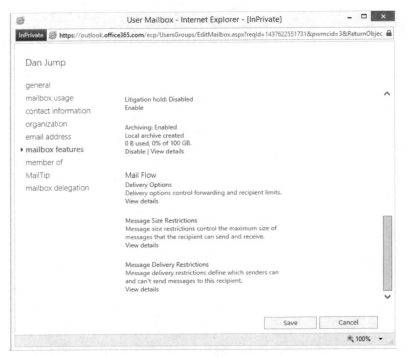

FIGURE 4-48 Enable Litigation Hold from Mailbox Features

5. On the Litigation Hold dialog box, enter the litigation hold duration. If the litigation hold is to be indefinite, ensure that you do not enter a number in this field. You can also provide a note about the litigation hold and a URL, which will be used to inform the user that their mailbox has been placed on hold. You can also provide a URL to provide the user with more information. Click Save to enact the litigation hold.

FIGURE 4-49 180-day Litigation Hold

6. Click Save on the User Mailbox Properties page, shown in Figure 4-50, to enact the litigation hold.

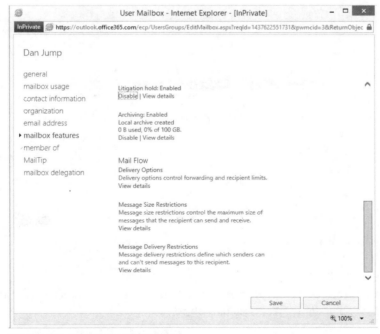

FIGURE 4-50 Litigation Hold Enabled

If the Office 365 user account associated with a mailbox that is placed on litigation hold is deleted, the mailbox is converted into an inactive mailbox. Inactive mailboxes store the contents of the deleted user's mailbox and will retain all mailbox items for the duration of the hold at the time when the hold was applied. For example, if a 90-day hold is placed on a mailbox, and the Office 365 user account is deleted five days later, then the contents of the inactive mailbox will be preserved for another 85 days. Inactive mailboxes are unable to receive new email messages and are not displayed in address books or other lists.

Remove litigation hold

Removing a user from litigation hold will mean that all deleted items that have exceeded their retention period will be purged. The original versions of items that have since been modified will also be deleted after the litigation hold is removed. Once the litigation hold is removed, the quota on the recoverable items folder will also return to 30 GB from 100 GB.

To remove a user from litigation hold, perform the following steps:

1. In the Recipients section of Exchange Admin Center, select the Mailboxes area and then select the mailbox of the user for whom you want to remove the litigation hold. Figure 4-51 shows the Dan Jump mailbox selected.

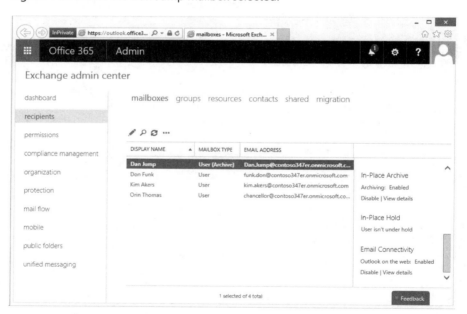

FIGURE 4-51 Dan Jump mailbox

2. Click the Edit (Pencil) icon.

3. In the Mailbox Features section of the Mailbox Properties dialog box, shown in Figure 4-52, click Disable under Litigation Hold: Enabled.

FIGURE 4-52 Disable Litigation Hold

4. In the Warning dialog box, warning you that you are about to disable litigation hold, shown in Figure 4-53, click Yes.

FIGURE 4-53 Warning

5. Click Save to apply the change to the user's mailbox.

Manage litigation hold with PowerShell

You use the Set-Mailbox Windows PowerShell cmdlet to place a mailbox on litigation hold. For example, to place the mailbox don.funk@contoso347er.onmicrosoft.com on indefinite litigation hold, issue the following command:

```
Set-Mailbox don.funk@contoso347er.onmicrosoft.com –LitigationHold $True
```

You can use the LitigationHoldDuration parameter to configure a duration for the litigation hold. For example, to place the kim.akers@contoso347er.onmicrosoft.com mailbox on litigation hold for 180 days, issue the following command:

```
Set-Mailbox kim.akers@contoso347er.onmicrosoft.com —LitigationHold $True
—LitigationDuration 180
```

You can use a combination of the Get-Mailbox and the Set-Mailbox cmdlets to put all of the mailboxes in the organization on litigation hold. You might need to do this if your organization is subject to litigation and the contents of all user mailboxes must be preserved. For example, to place all user mailboxes in the organization on hold for a period of 90 days, issue the following Windows PowerShell cmdlet:

```
Get-Mailbox -ResultSize Unlimited —Filter {RecipientTypeDetails -eq "UserMailbox"} |
Set-Mailbox -LitigationHoldEnabled $true -LitigationHoldDuration 90
```

You can remove a mailbox from litigation hold using the Set-Mailbox Windows PowerShell cmdlet. For example, to remove the litigation hold on the mailbox don.funk@contoso347er.onmicrosoft.com, issue the following command:

```
Set-Mailbox don.funk@contoso347er.onmicrosoft.com —LitigationHoldEnabled $False
```

> **MORE INFO** **LITIGATION HOLD**
>
> You can learn more about litigation hold at *https://technet.microsoft.com/en-us/library/ Dn743673(v=EXCHG.150).aspx*.

In-place hold

You configure in-place holds using the Compliance Center rather than configuring in-place holds on a per-mailbox basis. To create an in-place hold, perform the following steps:

1. Select the Compliance Management section of the Exchange Admin Center, as shown in Figure 4-54.

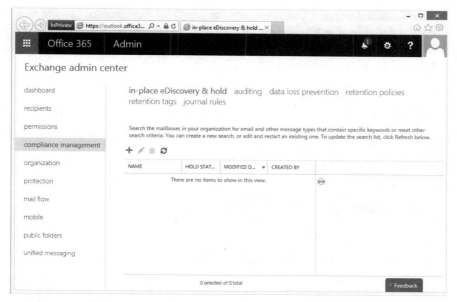

FIGURE 4-54 In-Place eDiscovery & Hold

2. Click the Plus (+) icon.

3. On the New In-Place eDiscovery & Hold page of the In-Place eDiscovery & Hold wizard, provide a name and click Next. Figure 4-55 shows the name set to Example-Hold.

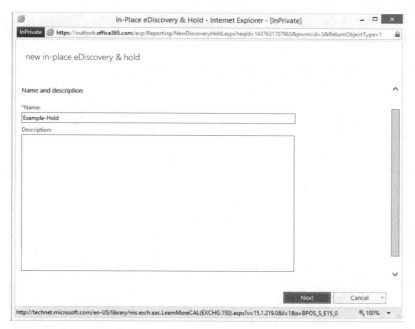

FIGURE 4-55 Example-Hold

4. On the Mailboxes page, choose whether to search all mailboxes or specific mailboxes. If you choose to search specific mailboxes, you add them by clicking the Plus (+) icon and then selecting them on the Select Mailbox dialog box, clicking Add, as shown in Figure 4-56, and then clicking OK.

FIGURE 4-56 Select mailboxes for in-place hold

5. Review the Mailboxes page to ensure that the appropriate mailboxes are selected, as shown in Figure 4-57, and then click Next.

FIGURE 4-57 Specify Mailboxes To Search

6. On the Search query page, you can include all content in the selected mailboxes, or choose to filter based on criteria. It is only possible to filter by criteria if the user creating the In-Place eDiscovery & Hold is a member of the Discovery Management role group. As shown in Figure 4-58, you can filter on the following options:

- Keywords
- Start Date
- End Date
- From
- To/CC/Bcc
- Message Types

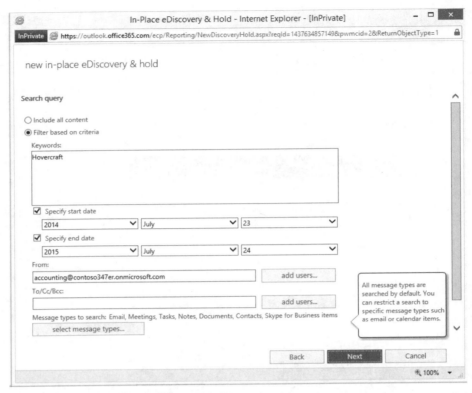

FIGURE 4-58 Search Query conditions

7. On the In-Place Hold settings page, select the Place Content Matching the Search Query in Selected Mailboxes on Hold, and specify whether the hold should be indefinite or should be held for a specific number of dates after their receive date. Figure 4-59 shows the configuration of an indefinite hold.

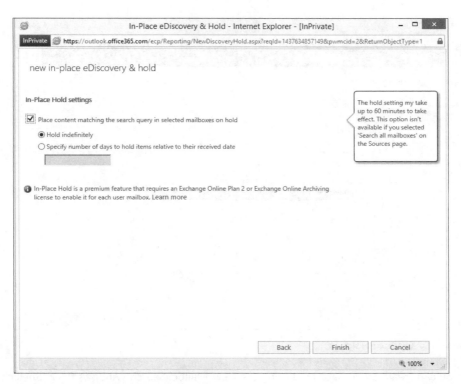

FIGURE 4-59 In-Place Hold Settings

8. Click Finish to create the hold.

To remove an in-place hold, select the in-place hold in the Compliance Management section of Exchange Admin Center, as shown in Figure 3-60, and then click the Delete (Trashcan/Recycle Bin) icon.

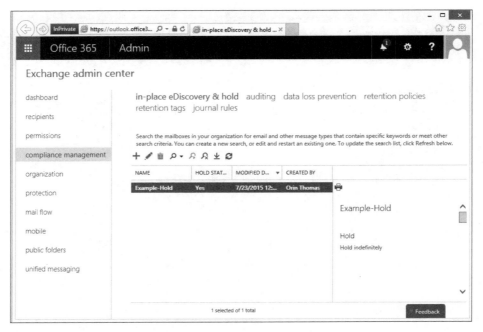

FIGURE 4-60 Example-Hold

You can create an in-place hold using the New-MailboxSearch Windows PowerShell cmdlet. For example, to create a new in-place hold of indefinite duration for all members of the Research distribution group for all messages relating to the terms "secret" and "hovercraft," issue the following command:

```
New-MailboxSearch -Name "Hold-Hovercraft" -SourceMailboxes Research -SearchQuery
"'Hovercraft' AND 'Secret'" -InPlaceHoldEnabled $True
```

You can disable an in-place hold using the Set-MailboxSearch Windows PowerShell cmdlet. For example, to disable the Hold-Hovercraft search, issue the command:

```
Set-MailboxSearch "Hold-Hovercraft" -InPlaceHoldEnabled $false
```

You use the RemovemailboxSearch cmdlet to remove an in-place hold. For example, to remove the "Hold-Hovercraft" in-place hold, issue the command:

```
Remove-MailboxSearch "Hold-Hovercraft"
```

> **MORE INFO IN-PLACE HOLD**
>
> You can learn more about in-place holds at *https://technet.microsoft.com/en-us/library/dd979797(v=exchg.150).aspx*.

Configure OWA access

Outlook Web App (OWA), also termed Outlook On The Web, allows users to access their Office 365 Exchange Online mailbox through a web browser. While a large number of Office 365 users will access their Exchange Online mailbox through the Outlook client software on their computer or mobile device, in some scenarios, such as when they are using a kiosk computer in an airport, they will want to access their mailbox through a web browser.

Allowing access to Office 365 Exchange Online mailboxes through OWA does provide users with convenience, but also exposes the organization to risk. Many users do not exercise due care when using computers in airports or Internet cafés. There are many instances where user credentials have been captured by malware installed on these computers provided for public use. These credentials can be used at a later point in time by attackers to access organizational data because they can gain access to OWA or even a user's Office 365 subscription. For this reason, many organizations disable OWA. As smartphone users are able to access Office 365 Exchange Online mailboxes through the Outlook app, available in each vendor's App Store, fewer users require access to OWA when away from their trusted computers.

To disable OWA, perform the following steps:

1. In the Recipients area of the Exchange Admin Center, select the user for which you want to disable ActiveSync. Figure 4-61 shows Dan Jump selected.

FIGURE 4-61 Select user for ActiveSync disable

2. Click the Edit (Pencil) icon.
3. In the Mailbox Features section, click Disable under Outlook On The Web: Enabled, as shown in Figure 4-62.

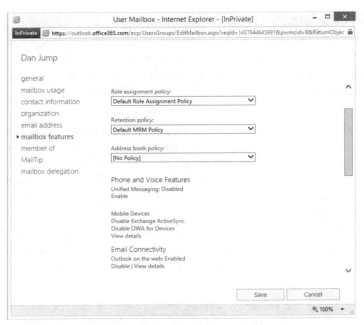

FIGURE 4-62 Disable Outlook On The Web

4. On the Warning dialog box, shown in Figure 4-63, click Yes.

FIGURE 4-63 Warning about disabling OWA

5. Click Save to save the changes to the Office 365 Exchange Online mailbox.

You can also disable or enable OWA from the list of mailboxes by clicking the text under Outlook on the Web in the list of users in Exchange Admin Center. For example, Figure 4-64 shows the Dan Jump mailbox selected. By clicking Enable under Outlook On The Web: Disabled, OWA would be re-enabled for the Dan Jump user account.

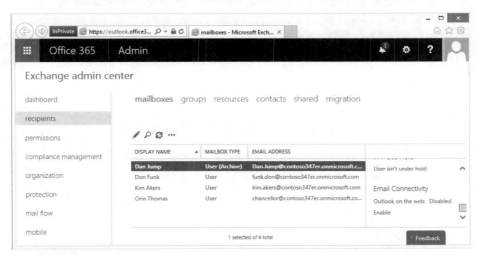

FIGURE 4-64 OWA disabled

You use the Set-CASMailbox Windows PowerShell cmdlet to enable and disable OWA on a per user basis. For example, to disable OWA for the dan.jump@contoso347er.onmicrosoft. com account, issue the command:

```
Set-CasMailbox dan.jump@contoso347er.onmicrosoft.com –OwaEnabled $False
```

You can use the Get-Mailbox cmdlet with the Set-CasMailbox cmdlet to disable OWA for all mailbox users. To do this, issue the following command:

```
Get-Mailbox -ResultSize Unlimited -Filter {RecipientTypeDetails -eq "UserMailbox"} |
Set-CasMailbox –OwaEnabled $False
```

To enable OWA for the dan.jump@contoso347er.onmicrosoft.com account, issue the command:

```
Set-CasMailbox dan.jump@contoso347er.onmicrosoft.com –OwaEnabled $True
```

Configure ActiveSync

ActiveSync is a protocol, primarily used by mobile devices, that allows access to email, calendar, contacts, and tasks. ActiveSync is enabled by default on Office 365 Exchange Online mailboxes. In some scenarios, you might want to disable ActiveSync.

To disable ActiveSync on a specific mailbox, perform the following steps:

1. In the Recipients area of the Exchange Admin Center, select the user for which you want to disable ActiveSync. Figure 4-65 shows Kim Akers selected.

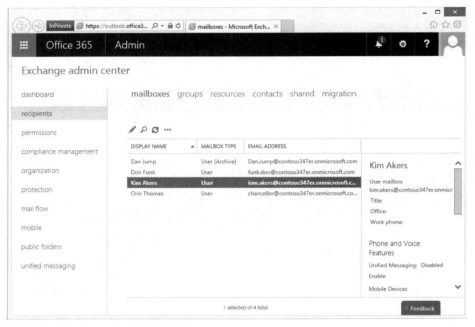

FIGURE 4-65 Preparing to disable ActiveSync

2. Click the Edit (Pencil) icon on the toolbar.

3. In the Mailbox Features section, shown in Figure 4-66, click Disable Exchange Active-Sync.

FIGURE 4-66 Disable ActiveSync

4. In the Warning dialog box, shown in Figure 4-67, click Yes.

FIGURE 4-67 Disable ActiveSync Warning

5. Click Save to close the User Mailbox properties page.

You can also disable and enable Exchange ActiveSync from the recipients list. To do this, select the recipient and in the details pane, select Enable Exchange ActiveSync or Disable Exchange ActiveSync. Figure 4-68 shows the option to enable Exchange ActiveSync for the Kim Akers user.

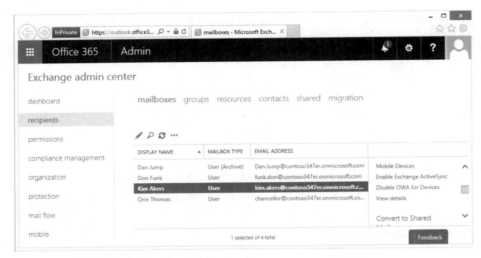

FIGURE 4-68 Enable ActiveSync from Mailboxes

You can use the Set-CASMailbox Windows PowerShell cmdlet to enable or disable Active-Sync. For example, to disable ActiveSync for the don.funk@contoso347er.onmicrosoft.com mailbox, issue the command:

```
Set-CASMailbox –Identity don.funk@contoso347er.onmicrosoft.com –ActiveSyncEnabled $False
```

You can use the Get-Mailbox cmdlet in conjunction with the Set-CasMailbox cmdlet to disable ActiveSync for all users in an organization. To do this, issue the command:

```
Get-Mailbox -ResultSize Unlimited -Filter {RecipientTypeDetails -eq "UserMailbox"} |
Set-CasMailbox –ActiveSyncEnabled $False
```

To enable ActiveSync for the don.funk@contoso347er.onmicrosoft.com mailbox, issue the command:

```
Set-CASMailbox –Identity don.funk@contoso347er.onmicrosoft.com –ActiveSyncEnabled $False
```

> **MORE INFO OFFICE 365 AND ACTIVESYNC**
>
> You can learn more about managing ActiveSync for Office 365 at *https://support.microsoft. com/en-us/kb/2795303*.

EXAM TIP

Remember the Windows PowerShell cmdlets used to configure and manage litigation hold.

Thought experiment
In-place hold at Tailspin Toys

In this thought experiment, apply what you learned about this objective. You can find answers to these questions in the "Answers" section at the end of this chapter.

You are looking at replacing the current practice of using litigation hold at Tailspin Toys when users are subject to discovery requests with instead switching to in-place hold. Management is especially interested in using the query functionality of in-place hold to locate items subject to discovery requests that are stored across multiple mailboxes. Management is also interested in what changes occur in terms of archive mailbox functionality when in-place hold is applied. With these issues in mind, answer the following questions:

1. Which Exchange Administrator role must a user be a member of to configure a query-based in-place hold?

2. When an in-place hold is applied on a mailbox, what is the new quota value assigned to the archive mailbox?

Objective summary

- Archived mailboxes can be accessed by clients running Outlook 2007 and later, as well as people running Outlook Web App on computers.

- Archive mailboxes cannot be accessed from mobile versions of Outlook and cannot be accessed from Outlook Web App when used from a mobile device web browser.

- Litigation hold is applied to an entire mailbox and preserves the contents of that mailbox until the duration of the litigation hold expires, including modified and deleted items.

- It can take up to 60 minutes for a litigation hold to be enforced by Exchange Online after an administrator enables the hold.

- You can enable litigation hold on a mailbox using the Set-Mailbox Windows PowerShell cmdlet.

- When litigation hold or in-place hold are enabled, the quota on the archive mailbox is increased to 100 GB from 30 GB.

- In-place hold differs from litigation hold in that only the items that meet the query condition will be protected, rather than all items in the mailbox.

- Only users who have been assigned membership of the Discovery Management role group can configure query-based in-place holds.

- In-Place hold is managed from Windows PowerShell using cmdlets with the Mailbox-Search noun and the InPlaceHold parameter.
- You can disable and enable Outlook Web App (OWA), also termed Outlook on the Web, through Exchange Admin Center or by using the Set-CasMailbox cmdlet with the OwaEnabled parameter.
- You can disable and enable ActiveSync through the Exchange Admin Center or by using the Set-CasMailbox cmdlet with the ActiveSyncEnabled parameter.

Objective review

Answer the following questions to test your knowledge of the information in this objective. You can find the answers to these questions and explanations of why each answer choice is correct or incorrect in the "Answers" section at the end of the chapter.

1. Which of the following Windows PowerShell cmdlets would you use to disable Active-Sync and Outlook Web App on several Office 365 Exchange Online mailboxes?

    A. Set-Mailbox

    B. Set-CasMailbox

    C. New-MailboxSearch

    D. Remove-MailboxSearch

2. Which of the following Windows PowerShell cmdlets would you use to enable litigation hold on an Office 365 Exchange Online mailbox?

    A. Set-CasMailbox

    B. New-MailboxSearch

    C. Set-Mailbox

    D. Set-MailboxSearch

3. You want to configure an in-place hold for all mentions of the phrase "project hover-craft" in all Exchange Online mailboxes in your organization. Which of the following Windows PowerShell cmdlets can you use to accomplish this goal?

    A. New-MailboxSearch

    B. Set-MailboxSearch

    C. Set-Mailbox

    D. Set-CasMailbox

4. Which of the following Windows PowerShell cmdlets can you use to disable, but not delete, an in-place hold?

    A. Set-CasMailbox

    B. Set-MailboxSearch

    C. Remove-MailboxSearch

    D. Set-MailboxSearch

5. Which of the following Windows PowerShell cmdlets can you use to delete an in-place hold?

   A. Set-CasMailbox

   B. Set-MailboxSearch

   C. Remove-MailboxSearch

   D. Set-MailboxSearch

Objective 4.4: Manage Skype for Business global external communications settings

This objective deals with managing tenancy level settings for Skype for Business. These settings allow you to manage, at the tenancy level, which external users Skype for Business clients are able to communicate with, including whether communication is allowed with the consumer version of Skype.

> **This objective covers the following topics:**
> - Manage external communication and domains
> - Manage Skype consumer connectivity
> - Customize meeting invitations
> - Disable push notifications

Manage external communication and domains

In the previous chapter, you read about how to manage external communication for Skype for Business Online users using the browser and the Skype for Business Admin Center, as shown in Figure 4-69.

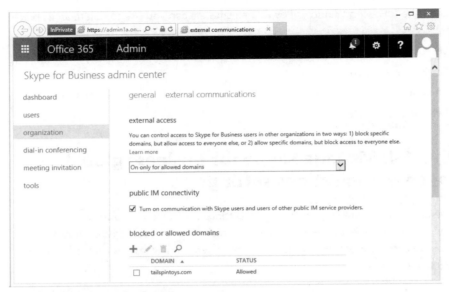

FIGURE 4-69 Public IM Connectivity

You can also use a set of Skype for Business Online specific Windows PowerShell cmdlets to manage external communication settings. These cmdlets are as follows:

- **New-CsEdgeAllowAllKnownDomains**   This cmdlet allows Skype for Business Online users to communicate with any domain, except those on the block list.
- **New-CsEdgeAllowList**   Use this cmdlet to configure the domains with which Skype for Business Online users can communicate. This cmdlet must be used in conjunction with the New-CsEdgeDomainPattern and Set-CsTenantFederationConfiguration cmdlets.
- **New-CsEdgeDomainPattern**   You use this cmdlet to modify the list of allowed or blocked domains, as string values cannot be passed directly to the cmdlets used to manage the list.
- **Get-CsTenantFederationConfiguration**   You can use this cmdlet to view information about the allowed domains and the blocked domains.

Managed allowed domain list

The following Windows PowerShell code allows users to only communicate with users in the tailspintoys.com and wingtiptoys.com domains.

```
$x = New-CsEdgeDomainPattern -Domain "tailspintoys.com"
$y = New-CsEdgeDomainPattern -Domain "wingtiptoys.com"
$newAllowList = New-CsEdgeAllowList -AllowedDomain $x,$y
Set-CsTenantFederationConfiguration -AllowedDomains $newAllowList
```

To remove a domain from the allowed list, you need to use a set of commands. First you need to place the current list of allowed domains in a variable:

```
$x = (Get-CsTenantFederationConfiguration).AllowedDomains
```

You then need to determine the number of the domain that you want to remove. You do this by issuing the variable as a command and then counting the number of lines until the domain that you want to remove, with the first line as zero. For example, if you had the following list output when you issued the variable as a command:

```
adatum.com
contoso.com
fabrikam.com
```

The domain contoso.com would be number 1 and adatum.com would be 0. Once you've determined which domain you want to remove, you issue the command $x.AllowedDomain. RemoveAt(Y), where Y is the number of the domain you want to remove. So if you wanted to remove fabrikam.com from the list, you would issue the command:

```
$x.AllowedDomain.RemoveAt(2)
```

You can repeat the process to remove other domains from the list. Once you've pruned all of the domains that you want to remove, you can then assign the list using the following command:

```
Set-CsTenantFederationConfiguration -AllowedDomains $x
```

The following command removes all domains from the current allow list:

```
$newAllowList = New-CsEdgeAllowList -AllowedDomain $Null

Set-CsTenantFederationConfiguration -Tenant -AllowedDomains $newAllowList
```

You can use the Get-CsTenantFederationConfiguration cmdlet to view the list of allowed domains by issuing the following command:

```
Get-CsTenantFederationConfiguration | Select-Object -ExpandProperty AllowedDomains |
Select-Object AllowedDomain
```

Manage blocked domain list

To add a domain to the blocked list, use the BlockedDomains parameter. For example, to add margiestravel.com to the list of blocked domains, issue the following command:

```
$x = New-CsEdgeDomainPattern "margiestravel.com"
Set-CsTenantFederationConfiguration -BlockedDomains @{Add=$x}
```

You can use the Get-CsTenantFederationConfiguration cmdlet to view the list of blocked domains by issuing the following command:

```
Get-CsTenantFederationConfiguration | Select-Object -ExpandProperty BlockedDomains
```

To remove the domain margiestravel.com from the domain blocked list, perform the following steps:

```
$x = New-CsEdgeDomainPattern "margiestravel.com"
Set-CsTenantFederationConfiguration –BlockedDomains @{Remove=$x}
```

You can remove all domains from the blocked domain list by issuing the following command:

```
Set-CsTenantFederationConfiguration –BlockedDomains $Null
```

> **MORE INFO MANAGE EXTERNAL COMMUNICATION**
>
> You can learn more about managing external communication using Windows PowerShell for Skye for Business Online at *https://technet.microsoft.com/en-us/library/dn362813(v=ocs.15).aspx*.

Manage Skype consumer connectivity

As you read about in the last chapter, you can use the Turn On Communication With Skype Users And Users Of Other Public IM Service Providers option, found in the External Communications area of the Skype for Business Admin Center, as shown in Figure 4-70, to allow or block Skype for Business users from communicating with Skype users.

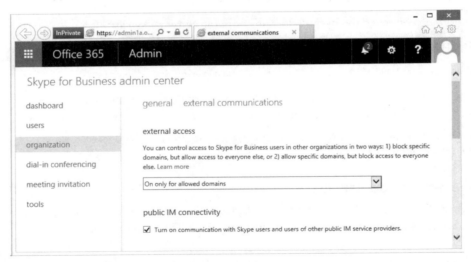

FIGURE 4-70 Allow Skype communication

You can use the Set-CsTenantFederationConfiguration cmdlet to also disable and enable public IM connectivity. The following command enables public IM connectivity:

```
Set-CsTenantFederationConfiguration –AllowPublicUsers $True
```

Once you've enabled public IM connectivity, you can allow or block specific providers. You do this with the Set-CsTenantPublicProvider cmdlet. When using this cmdlet, you must specify the tenant identifier. You can determine the tenant ID using the following command:

```
Get-CsTenant | Select-Object TenantID
```

Once you have the tenant ID, you can enable connectivity to Skype using the following command:

```
Set-CsTenantPublicProvider -Tenant "TenantID" -Provider "Skype"
```

The following command disables public IM connectivity:

```
Set-CsTenantFederationConfiguration –AllowPublicUsers $False
```

> **MORE INFO** **PUBLIC IM PROVIDER CONNECTIVITY**
>
> You can learn more about allowing access to public IM providers at *https://technet.micro-soft.com/en-us/library/dn362809(v=ocs.15).aspx*.

Customize meeting invitations

You can customize meeting invitations, including a logo, help URL, legal URL, and meeting footer text. The logo can be up to 188 pixels by 30 pixels in size and can be in JPG or GIF format. By default, meeting invitations are not customized.

To configure custom meeting invitations, perform the following steps:

1. Select the Meeting Invitation section in the Skype for Business Admin Center.
2. Provide information in the following areas, as shown in Figure 4-71:

   - **Logo URL**   The URL of a JPG or GIF file no larger than 188 pixels by 30 pixels.
   - **Help URL**   The URL of documentation providing assistance to meeting attendees.
   - **Legal URL**   The URL of any legal information necessary for meeting attendees to be aware of.
   - **Footer Text**   Text that will be included in the footer of any meeting invitation.

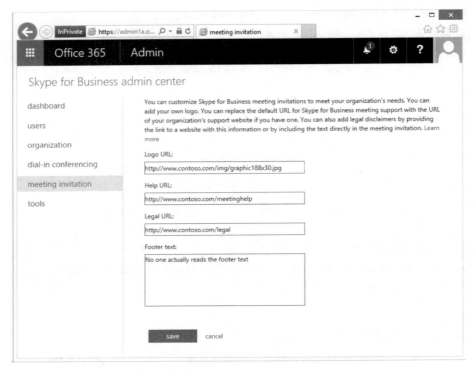

FIGURE 4-71 Custom Meeting Invitation

> **MORE INFO** **CUSTOMIZE MEETING INVITATIONS**
>
> You can learn more about customizing Skype for Business Online meeting notifications at *https://support.office.com/en-us/article/Customize-meeting-invitations-9af52080-dd56-4b66-b056-41ed1a7aaae3*.

Disable push notifications

Push notification allows alerts about incoming and missed instant messages to be displayed whenever the user is not actively using Skype for Business on their phone or tablet. Push notifications are enabled by default in Skype for Business. Users are able to disable them through the options in the Skype for Business client on their own device. If you want to disable push notifications, users will receive alerts about incoming and missed instant messages the next time they use the Skype for Business client on their mobile device.

To disable push notifications, perform the following steps:

1. Select the Organization section in the Skype for Business Admin Center.

2. Ensure the General section is selected.

3. Under Mobile Phone Notifications, shown in Figure 4-72, remove the check next to each of the notification types that you would like to remove.

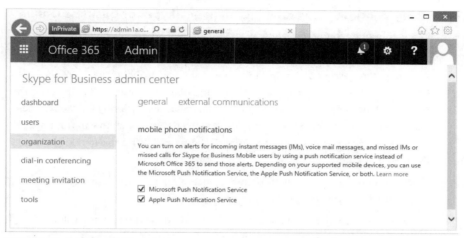

FIGURE 4-72 Push Notifications

4. Click Save to apply the changes.

You use the Set-CsPushNotificationConfiguration cmdlet to enable or disable the push notification service. To disable the Apple and Microsoft Push notification services, issue the following command:

```
Set-CsPushNotificationConfiguration -EnableApplePushNotificationService $False
-EnableMicrosoftPushNotificationService $False
```

You can disable the push notification for one service whilst keeping the push notification for the other service running. For example, to disable the Microsoft push notification service, but enable the Apple push notification service, issue the following command:

```
Set-CsPushNotificationConfiguration -EnableApplePushNotificationService $True
-EnableMicrosoftPushNotificationService $False
```

> **MORE INFO PUSH NOTIFICATIONS**
>
> You can learn more about configuring push notifications at *https://support.office.com/en-us/article/Turn-off-mobile-phone-notifications-2de47013-4f09-493c-abc5-372f56ad69e3*.

Thought experiment
Using Windows PowerShell to manage Skype for Business Online

In this thought experiment, apply what you learned about this objective. You can find answers to these questions in the "Answers" section at the end of this chapter.

You are in the process of configuring Skype for Business Online using Windows PowerShell. You are interested in configuring public IM connectivity, disabling the Apple push notification service, and removing all of the currently blocked domains from the blocked domain list. To do this, you need to research the appropriate Windows PowerShell commands to accomplish these tasks. With this in mind, answer the following questions:

1. Which Windows PowerShell command, including parameters and values, would you use to disable public IM connectivity?

2. Which Windows PowerShell command, including parameters and values, would you use to disable the Apple push notification service?

3. Which Windows PowerShell command, including parameters and values, would you use to remove all domains from the blocked domains list?

Objective summary

- Use the New-CsEdgeAllowAllKnownDomains cmdlet to allow Skype for Business Online users to communicate with any domain, except those on the blocked list.

- Use the New-CsEdgeAllowList cmdlet to configure the domains with which Skype for Business Online users can communicate. This cmdlet must be used in conjunction with the New-CsEdgeDomainPattern and Set-CsTenantFederationConfiguration cmdlets.

- Use the New-CsEdgeDomainPattern to modify the list of allowed or blocked domains.

- Use the Get-CsTenantFederationConfiguration to view information about the allowed domains and the blocked domains.

- You can use the Set-CsTenantFederationConfiguration cmdlet to also disable and enable public IM connectivity.

- You can customize meeting invitations, including a logo, help URL, legal URL, and meeting footer text.

- Skype for Business push notification allow alerts about incoming and missed instant messages to be displayed whenever the user is not actively using Skype for Business on their phone or tablet.

- You can disable push notifications for the Microsoft and Apple Push notification service through the Skype for Business Admin Center or by using the Set-CsPushNotification-Configuration.

Objective review

Answer the following questions to test your knowledge of the information in this objective. You can find the answers to these questions and explanations of why each answer choice is correct or incorrect in the "Answers" section at the end of the chapter.

1. Which of the following Windows PowerShell cmdlets do you use to allow Skype for Business Online users to communicate with any domain, except those on the block list?

   A. New-CsEdgeAllowAllKnownDomains

   B. New-CsEdgeAllowList

   C. New-CsEdgeDomainPattern

   D. Get-CsTenantFederationConfiguration

2. Which of the following Windows PowerShell cmdlets do you use to view information about currently allowed or blocked domains across the tenancy for Skype for Business Online?

   A. New-CsEdgeAllowAllKnownDomains

   B. Set-CsPushNotificationConfiguration

   C. Set-CsTenantFederationConfiguration

   D. Get-CsTenantFederationConfiguration

3. Which of the following Windows PowerShell cmdlets do you use to enable and disable public IM connectivity across the tenancy in Skype for Business Online?

   A. Set-CsPushNotificationConfiguration

   B. Set-CsTenantFederationConfiguration

   C. New-CsEdgeDomainPattern

   D. Get-CsTenantFederationConfiguration

4. Which of the following Windows PowerShell cmdlets would you use to disable the Apple push notification service for Skype for Business Online?

   A. Set-CsTenantFederationConfiguration

   B. Get-CsTenantFederationConfiguration

   C. New-CsEdgeAllowAllKnownDomains

   D. Set-CsPushNotificationConfiguration

5. Which of the following Windows PowerShell cmdlets is used in the process of modifying the list of allowed or blocked domains for Skype for Business Online? (Choose all that apply.)

   A. New-CsEdgeDomainPattern

   B. New-CsEdgeAllowAllKnownDomains

   C. Set-CsPushNotificationConfiguration

   D. Set-CsTenantFederationConfiguration

Answers

This section contains the solutions to the thought experiments and answers to the objective review questions in this chapter.

Objective 4.1: Thought experiment

1. Edit the default spam filter policy and alter the Spam action to Quarantine message.
2. Edit the international spam settings of the default spam filter policy and specify the Esperanto language and the New Zealand country or region.
3. Use the Release-QuarantineMessage cmdlet with the ReleaseToAll parameter to release a message currently in quarantine to all recipients.

Objective 4.1: Review

1. **Correct answer:** B

   A. **Incorrect:** Use the Set-MalwareFilterPolicy cmdlet to modify malware filter policy settings.

   B. **Correct:** Use the Get-MalwareFilterPolicy cmdlet to view malware filter policy settings.

   C. **Incorrect:** Use the Set-MalwareFilterRule cmdlet to edit an existing malware filter rule.

   D. **Incorrect:** Use the Get-MalwareFilterRule cmdlet to view an existing malware filter rule.

2. **Correct answer:** D

   A. **Incorrect:** Use the Remove-MalwareFilterPolicy cmdlet to remove a custom filter policy.

   B. **Incorrect:** Use the Remove-MalwareFilterRule cmdlet to remove a rule. This does not suspend the rule, it removes it entirely.

   C. **Incorrect:** Use the Remove-HostedContentFilterPolicy to remove a custom spam filter policy.

   D. **Correct:** Use the Disable-MalwareFilterRule to turn off a malware filter rule without removing it.

3. **Correct answer:** A

   A. **Correct:** Use the Remove-HostedContentFilterPolicy to remove a custom spam filter policy.

   B. **Incorrect:** Use the Disable-MalwareFilterRule to turn off a malware filter rule without removing it.

   C. **Incorrect:** Use the Remove-MalwareFilterRule cmdlet to remove a malware filter rule.

   D. **Incorrect:** Use the Remove-MalwareFilterPolicy cmdlet to remove a custom malware filter policy.

4. **Correct answer:** C

   A. **Incorrect:** Use the New-HostedContentFilterPolicy cmdlet to create a new custom spam filter policy.

   B. **Incorrect:** Use the Get-MalwareFilterRule cmdlet to view an existing malware filter rule.

   C. **Correct:** Use the Get-HostedContentFilterPolicy cmdlet to view existing spam filter settings.

   D. **Incorrect:** Use the Get-MalwareFilterPolicy cmdlet to view malware filter policy settings.

5. **Correct answer:** B

   A. **Incorrect:** Use the New-HostedContentFilterPolicy cmdlet to create a new custom spam filter policy.

   B. **Correct:** Use the New-MalwareFilterPolicy cmdlet to create a new custom malware filter policy.

   C. **Incorrect:** Use the Enable-MalwareFilterRule cmdlet to turn on a malware filter rule.

   D. **Incorrect:** Use the Set-MalwareFilterPolicy cmdlet to modify malware filter policy settings.

6. **Correct answer:** B

   A. **Incorrect:** Use the Set-MalwareFilterRule cmdlet to edit an existing malware filter rule.

   B. **Correct:** Use the Enable-MalwareFilterRule cmdlet to turn on a malware filter rule.

   C. **Incorrect:** Use the New-HostedContentFilterPolicy cmdlet to create a new custom spam filter policy.

   D. **Incorrect:** Use the New-MalwareFilterRule cmdlet to create a new filter rule that can be applied to a custom policy.

7. **Correct answer:** A

   A. **Correct:** Use the Remove-MalwareFilterRule cmdlet to remove a malware filter rule.

   B. **Incorrect:** Use the Remove-HostedContentFilterPolicy to remove a custom spam filter policy.

   C. **Incorrect:** Use the Remove-MalwareFilterPolicy cmdlet to remove a custom malware filter policy.

   D. **Incorrect:** Use the Disable-MalwareFilterRule to turn off a malware filter rule without removing it.

8. **Correct answer:** D

   A. **Incorrect:** Use the New-MalwareFilterPolicy cmdlet to create a new custom malware filter policy.

   B. **Incorrect:** Use the New-MalwareFilterRule cmdlet to create a new filter rule that can be applied to a custom policy.

   C. **Incorrect:** Use the Set-HostedConnectionFilterPolicy cmdlet to configure the connection filter policy settings. This cmdlet includes the IPAllowList and IPBlockList parameters.

   D. **Correct:** Use the New-HostedContentFilterPolicy cmdlet to create a new custom spam filter policy.

9. **Correct answer:** A

   A. **Correct:** Use the Set-HostedConnectionFilterPolicy cmdlet to configure the connection filter policy settings. This cmdlet includes the IPAllowLIst and IPBlockList parameters.

   B. **Incorrect:** Use the Get-HostedContentFilterPolicy cmdlet to view existing spam filter settings.

   C. **Incorrect:** Use the Set-MalwareFilterPolicy cmdlet to modify malware filter policy settings.

   D. **Incorrect:** Use the Set-MalwareFilterRule cmdlet to edit an existing malware filter rule.

10. **Correct answer:** B

   A. **Incorrect:** Use the Set-MalwareFilterPolicy cmdlet to modify malware filter policy settings.

   B. **Correct:** Use the Set-MalwareFilterRule cmdlet to edit an existing malware filter rule.

   C. **Incorrect:** Use the Set-HostedConnectionFilterPolicy cmdlet to configure the connection filter policy settings. This cmdlet includes the IPAllowLIst and IPBlockList parameters.

   D. **Incorrect:** Use the Get-MalwareFilterPolicy cmdlet to view malware filter policy settings.

Objective 4.2: Thought experiment

1. The first step in an IMAP migration is to create user accounts in Office 365 that correspond to the on-premises IMAP accounts that must be migrated.

2. Once synchronization is successful and periodic synchronization is proceeding without problem, the administrator should update MX records to point to Exchange Online.

3. The tenant administrator should delete the IMAP migration batches after mail flow is occurring successfully to Exchange Online and not the on-premises IMAP messaging system.

Objective 4.2: Review

1. **Correct answer:** C

   A. **Incorrect:** Cutover migration is suitable if your on-premises environment has Exchange Server 2007, Exchange Server 2010, or Exchange Server 2013 and you have less than 2,000 and you do not want to perform on-premises account management.

   B. **Incorrect:** Staged migration is suitable if you have an on-premises deployment of Exchange 2007 deployment with any number of user accounts. This method is appropriate independently of whether or not you want to perform on-premises or cloud-based user account management.

   C. **Correct:** Remove move migrations are appropriate if you have more than 2,000 user accounts, have Exchange 2007, Exchange 2010, and Exchange 2013 as the on-premises environment, and you want to have cloud-based user management.

   D. **Incorrect:** Use an IMAP migration if you have a non-Exchange on-premises messaging solutions.

2. **Correct answer:** B

   A. **Incorrect:** Remove move migrations are appropriate if you have more than 2,000 user accounts, have Exchange 2007, Exchange 2010, and Exchange 2013 as the on-premises environment, and you want to have cloud-based user management.

   B. **Correct:** Use an IMAP migration if you have a non-Exchange on-premises messaging solutions.

   C. **Incorrect:** Staged migration is suitable if you have an on-premises deployment of Exchange 2007 deployment with any number of user accounts. This method is appropriate independently of whether or not you want to perform on-premises or cloud-based user account management.

   D. **Incorrect:** Cutover migration is suitable if your on-premises environment has Exchange Server 2007, Exchange Server 2010, or Exchange Server 2013 and you have less than 2,000 and you do not want to perform on-premises account management.

3. **Correct answer:** C

   A. **Incorrect:** Use an IMAP migration if you have a non-Exchange on-premises messaging solutions.

   B. **Incorrect:** Remove move migrations are appropriate if you have more than 2,000 user accounts, have Exchange 2007, Exchange 2010, and Exchange 2013 as the on-premises environment, and you want to have cloud-based user management.

   C. **Correct:** Staged migration is suitable if you have an on-premises deployment of Exchange 2007 deployment with any number of user accounts. This method is appropriate independently of whether or not you want to perform on-premises or cloud-based user account management.

   D. **Incorrect:** Cutover migration is suitable if your on-premises environment has Exchange Server 2007, Exchange Server 2010, or Exchange Server 2013 and you have less than 2,000 and you do not want to perform on-premises account management.

4. **Correct answer:** D

   A. **Incorrect:** Staged migration is suitable if you have an on-premises deployment of Exchange 2007 deployment with any number of user accounts. This method is appropriate independently of whether or not you want to perform on-premises or cloud-based user account management.

   B. **Incorrect:** Remove move migrations are appropriate if you have more than 2,000 user accounts, have Exchange 2007, Exchange 2010, and Exchange 2013 as the on-premises environment, and you want to have cloud-based user management.

   C. **Incorrect:** Use an IMAP migration if you have a non-Exchange on-premises messaging solutions.

   D. **Correct:** Cutover migration is suitable if your on-premises environment has Exchange Server 2007, Exchange Server 2010, or Exchange Server 2013 and you have less than 2,000 and you do not want to perform on-premises account management.

Objective 4.3: Thought experiment

1. A user must be a member of the Discovery Management Exchange Administrator role to be able to configure a query-based in-place hold.

2. When an in-place hold or litigation hold is applied on a mailbox, the archive mailbox quota is increased from 30 GB to 100 GB.

Objective 4.3: Review

1. **Correct answer:** B
    - A. **Incorrect:** Set-Mailbox can be used to enable litigation hold.
    - B. **Correct:** Set-CasMailbox can be used to enable or disable ActiveSync and Outlook Web App.
    - C. **Incorrect:** New-MailboxSearch can be used with the InPlaceHoldEnabled parameter to enable an in-place hold.
    - D. **Incorrect:** Remove-MaillboxSearch can be used to remove an In Place Hold.

2. **Correct answer:** C
    - A. **Incorrect:** Set-CasMailbox can be used to enable or disable ActiveSync and Outlook Web App.
    - B. **Incorrect:** New-MailboxSearch can be used with the InPlaceHoldEnabled parameter to enable an in-place hold.
    - C. **Correct:** Set-Mailbox can be used to enable litigation hold.
    - D. **Incorrect:** Set-MailboxSearch can be used to disable an in-place hold.

3. **Correct answer:** A
    - A. **Correct:** New-MailboxSearch can be used with the InPlaceHoldEnabled parameter to enable an in-place hold.
    - B. **Incorrect:** Set-MailboxSearch can be used to disable an in-place hold.
    - C. **Incorrect:** Set-Mailbox can be used to enable litigation hold.
    - D. **Incorrect:** Set-CasMailbox can be used to enable or disable ActiveSync and Outlook Web App.

4. **Correct answer:** B
    - A. **Incorrect:** Set-CasMailbox can be used to enable or disable ActiveSync and Outlook Web App.
    - B. **Correct:** Set-MailboxSearch can be used to disable an in-place hold.
    - C. **Incorrect:** Remove-MailboxSearch can be used to remove an In Place Hold.
    - D. **Incorrect:** Set-MailboxSearch can be used to disable an in-place hold.

5. **Correct answer:** C
    - A. **Incorrect:** Set-CasMailbox can be used to enable or disable ActiveSync and Outlook Web App.
    - B. **Incorrect:** Set-MailboxSearch can be used to disable an in-place hold.
    - C. **Correct:** Remove-MailboxSearch can be used to remove an In Place Hold.
    - D. **Incorrect:** Set-MailboxSearch can be used to disable an in-place hold.

Objective 4.4: Thought experiment

6. You would use the Set-CsTenantFederationConfiguration –AllowPublicUsers $False command to disable public IM connectivity.

7. You would use the Set-CsPushNotificationConfiguration –EnableApplePushNotifica-tionService $False command to disable the Apple push notification service.

8. You use the Set-CsTenantFederationConfiguration -BlockedDomains $Null command to remove all domains from the blocked domains list.

Objective 4.4: Review

1. **Correct answer:** A

   A. **Correct:** You can use the New-CsEdgeAllowAllKnownDomains cmdlet to allow Skype for Business Online users to communicate with any domain, except those on the block list.

   B. **Incorrect:** Use the New-CsEdgeAllowList cmdlet to configure the domains with which Skype for Business Online users can communicate. This cmdlet must be used in conjunction with the New-CsEdgeDomainPattern and Set-CsTenantFederation-Configuration cmdlets.

   C. **Incorrect:** You can use the New-CsEdgeDomainPattern to modify the list of al-lowed or blocked domains.

   D. **Incorrect:** You can use the Get-CsTenantFederationConfiguration to view informa-tion about the allowed domains and the blocked domains.

2. **Correct answer:** D

   A. **Incorrect:** You can use the New-CsEdgeAllowAllKnownDomains cmdlet to allow Skype for Business Online users to communicate with any domain, except those on the block list.

   B. **Incorrect:** You can use the Set-CsPushNotificationConfiguration cmdlet to config-ure push notification settings.

   C. **Incorrect:** You can use the Set-CsTenantFederationConfiguration cmdlet to also disable and enable public IM connectivity. You can also use this cmdlet to set the allowed and blocked domains lists.

   D. **Correct:** You can use the Get-CsTenantFederationConfiguration to view informa-tion about the allowed domains and the blocked domains.

3. **Correct answer:** B

   A. **Incorrect:** You can use the Set-CsPushNotificationConfiguration cmdlet to config-ure push notification settings.

   B. **Correct:** You can use the Set-CsTenantFederationConfiguration cmdlet to also disable and enable public IM connectivity. You can also use this cmdlet set the al-lowed and blocked domains lists.

   C. **Incorrect:** You can use the New-CsEdgeDomainPattern to modify the list of al-lowed or blocked domains.

   D. **Incorrect:** You can use the Get-CsTenantFederationConfiguration to view informa-tion about the allowed domains and the blocked domains.

4. **Correct answer:** D

   A. **Incorrect:** You can use the Set-CsTenantFederationConfiguration cmdlet to also disable and enable public IM connectivity. You can also use this cmdlet set the al-lowed and blocked domains lists.

   B. **Incorrect:** You can use the Get-CsTenantFederationConfiguration to view informa-tion about the allowed domains and the blocked domains.

   C. **Incorrect:** You can use the New-CsEdgeAllowAllKnownDomains cmdlet to allow Skype for Business Online users to communicate with any domain except those on the block list.

   D. **Correct:** You can use the Set-CsPushNotificationConfiguration cmdlet to configure push notification settings.

5. **Correct answers:** A and D

   A. **Correct:** You can use the New-CsEdgeDomainPattern to modify the list of allowed or blocked domains.

   B. **Incorrect:** You can use the New-CsEdgeAllowAllKnownDomains cmdlet to allow Skype for Business Online users to communicate with any domain except those on the block list.

   C. **Incorrect:** You can use the Set-CsPushNotificationConfiguration cmdlet to config-ure push notification settings.

   D. **Correct:** You can use the Set-CsTenantFederationConfiguration cmdlet to also disable and enable public IM connectivity. You can also use this cmdlet set the al-lowed and blocked domains lists.

Index

A

ACEs. *See* Access Control Entries (ACEs)
activation management
  Office 365 ProPlus 8–13
  Office for Mac 19–23
ActiveSync
  configuration of 295–298
  disabling 295–298
Add A Domain page 217
Add Allowed Domain dialog box 248
Add Blocked Domain dialog box 246–247
Add-MailboxPermission cmdlet 175
Add-RecipientPermission cmdlet 170
address books
  adding external contacts to 183–184
administrator privileges 5
administrators
  OneDrive for Business 132–134
  site collection 99–101
Agents worksheet 58
Allow Anonymous Attendees To Dial-Out option 221
allowed domain list 302–303
Allowed IP Address WebPage Dialog 240–241
anonymous sharing 129
anti-malware notifications 231–233
anti-malware policies 229–239
  anti-malware notifications 231–233
  creating 235–238
  default 233–235
  Enable-MalwareFilterRule cmdlet 239
  Get-MalwareFilterPolicy cmdlet 238
  malware detection response settings 230–231
  New-MalwareFilterPolicy cmdlet 238
  New-MalwareFilterRule cmdlet 238
  Remove-MalwareFilterPolicy cmdlet 238
  Set-MalwareFilterPolicy cmdlet 238

  Set-MalwareFilterRule cmdlet 239
  Windows PowerShell cmdlets 238–239
anti-spam policies
  advanced policy options 250–252
  allow lists 246–247
  applying 253–254
  block lists 244–246
  bulk actions 243–244
  connection filter policies 239–242
  international spam 248–251
  Outbound Spam policy 254–256
  Quarantine 256–257
  spam confidence levels 252–253
  spam filter policies 242–254
  Windows PowerShell cmdlets 254
Apple App Store 6–7
Applied To setting 235, 253
Apply Sensitive Word List 252
App Store 134–135
App-V package 30
Archive Mailbox dialog 199–200
archives
  accessing 273
  client requirements for 273–277
  enabling personal 196–201
  importing PST files 275–278
  transferring items to 273–274
Auto Account Setup page 65

B

blocked domain list 303–304
BlockedDomains parameter 303
blocked IP address ranges 240
Blocked IP Address webpage dialog box 240
blocked sender list 245

319

I

J

K

L

M

About the author

 ORIN THOMAS is an MVP, a Microsoft Regional Director, an MCT and has a string of Microsoft MCSE and MCITP certifications. He has written more than 30 books for Microsoft Press on topics including Windows Server, Windows Client, Azure, System Center, Exchange Server, Security, and SQL Server. He is an author at PluralSight and is a contributing editor at *Windows IT Pro* magazine. He has been working in IT since the early 1990's and regularly speaks at conferences in Australia and around the world. Orin founded and runs the Melbourne System Center, Security, and Infrastructure Group and is completing a Doctorate in Information Technology at Charles Sturt University. You can follow him on twitter at *http://twitter.com/orinthomas*.

Free ebooks

From technical overviews to drilldowns on special topics, get *free* ebooks from Microsoft Press at:

www.microsoftvirtualacademy.com/ebooks

Download your free ebooks in PDF, EPUB, and/or Mobi for Kindle formats.

Look for other great resources at Microsoft Virtual Academy, where you can learn new skills and help advance your career with free Microsoft training delivered by experts.

Now that you've read the book...

Tell us what you think!

Was it useful?
Did it teach you what you wanted to learn?
Was there room for improvement?

Let us know at http://aka.ms/tellpress

Your feedback goes directly to the staff at Microsoft Press,
and we read every one of your responses. Thanks in advance!